Transmitting the Spirit

Transmitting the Spirit

Religious Conversion, Media, and Urban Violence in Brazil

Martijn Oosterbaan

The Pennsylvania State University Press
University Park, Pennsylvania

Parts of chapter 2 appeared in "Sonic Supremacy: Sound, Space and the Politics of Presence in a Favela in Rio de Janeiro," *Critique of Anthropology* 29, no. 1 (2009): 81–104.

An earlier version of chapter 3 appeared in "Mass Mediating the Spiritual Battle: Pentecostal Appropriations of Mass Mediated Violence in Rio de Janeiro," *Material Religion* 1, no. 3 (2005): 358–85.

Parts of chapter 5 appeared in the article "Spiritual Attunement: Pentecostal Radio in the Soundscape of a Favela in Rio de Janeiro," *Social Text* 26, no. 3 (2008): 123–45.

Copyright © 2017 Martijn Oosterbaan
All rights reserved
Printed in the United States of America
Published by The Pennsylvania
State University Press,
University Park, PA 16802-1003

The Pennsylvania State University Press is a member of the Association of American University Presses.

It is the policy of The Pennsylvania State University Press to use acid-free paper. Publications on uncoated stock satisfy the minimum requirements of American National Standard for Information Sciences—Permanence of Paper for Printed Library Material, ANSI Z39.48–1992.

Library of Congress Cataloging-in-Publication Data

Names: Oosterbaan, Martijn, 1975– , author.
Title: Transmitting the spirit : religious
    conversion, media, and urban violence in
    Brazil / Martijn Oosterbaan.
Description: University Park, Pennsylvania :
    The Pennsylvania State University Press,
    [2017] | Includes bibliographical refer-
    ences and index.
Summary: "Examines Pentecostalism, media,
    society, and culture in the turbulent
    favelas of Brazil. Explores both the evolv-
    ing role of religion in Latin America and
    the proliferation of religious ideas and
    practices in the postmodern world"—
    Provided by publisher.
Identifiers: LCCN 2017006195 | ISBN
    9780271078434 (cloth : alk. paper) | ISBN
    978-0-271-07844-1 (pbk. : alk. paper)
Subjects: LCSH: Pentecostalism—Brazil.
    | Mass media—Brazil. | Mass media—
    Religious aspects—Pentecostal churches.
    | Conversion—Pentecostal churces. |
    Slums—Brazil—Rio de Janeiro. | Urban
    violence—Brazil.
Classification: LCC BR1644.5.B6 O57 2017 |
    DDC 270.8/20981—dc23
LC record available at https://lccn.loc.
gov/2017006195

In loving memory of Henk Oosterbaan

In every corner of the city there is a favela,
In every corner of the favela there is a *traficante*
And there is always a *traficante* who has a mother who is a *crente*
Who prays for her son desperately
Tired of weeping, of fighting, of suffering,
She believes that one day he will repent
And remember everything that she taught him,
Return to his origins or what is left of it . . .

—**DJ ALPISTE,** "VENCER O MAL" (OVERCOME EVIL)

Contents

Acknowledgments

Many people helped me to write this book, and there are some I wish to thank explicitly here. I thank Zelinda for inviting me to stay at her place and helping me find my way in Rio de Janeiro and Marcus for taking me up the morro the first time. Settling on the morro would have been nearly impossible without the help of Ismael. Of all those who have helped me during my fieldwork I would like to mention specifically Bezerra, Josémar, Paulo, and Fátima. Several people I met during the years of fieldwork will always remain immensely dear to me: Claudio and Elisete, Didi, Deize, Juliana and Pará, Bam Bam and Enrique, Denilda and Josenil, Branco, Yara, Demilson, Poty, Orlando, and Yara. I would also like to thank the people of the research group Religion and Society at the University of Amsterdam—Peter van der Veer, Peter Pels, Patricia Spyer, Peter van Rooden, and specifically Gerd Baumann—you showed me the way to go. Of the AISSR mentors, Peter Geschiere has been a great inspiration; I do not know many with such dedication. This book is undoubtedly the result of the years of cooperation with "the extended Pionier family": Mattijs van de Port, Rafael Sánchez, Stephen Hughes, Charles Hirschkind, Brian Larkin, Meg McLagan, Jeremy Stolow, Marleen de Witte, Francio Guadeloupe, Lotte Hoek, Zé d'Abreu, Miriyam Aouragh, and Carly Machado. I learned so much from all of you. Christian Bröer, your intellectual curiosity is an inspiration. Michiel Baud and Geert Banck have helped me to think of Brazil in a broader Latin American perspective and have encouraged me enormously. Thank you, Birgit Meyer, for giving me the chance to pursue this path and for all you have done for me. In Rio de Janeiro, Clara Mafra helped me to find the right direction, and Patricia Birman generously aided me practically and intellectually. Her home felt like a refuge, and I have benefited greatly from her knowledge of Brazilian anthropology. At Utrecht University I found many inspiring colleagues, of whom I would like to thank specifically Patrick Eisenlohr, Ton Robben, Yvon van der Pijl, and Kootje Willemse. Stephan Lanz, Kathrin Wildner, Rivke Jaffe and Martine Prange, thank you for your wonderful cooperation. I wish to thank my dear parents—Henk and Ineke—and my family for their support and love: Koen and Saskia, Immy, Olfertjan and Inge, Anne and Bram, Mieneke, Dick and Erika, Niels and Hanna, Marie-José, and Guurtje. Last but not least, I want to thank Daphne, Isis, and Julius—it is great to be with you.

Introduction

The sports area of the favela Roda do Vento was bustling with people awaiting the beginning of the last evening of the *cruzada evangelista* (evangelical crusade).[1] The concrete field, generally used as a soccer pitch, was full with white plastic chairs, facing a provisional stage supporting a pulpit and massive loudspeakers at both sides. Behind the stage, a large film screen had been attached to the wired fence surrounding the pitch. The program of the evening was promising. Two well-known female *gospel*[2] singers—Flordelis and Elaine Martins—were headlining the event, and Pastor Anderson do Carmo—a renowned preacher—was to deliver a sermon to close it off.

At the entrance of the pitch, inhabitants of the community were selling T-shirts and DVDs of the first night of the cruzada, just one day ago. As the vendors assured, that first night had been tremendous. The high point of the night had been the testimony of Pastor Demétrio Martins, born and raised in the Complexo do Alemão, one of the most infamous favela complexes of Rio de Janeiro. According to the vendors, the pastor had recounted in detail how his career as a gang member of the Comando Vermelho (CV; Red Command) pushed him further and further along the road of violence and misery until he was shot during an armed confrontation with rival gang members. It was then that he decided to accept Jesus and preach so he could save others from a life of crime and insecurity.

The vendor had won my attention not in the least because the Complexo do Alemão had been in the news continually in Rio de Janeiro in 2011. In that year, the Brazilian military spectacularly invaded the complex to rid the favelas of the heavily armed members of the CV. One of the news broadcasts dedicated to the military operation showed soldiers planting a Brazilian flag atop the highest hill of the complex to exemplify that the place—once in the hands of the CV—had been "reconquered" by the state.

Convinced by the sales pitch of the vendor, I bought a DVD and entered the cruzada area. As the program promised, the performances were overwhelming indeed. Flordelis—born and raised in Jacarezinho, a favela nearby—delivered her *testemunho* (testimony).[3] In an emotional tone, she narrated her struggle to acquire legal custody over the fifty underprivileged children she had taken into her home in Jacarepaguá in the western region of Rio de Janeiro. Many of the children had traumatic encounters with the violence, addiction, and poverty that can be part of favela life. Her testimony was touching, but the songs she performed were even more gripping. In particular the powerful pop ballad "Deus no Controle" (God in control) moved the crowd; when she ended, both she and many people in the audience were shouting out hallelujahs and speaking in tongues.

As if to prove that God had blessed her equally, Elaine Martins also delivered a performance that was received enthusiastically. Elaine—a tall black woman from Rio de Janeiro—began with a slow yet forceful ballad, "Muda O Meu Coração" (Change my heart). Her imposing voice—matched by her emotional facial expressions, projected on the screen behind her—was met by shouts from the crowd. Before starting her second song, Elaine spoke in a preaching tone of her own life as a child in the Complexo do Alemão. Her own brother had died as a result of his involvement with the drug gangs, and she had also almost been led astray until God spoke to her and rescued her from the perils of favela life.

In awe, I left the pitch to see what was going on in the vicinity. It was dark, but it was clear that not all the inhabitants of the community were at the cruzada; there was a lot of movement of inhabitants minding their day-to-day business. Maria, a friend, approached and told me that many boys from the local gang had gathered a bit farther down the road, not in plain sight but close enough to hear the amplified voices of the event. I headed back to observe the closing sermon of Pastor Anderson do Carmo and then went home.

Two weeks after the cruzada I interviewed Emerson, an inhabitant of Roda do Vento, the favela where the cruzada had taken place. Emerson, a self-identified *evangélico* (evangelical),[4] told me that seven years before, when he was head of a *bonde* (gang) operating in the favela, a similar cruzada had led him to the path of transformation:

It was during a cruzada like that one that I offered my life to Jesus. . . . I was with the bonde, everyone was armed. We were close to the event, listening. And at that moment those gospel music songs were reaching me, entering my heart. At the end of the cruzada they called people to come forward and pray and I went. I pulled off my backpack and laid down my weapons and I went to receive a prayer. At that very moment I received the Holy Spirit; total remission. Nothing had been able to fulfill me till then, not the drugs, not the *baile funk* [popular dances in the favelas], the liquor, the flirting, nothing had fulfilled me the way the presence of God did at that moment.[5]

Religion remains one of the most salient identity markers and cultural traits of the world. Moreover, as the example above illustrates, people of contemporary religious movements make ample use of socio-technological possibilities to exchange audiovisual material, to reproduce particular religious lifestyles, and to persuade people to convert to specific religious traditions. In this volume I argue that the question of why these religious ideas and practices thrive in a postmodern world can only be answered when we understand how media shape everyday cultural life and how religious ideas and practices are related to mediated life-worlds. To make this argument, this book focuses on Pentecostalism in urban Brazil.

Pentecostalism is one of the most rapidly expanding religious-cultural forms in the world. While Pentecostal movements around the globe display variety, they nevertheless exhibit a striking similarity of practices and cosmologies. Pentecostalism stresses gifts (*charismata*) of the Holy Spirit such as faith healing and speaking in tongues (*glossolalia*). Largely, its practitioners see the devil and his demons as agents who try to win the hearts and minds of humans and lead them to death and destruction. The existence of such evil enforces the so-called duality of the Pentecostal worldview (Droogers 2001, 46): the belief that the world is divided between those who follow God and those who follow the devil. Given this duality, the acceptance of Jesus as one's Savior is seen as a fundamental conversion by which to achieve happiness in this life and salvation in the hereafter.

One of the most intriguing questions related to religion and globalization is why Pentecostalism and similar Charismatic Christian movements have rapidly become the most popular religious movements in the world.[6] The Brazilian census of 2010 showed that 22 percent of the population described itself as evangélico, an increase of approximately 61 percent in ten years. The term *evangélicos* is used to denote the broader collection of (Protestant) Christians in Brazil.[7] Nevertheless, the majority of Brazil's 42.3 million evangélicos can be identified as Pentecostal.[8] How can we explain such a cultural transformation? In this book I hope to convince readers that the answer to this question lies in Pentecostalism's remarkable capacity to incorporate both religious *and* nonreligious cultural forms that shape the daily life of people. To make this point, the present work explores the nexus between Pentecostalism, media, and (in)security in the favelas of Rio de Janeiro, Brazil.

Researchers who explore the popularity of Pentecostalism have analyzed its attractiveness in relation to socioeconomic circumstances and existing religious contexts. In a global context, Pentecostalism is understood as a religious system that breaks with traditional cultural forms to excavate space for a new form of subjectivity (Meyer 1999; Robbins 2004). While several scholars have argued that, in fact, Pentecostalism's secret of success lies in its capacity to both break with existing native cosmologies and incorporate them in the new religious framework, I argue that we should go beyond an exclusive focus on so-called native (traditional) religious and cultural forms that are reproduced in the Pentecostal frameworks and understand that Pentecostalism incorporates with unprecedented ease traditional *and* contemporary, native *and* global, popular cultural forms.

In his influential essay on the global increase of slums, Mike Davis (2004, 32) has argued that the Pentecostal movement can be seen as "the single most important cultural response to explosive and traumatic urbanization" in Latin America. Though Davis, in my opinion, is right to underscore the connection between Pentecostalism and the socioeconomic conditions of the urban areas under scrutiny, the steady increase of Pentecostal adherents cannot be described merely in terms of a religious response to material changes, violence, or relative deprivation. Such a description would do little justice to the intricate relations among religion, culture, and politics or to the cultural differences among Latin American cities.

Pentecostalism has become ubiquitous in the favelas of Rio de Janeiro, which are urban settlements often built on occupied land. The brick and concrete houses, built close to and on top of one another, form large residential areas that generate their own formal and informal economies. These self-built neighborhoods display many similarities with urban settlements in other Latin American countries—think of the periphery of Caracas, for example. Nevertheless, favelas have their own particularities. For instance, favelas are characterized by specific extralegal violent organizations (such as the Comando Vermelho) that display particular historical relations with state institutions and particular enmeshments with cultural expressions such as baile funk.

Research among inhabitants of several favelas in Rio de Janeiro revealed that 97 percent of the favela households had a television set (Perlman 2010).

The ubiquitous presence of mass media in favelas challenges the assumption that we can analyze the spread of Pentecostalism in favelas without taking into account its relation to popular media. Not only should we recognize that mass media co-constitute social identities, dreams, and actions of people in all parts of the world, but we should also acknowledge that in Latin America media have become "part of the basic fabric of urbanity" (Martín-Barbero 2002, 27).

A number of important writers who have investigated the cultural translations that have taken place under the guise of missionary projects in times of colonialism have described the transformations in subject positions that were crafted during the colonial encounter in terms of "conversion to modernities" (Van der Veer 1996). *Transmitting the Spirit* maintains the insights of these writers but argues that contemporary conversions to Christianity must be understood in light of a fragmentation and pluralization of social life. Contemporary religious conversions occur in heterogeneous religious arenas and—equally important—such conversions take place amid a plethora of lifestyles based on global religious and nonreligious cultural trends, sustained by mass media. This begs the question: what entails conversion in these contexts?

As will become clear, I think it is best when we understand conversion in these contexts as *hypermediated*. The term "hypermediated conversion" serves to indicate that contemporary Pentecostal aspirations of self-transformation display certain similarities with modern conversion dynamics that accompanied the cultural ruptures during the global spread of Christianity—as, for instance, described by Peter van der Veer (1996), Birgit Meyer (1999), and Webb Keane (2007). However, current conversions take place in a context of cultural plurality and mediatization of everyday life that complicates the stability of such self-transformations and asks for a continuous reworking of the self and of popular cultural products and practices.

The life-worlds in which Pentecostalism generally operates are riddled with different cultural practices, images, lifestyles, and stories, reproduced and amplified by means of different media. While Pentecostalism often presents itself as the most powerful counterforce to immoral popular culture, Pentecostalism, in fact, is presented *intertextually*, *interoptically*, and *interacoustically* with and in relation to religious and nonreligious television shows, newspaper articles, radio programs, and music recordings. The meaning and attraction of Brazilian gospel music—itself a hybrid mixture of genres—is intricately related to the amplified sound of *samba* and baile funk and the lifestyles and cultural expressions attached to them. The Pentecostal message of salvation is delivered in Pentecostal magazines that remediate televised images of city violence, and the work of the devil is clarified with reference to the enormously popular *telenovelas* (soap operas). Last but not least, Pentecostal politicians simultaneously present themselves as credible leaders and as charismatic gospel singers who are able to move people emotionally.

As I will show in this volume, Pentecostalism acquires its distinctive form and appeal in relation to the other forms of popular culture that circulate in Brazilian society, and it also offers a variety of techniques to purify these popular cultural forms in order to make them accessible for Christian consumption. These purifying techniques involve both an elaborate reworking of the self (Mahmood 2005; Marshall 2009) and a reformation of the popular cultural products to rid them of their demonic content. Vice versa, Pentecostal and Charismatic cultural expressions are transformed to make them accessible to a larger audience.

As *Transmitting the Spirit* contends, Pentecostal movements are able to connect politics, entertainment, and religion in an unprecedented fashion because they progressively appropriate and recategorize popular cultural forms according to their cosmology. Pentecostalism's dialectic symbiosis[9] with popular consumer and entertainment culture, driven by the projected separations between sacred and profane domains of life, allows for an unanticipated and unequaled incorporation of popular images, sounds, and embodied experiences without losing much, if any, of its defiant characteristics. Pentecostalism has become immensely popular because it offers its followers a relatively unambiguous socioreligious identity in a turbulent social world while it projects itself at the center of global flows of power, wealth, and information. The discursive opposition to demonic expressions, deemed to be connected to a host of religious, political, and cultural practices, creates pathways for a persuasive assimilation of a plethora of cultural forms that are generally not considered "religious" *an sich* yet end up being pulled into the powerful current of global Pentecostalism.

Pentecostalism and Brazilian Society

The past twenty to thirty years of Brazilian history display a remarkable change in the religious and political field. After decades of military rule, the direct presidential elections of 1989 can be regarded a landmark in Brazilian political history, as they exemplified a variety of societal changes (Fausto 1999). Without being able to fully flesh out all the interconnections in this volume, it is important to note that the *abertura* (opening)—the gradual diminishment of authoritarian rule in the 1980s—went hand in hand with two major societal changes that are at the heart of this book: the rise in number of Pentecostal and neo-Pentecostal believers, often at the expense of self-defined Catholic believers (cf. Birman and Leite 2000; Lehmann 1996), and the society-wide expansion of what Kees Koonings and Dirk Kruijt (2004) have called the "new violence" of Latin America.

Though certainly not reducible to it, the rise of Pentecostal adherents is related to the position of the Roman Catholic Church in Brazil during and after the period of military rule (1964–85). For a long time Brazil has been portrayed as the country with the highest number of Catholic adherents in the world (Birman and Leite 2000). This image, though still prevailing in some descriptions of the country, cannot conceal transformations in the religious landscape. In the past thirty years, the number of Brazilians who identify themselves as Roman Catholics has declined. The Brazilian census of 2010 showed that the number of Roman Catholics in Brazil had decreased from 125 million in 2000 to 123.3 million in 2010. In relation to the population growth, this decline is significant. In 2000 the Roman Catholic population represented 73.6 percent of Brazil's total population, but in 2010 that percentage had dropped to 64.6 percent.[10]

The decline is partly related to the changes within the Roman Catholic Church in Latin America during the 1970s and 1980s (Mainwaring 1986). Influenced by liberation theology, the Roman Catholic Church generally "opted for the poor" and sought to narrow the gap between the clergy and the ordinary members, among others, by means of the creation of Catholic Christian Base Communities (CEBs).[11] In Brazil, the popularity of the CEBs was tied to political repression by the hands of the military rulers and the oppositional stance of the Catholic Church against their authoritarianism. Despite siding with the conservative forces at the moment of the military takeover, the Catholic Church supported progressive political movements in the years thereafter.

Though influential in bringing about political change from below, the CEBs lost much of their appeal and force after the democratic turn. As John Burdick (1993) has described, some of the progressive aspirations of the CEBs materialized with the creation of civil institutions that, in a way, made them redundant. However, Burdick also demonstrates that many of the desires of the people who supported the CEBs were never fully translated in the practices of these communities. Among those was the desire for a genuine spiritual experience of rupture and self-transformation. According to Burdick, the Catholic Church presented no such spiritual scheme and, in addition, reached out unevenly to the literate segments of the population, leaving many of the illiterate segments feeling underrepresented. Alberto Antoniazzi (1994) makes a similar point when he writes that the Catholic Church did not offer the kind of religious practices that are part of the popular religious field in Brazil and that connect mundane, everyday problems to "therapeutic" spiritual experiences.

Such an interpretation is strengthened by the rise of the Catholic Charismatic Renewal (CCR) movement in Brazil. According to Thomas Csordas (2009, 73), the CCR movement originated in the 1970s within the Roman Catholic Church in the United States, "synthesizing elements of Catholicism and Pentecostalism, with ecumenical leanings and a tropism toward development of intentional communities." Though the Brazilian census data do not distinguish between the different Roman Catholic movements, Prandi and Pierucci (1995) estimated the number of CCR devotees in Brazil to be 3.8 million in 1994, indicating the popularity of the movement at the time.

The second societal change important to understanding the appeal of Pentecostal movements in Brazil is the rise of a new kind of urban violence in many of the Brazilian cities after the abertura. Brazilians had suffered considerable state violence during the military rule that started in 1964 and ended in 1985. State repression and torture reached its peak in the years between 1968 and 1974. The gradual liberalization that started in 1974 led to a new constitution in 1988 and direct presidential elections in 1989.

Unfortunately, the end of authoritarian rule did not end urban violence in Brazil. As Desmond Enrique Arias and Daniel Goldstein (2010) have aptly described, the democratic turn and consolidation of many Latin American societies present a striking paradox. Whereas many Latin American countries built up democratic institutions designed to secure the civil rights of their populations, in fact violence did not decline, and large segments of the population are exposed to high levels of insecurity. In my opinion, Kees Koonings and Dirk Kruijt (2004, 6) have also put it well: "One of the most noteworthy characteristics of contemporary Latin American societies is the de facto coexistence of formal constitutionalism, (electoral) democracy and an often vibrant civil society on the one hand, and the use of force to stake out power domains or pursue economic or political interests on the other." In Brazil, as in other countries, the causes of the perseverance of armed violence are strongly related to limited state investments in public security and high economic inequality (Gay 2010). Especially in the large Brazilian cities, home to millions of people living in slums, multilayered formal/informal groups such as *comandos* (networks of drug gangs) and *milícias* (Mafia-like organizations) compete over territories, assets, and power.[12] While the Brazilian nation still has a popular appeal to many of its inhabitants, the state frequently fails as guardian and protector of the less privileged. According to Teresa Caldeira and James Holston (1999, 694), Brazil can therefore best be described as a "disjunctive democracy," one in which the civil component of citizenship is at odds with citizens' formal rights and duties. We will return to some of the details of the disjunctive elements of favela life in the next chapter, but here it is worth highlighting that the "new violence"—as Koonings and Kruijt (2004) have coined it—has left many Brazilian citizens feeling abandoned.

Though certainly not the only two—or the most important—transformations in Brazil, these historical currents are important to understanding the rising appeal of Pentecostal and evangelical movements in Rio de Janeiro and the connections between religion, media, and daily life. Before demonstrating in more detail how they are connected in the following chapters, it is important to note that the increase in Pentecostal adherents was and is reflected in the political presence of Pentecostalism in Brazil as well.

Pentecostalism and Politics in Brazil

In the past decades many political candidates affiliated with Pentecostal churches have campaigned for legislative positions in Brazil, and many of these candidates have been elected. The *bancada evangélica* (evangelical caucus), which had forty-four members in the chamber of federal deputies in 1998, presented ninety-six evangelical members after the 2014 elections.[13]

Among the members of this caucus, the associates of the neo-Pentecostal church Igreja Universal do Reino de Deus (IURD) and the Pentecostal church Assembleia de Deus have drawn much attention.[14] The Igreja Universal, founded in 1977 in Rio de Janeiro by its charismatic leader Edir Macedo, has developed into a strongly organized, hierarchical mega-church. On July 31, 2014, at the inauguration ceremony of the new headquarters of the Igreja Universal in São Paulo—the "Temple of Solomon"—Dilma Rousseff, president of Brazil at the time, sat next to Macedo.[15] Marcelo Crivella, nephew of Macedo and prominent member of the Igreja Universal, was elected senator for the state of Rio de Janeiro in 2002 and mayor of the city of Rio de Janeiro in 2016. According to the census of 2010, the church had 1.87 million affiliates in Brazil.

Of the varied Pentecostal churches that deliver political candidates for state and federal elections in Brazil, the Igreja Universal has become the most visible.[16] Over the last thirty years it has built many huge *cated-rais* (cathedrals) throughout Brazil. Macedo bought one of the six national public television broadcast networks, Rede Record, in 1989. The church operates a vast network of websites, its own publishing house, and a record company. It publishes the weekly newspaper *Folha Universal* (Universal paper) and owns several radio stations that broadcast twenty-four hours a day. Besides its growth in Latin America, the Igreja Universal has expanded swiftly into other continents in the last few decades.[17] In fact, according to Paul Freston (2005, 33), few other Christian denominations from the Third World have been "exported so successfully and rapidly." According to its own website, the Igreja Universal is present in nearly one hundred countries.[18]

Although the Igreja Universal is emblematic of the new intersections among commerce, religion, media, and politics, this does not mean that it has the largest following or that other evangelical churches have not transformed as a result of shifts in the religious field. Other (older) Pentecostal denominations such as the Assembleia de Deus and the Congregação Cristo no Brasil have more affiliates and have also grown substantially in the past few decades.[19] According to the census of 2010, the Assembleia de Deus had 12.4 million followers in Brazil and was thus the Pentecostal denomination with the largest following.[20] It was founded in 1911 by two Swedish missionaries in Belém in the state of Pará and has since expanded gradually throughout Brazil. In 2010 and 2014, Marina Silva, *pastora* of the Assembleia de Deus, finished in third place in the presidential elections.

The Igreja Universal and the Assembleia de Deus—both prominent in this book—display marked differences. The Igreja Universal is governed from the top down and has systematized its rituals across time and space, creating a highly recognizable uniformity in appearance and routines. This stands in contrast to the Assembleia de Deus, which consists of "local moral communities" (Mafra 2002, 41) that operate independently. As Paul Freston (1995, 123) explains, "The system of government is oligarchical, grouped in lineages around *caudilho*-type *Pastores-presidentes*. The AG [Assemblies of God] is a complex web of (geographically intertwined) networks of mother-churches and dependent churches." Despite the differences, we should be mindful not to describe the followers of these churches as two isolated, self-contained groups. Although one could describe the relatively "young" Igreja Universal as an example of the "evolution" of Pentecostal churches in postmodern times (Campos 1997), this does not mean that the "traditional" Pentecostal churches are not transforming as well.

The religious/political transformation in Brazil is recurrently explained with reference to the growth of Pentecostal media.[21] It is broadly recognized that mediatized performances of charismatic evangelical politicians have stirred up the political landscape of Brazil, especially because the Pentecostal churches generally display an aggressive attitude toward Afro-Brazilian religious practices and Catholicism.[22] The Igreja Universal in particular has developed new media formats that have shifted the position and character of popular sacred entities and objects according to their cosmological duality. Most important are the "staged" expulsions of demons during massive church services, which are mass mediated via the Internet, television, magazines, and newspapers.[23]

One of the central rituals in the Igreja Universal is the *sessão de descarrego*.[24] This weekly church session consists of highly ritualized mass exorcisms in which people are invited to enact their self-empowerment and to change their social and economic conditions with the help of the Holy Spirit. These public performances of exorcism serve as visualizations of hitherto invisible forces, as Eric Kramer (2005, 115) has shown: "Exorcism as spectacle invites the congregation to enter into a transactive realm of the spirit. This process articulates value transformations through images grounded in the appropriation of local cultural discourses and forms of popular religiosity." Through the practice of exorcism, the church simultaneously identifies and expels the roots of evil and offers direct spiritual interventions in situations of relative poverty and violence, common for many urban spaces in Brazil.

The mass mediatization of expulsions has thoroughly shifted the relations between religious institutions in Brazil. Rather than discarding Afro-Brazilian religious beliefs and practices, the Igreja Universal incorporates the spiritual entities worshiped in Candomblé and Umbanda and represents them as demons. Misfortune and misery are thus broadcast as consequences of Afro-Brazilian religious practices. The demons, or *encostos*,[25] are held responsible for physically harming the individuals they possess and are accountable for hindering them from achieving fortune and happiness in this life and salvation in the hereafter.

While the spiritual warfare of the Igreja Universal and the Assembleia de Deus is mostly directed against Afro-Brazilian religious practices, the Catholic Church is another prominent adversary. Both Pentecostal churches forcefully oppose the presumed idolatry of Catholic saints. The most famous public incident is known as the *chute na santa*—the kicking of the saint. During a television broadcast, a pastor of the Igreja Universal desecrated a plaster statue of the Catholic patron saint of Brazil, Nossa Senhora Aparecida.

Several authors have argued that the assault on the statue was not merely an attack on a Catholic icon, but an attack on the cultural hegemony of Catholicism in Brazil (Kramer 2001a; Birman and Lehmann 1999). Besides this frontal attack on a Catholic saint, Pentecostal organizations throughout Brazil have criticized many popular cultural practices that are considered part of the national identity, such as samba and carnival.[26] Instead of portraying these practices as the epitome of "Brazilianness" and of national pride, Pentecostal organizations connected these cultural practices to the social and personal problems of the Brazilian population at large.

The visible connection between Pentecostalism and politics in Brazil—coupled with the aggressive attitude of Pentecostal preachers toward Brazilian cultural heritage—has raised many critical voices in the past decades. A considerable fraction of the commentators portray mass media as powerful tools of evangelical churches to manipulate citizens to vote for religious leaders.[27] Discussions about the broadcasts of evangelical politicians are related to pertinent normative debates about the place of religion in contemporary societies. While these discussions are important, not least because they are part of the distribution of power in society, as Talal Asad (2003) has argued forcefully, my concern in this volume lies less with political theory and more with presumptions about the workings of mediatized religion in relation to the mobilization of people.

The present work on Pentecostalism, media, and urban conflict in Brazil does not follow the assumption that religion will or should gradually disappear from the public sphere, but takes as a point of departure the question of how religious movements use media to address audiences and how the presence of these media influences the formation of collective identities and sensorial communities that affect political sensitivities in diverse ways.[28]

Religion, Media, and Conversion

To clarify the growing constituency of Pentecostal politicians in Brazil, many of the studies on Brazilian Pentecostalism focus on the institutional developments within the Pentecostal churches in relation to the newly acquired media channels and political projects.[29] In itself this approach demonstrates a welcome step forward compared to studies that described the relation between "religion" and "modern media" in anachronistic terms. As a number of authors have argued in the past ten years, many religious movements have been eager to appropriate media for proselytism and communication, and it is important to investigate the consequences of this intermarriage.[30]

With regard to Brazilian Pentecostalism, however, analysis is often centered on content analysis of the mass media, on the religious doctrines, and on the political endeavors of pastors and other church leaders. As much as these are needed to understand doctrinal positions and institutional changes, such analyses can only partly explain the popularity of charismatic evangelical leaders. Many of the works do not specify which people are attracted to Pentecostal ideas and practices or explain how these practices relate to their day-to-day life. Taking into account that many of the adherents of Pentecostal churches live in Brazilian favelas, we should also attempt to understand what life in a favela looks like.

The first time I walked through a favela, during my first stay in Rio de Janeiro in 2001, I was overtaken by the cacophony of sounds emanating from different locales. Loud music from small shops and amplified sermons produced the characteristic sonic environment. During the walk I occasionally passed armed youngsters of the comando who checked me out and let me pass. All the living rooms I saw that day featured TV sets that oscillated between background noise and foreground presence, temporarily interrupting our conversations. I remembered asking myself, how do people relate to all these different media? And what place do Pentecostal media attain in this landscape?

As this work argues, the nexus between media, religion, and audiences should not be analyzed with only propaganda or effect models in mind. While it is tempting to think of the relation between media and religion in terms of proselytism—especially since religious media so often represent this image themselves—mere presence in the media does not mean that people will attend churches; other social and cultural aspects are at play as well (Novaes 2002). Surely, media help people become acquainted with the doctrines, the language, and the style of Pentecostalism, but such knowledge in itself is only one part of the many influences that may or may not eventually lead people to attend a Pentecostal church service. People may hear of a particular church on television or radio, but a visit to a particular church generally follows an invitation from friends, family, or neighbors (82). The familiarization with a particular Pentecostal doctrine or church often happens after personal contact with people who evangelize *corpo a corpo* (body to body), as Machado and Fernandes have put it (1998).

The depiction of the cruzada evangelista in the favela gives but one small depiction of how Pentecostal churches use mass media beyond broadcasting sermons or staged exorcisms. By means of different media, Pentecostal churches connect their cosmologies and practices to a host of other phenomena of contemporary society and seek to instill in their audience particular emotional states and points of identification. As exemplified by Emerson—who was deeply touched by a cruzada evangelista and decided to leave the gang he was part of—people in the favelas of Rio de Janeiro generally relate to narratives and images of crime, violence, and suffering because they have personal knowledge of it.

Yet a closer inspection of Emerson's words reveals that more is at play. First, the music of Elaine Martins that has touched him profoundly may carry an evangelical message, but the rhythm and melody of her songs resemble those of pop records that have no explicit Christian character. In other words, the persuasive form of the music cannot exclusively be described in religious terms. Moreover, Emerson juxtaposes the music of Elaine Martins and the reception of the Holy Spirit to baile funk parties that could not fulfill him the way the Spirit did, signaling that both operate at an emotional level yet also speak to each other as opposites. What are we to make of these enmeshments and oppositions of forms and meanings that played such an important part in Emerson's decision to give up his life as a gang member?

This ethnography, based on fieldwork in a number of favelas in Rio de Janeiro between 2001 and 2016, tries to answer these questions. I use insights from anthropology, cultural analysis, and religious and media studies in an effort to write thick description "with a difference" (Appadurai 1996, 55). Based on approximately fifty recorded interviews, many church visits, daily talks, and—above all—accounts of media-related practices of favela inhabitants, this ethnography shows that Pentecostal media are intertextually and interexperientially related to a host of other popular media and cultural forms. As will become clear, even though Pentecostalism is often framed in opposition to other media and cultural phenomena, Pentecostal transmissions are in fact habitually produced in close symbiosis with those media forms.

The book stems from and contributes to current discussions in the field of religious studies and media theory. Instead of understanding technology and religion as discrete domains, Hent de Vries (2001) has argued that religion can be comprehended as a practice of mediation (see also Meyer 2009). While such a conceptualization harbors the risk of conflating different ideas of mediation, as Charles Hirschkind has argued (2011), this insight has urged anthropologists to research the relations between the form and content of religious media. As a number of scholars have recently argued, religious deployment of media has often been guided by a quest for transcendence.[31] Religious groups take up and develop (media) technologies not merely to distribute a message or doctrine but also to reproduce the sensation of an unmediated contact with or experience of the divine.

This book analyzes the media technologies and formats that Brazilian Pentecostal movements use to communicate divine presence, and it argues that Pentecostalism itself is fundamentally altered by these adoptions. As Pentecostals incorporate specific media (music, television formats, etc.), people become responsive to specific sensory perceptions that signal and authenticate divine presence. By investigating closely the religious disciplines and experiences of people in the favelas of Rio de Janeiro, the chapters in this volume describe through which media practices "enchantment manifests itself" (Pinney 2001, 157).

Notwithstanding the importance of divine presence, we should not forget to pay attention to the perceived manifestations of evil through media technologies. As this work will show, positive divine presence manifests itself primarily through Brazilian evangelical music (worship), but demonic presence often manifests itself in telenovelas, popular music, and reality shows (e.g., *Big Brother Brasil*). Furthermore, the perceived borders between divine and demonic media are closely related to the differences between social identities in the favelas.

The detailed attention to changing notions of good and evil media as a result of social transformations in Rio de Janeiro demonstrates how "sensational forms" (Meyer 2010) interact with semiotic ideologies (Keane 2007), but also takes seriously William Mazzarella's (2004, 353) critique that anthropologists rarely acknowledge that mediation "precedes what we commonly recognize as 'media'; that, in fact, local worlds are necessarily already the outcome of more or less stable, more or less local social technologies of mediation." This insight pushes us to go beyond "media-effect models" looming in the background and helps us see that different media technologies form part of a complex "communicative ecology" (Slater and Tacchi 2004).

This broader understanding of media connects well to Stig Hjarvard's (2008) argument that we can only understand the current functioning of religion in the world when we recognize that media in general have come to play a pivotal role in structuring social life. This argument serves as inspiration to go beyond narrow interpretations of the relation between religion and media. As the brief description of Emerson's experiences indicates, we can only understand why and how Pentecostal organizations have acquired popular appeal in Brazil—specifically in large cities such as Rio de Janeiro—when we place the Pentecostal media in relation to other media and to the daily lives of the people who live in the urban spaces where these media circulate.[32]

These observations lead us to the insight that we cannot take the Pentecostal discourse on the relation between media and conversion at face value. Although Pentecostal churches regularly present the idea that particular evangelical broadcasts lead individual people to accept Jesus and often suggest that this decision was instantaneous and permanent, this book sets out to show that this is not how the reception of Pentecostal media works in practice. Media reception in the favelas is inherently social, and listening and watching media are part of the performative constitution of religious identity. Such a conceptualization of religious identity helps us understand which social forces co-constitute the drives of people to follow particular doctrines. In the favelas, people play Christian music because they feel in touch with God but also to signal their neighbors that they are firm believers and cannot be persuaded to follow the voice of the devil and engage in immoral or criminal behavior. Favela inhabitants who are attracted by the moral message of Pentecostalism generally express a shared attitude with respect to the popular media in the favelas. Media that were hitherto seen as harmless are now regarded as a powerful confirmation of the presence of the devil in daily life. People encourage one another to question the content of the telenovelas whose protagonists cheat, lie, and steal, and they point one another to the apparent links between samba music and illicit pleasures that eventually lead to misery and grief.

While ethnographically grounding the claim that discrete findings about content or effects are not as important as the "process of reception, where meanings are intended, attributed, made, and exchanged in the context of media audience practice" (Hoover 2002, 29), this work also demonstrates that we should move beyond a narrow notion of "interpreting audiences" (Moores 1993; Dant 2012). Especially in the case of Pentecostalism, in which doctrines and practices are centered on the body, the Holy Spirit, and corporeal experiences, we cannot describe the relationship between Pentecostals and television simply in terms of "reading." As the book shows, watching television involves what Christopher Pinney (2001, 158) has coined as "corpothetics": "the sensory embrace of images, the bodily engagement that most people (except Kantians and modernists) have with artworks." Pentecostal adherents watch television but remain alert not to be "aroused" by the devil or "poked" by the Holy Spirit.

Though the work of authors such as Christopher Pinney (2001) and David Morgan (2005) are sources of great inspiration, their work generally focuses on visual media and on practices of looking, whereas music is also a very important element of Pentecostalism.[33] In the contemporary Brazilian context, music is the cultural form par excellence through which Pentecostal culture is remediated. Successful Pentecostal radio and television programs, magazines, or websites are often related to the Brazilian gospel music industry (Mendonça 2008, 229). It is thus very important to include in the analysis the "corpothetics" of people's perceptions of sound and music.

The Space Between

This book is the result of my interest in questions related to the global popularity of Pentecostalism in relation to the anthropology of religion, as well as my desire to understand better what life in the favelas of Rio de Janeiro is like. Favelas form an important part of talk among residents of Rio de Janeiro (and beyond), not least because favelas are featured in news broadcasts, movies, and television shows and are portrayed as places where violent confrontations occur frequently. Sadly, favela residents are often portrayed as criminals and hustlers. Simultaneously, favelas are shown to be places where one encounters some of the "authentic" Brazilian cultural traditions, such as samba, and where one can find the true social spirit of Brazil—the places where people celebrate life together and carry its burdens collectively. My fascination with these seemingly contradictory descriptions of favela life supported my choice to do fieldwork in the favelas described in this book. I was drawn both by these accounts of favela life and by my disbelief that these positive and negative stereotypes could represent how things really were.

As I learned, favela life is much richer, and even though this book deals with some of the topics that often come to the fore in the media, I have done my best to picture the richness and depth that one encounters. My first excursions in the favela Visionário are exemplary of some of the structural features of favela life that have intrigued me ever since I started this work. During that first visit to the favela I met Pastor Abrahão of a small Assembleia de Deus church, who kindly suggested that I return to Visionário and participate in his church services. Not knowing if the local men of the Comando Vermelho would allow me to live in and pass through the favela, I learned that my affiliations with a local pastor and with evangelical congregants of his church cleared their suspicions that I was interfering with their business, although it was only later that I pieced together how this had worked.

After I had participated in a number of church services, I found a small apartment for rent in the Visionário. Weeks after having moved there, I accompanied the sister of one of the congregants to a local baile funk. I was excited but also mildly anxious about going because some congregants told me that *crentes* (believers) should not frequent bailes anymore, and I was unsure how the congregants would react. The baile kicked off way past midnight. I thought the music was great, and my chaperone mostly laughed about my awkward style of dancing. One week later, Robson—a young congregant of Abrahão's church—approached me after a church service. As Robson had told me during one of my first church visits, he had been shot in the leg by a policeman during a gunfight a couple of months before my arrival. Grateful that he had survived, he decided to join Abrahão's church to be closer to God. Since I erroneously took for a fact the stark oppositions between people of God and people of the world—presented to me during the first couple of church services—I had assumed Robson would no longer attend bailes, let alone hang out with people of the local comando. However, when Robson approached me a week after my first baile, he told me smilingly, "You don't need to worry, Martijn, I have straightened it all out." Apparently Robson had been at the baile with the local leaders of the Comando Vermelho. They had seen me and had wondered what I was doing in the favela. At that moment Robson had intervened and told them I was "okay," indicating that I was not a threat. I thanked Robson and asked him how he reconciled going to the baile with his efforts to encounter God in light of the doctrines of the church. He replied that instead of breaking with his past abruptly—as many congregants urged—he was taking it slowly. Gradually he would make the changes that would bring him closer to God.

Though I cannot be sure, Robson's intervention at the baile probably made things much easier for me. Strikingly, Robson stopped frequenting the church after a couple of months, and after that I saw him mostly in the presence of comando members. The sequence of events has stayed with me over the years: learning that my presumption was wrong and finding out that Robson occupied a kind of liminal position between leaving the ranks of the CV and joining the church gave me insight into the complexity of life in Rio's favelas, the forces at work, and the differences between the worlds presented in church and daily life.

Pentecostal narratives and practices are appealing to many favela residents because they picture the world in black and white in an environment with many shades of gray, yet one in which choices can have severe consequences. Robson was attracted to the Pentecostal promise to start a new life as a born-again member after he was shot, yet he was not willing to break with the life he had lived. Though not all stories I noted during the years of research in Rio de Janeiro involved personal accounts of armed violence, there were plenty of other people who straddled the life they lived and the life they imagined. This book is also an attempt to understand these stories in the context of the complexities and hardships of favela life.

Overview of the Book

The first three chapters of this volume examine Pentecostal/evangelical ideas and practices in relation to the urban space, the mediated soundscape, and the visual representations of violence and conflict in the city. These chapters will provide the necessary background for the following three chapters, which will elucidate the concept "hypermediated conversion" by way of an analysis of the nexus of Pentecostalism, daily environment, and mass media.

Chapter 1 gives an account of the particular relations between the state and the favelas and describes the popularity of the Pentecostal churches. The churches present alternative identities in the face of social stigma but demand from their members strict moral codes of conduct. Whereas we should understand the practice and ideology of the churches as a form of governmentality, the members reproduce some of the stigmas and power structures they seek to counter. This chapter prepares the ground for a more elaborate description of self-discipline and transformation in chapter 4.

The second chapter demonstrates that the soundscape of the favelas reflects and constitutes the different social groups present. Pentecostal sound and music is deemed so important to the people who attend Pentecostal churches because the music signals a confirmation of their *status aparte* amid the other inhabitants. Evangélicos oppose their "godly" sound and music to the worldly sounds of their neighbors and try to transmit the Holy Spirit in order to persuade other inhabitants to follow their faith.

Chapter 3 shows how the Pentecostal discourse of peace and redemption is related to mass media that portray Rio de Janeiro as an evil city. Pentecostal churches employ various visual tropes to enforce a Pentecostal imagination of the *batalha espiritual* (spiritual battle), the metaphysical battle between God and the devil. Pentecostal interpretations of society are framed intertextually. Pentecostal movements seize and adopt images and narratives of urban violence and intertextually transform stark oppositions presented in mainstream media into earthly manifestations of a transcendental battle between holy and diabolic forces.

The fourth chapter describes the apparent homology between individual deliverance practices and the purification of the spaces in the favelas. Pentecostal churches are able to sustain the homology by convincing people that a spiritual battle between God and the devil is taking place. Many evangélicos are convinced that the violence of the *tráfico* (drug trafficking) is related to Afro-Brazilian religious practices. In response to the presence of the comandos in the favelas, adherents of the Pentecostal churches offer a discourse of peace and redemption. Possible conversion from "being of the world" to "being in the world" reproduces a *status aparte* of evangélicos in the favelas. Conversion narratives restructure the representation of the life path of adherents in such a way that a break is imagined between old and new identities. The theoretical exposé about conversion in this chapter clears the path for an understanding of conversion as hypermediated.

Chapter 5 deals with the listening practices of people in the favelas and their accounts of the importance of music/radio. This chapter shows that tuning into evangelical radio stations and playing gospel music is the outcome of the desire to be "in touch" with God and the result of the social pressures to maintain the *status aparte* in the favela. This implies that media technologies are an essential part of the process of conversion. Tuning in to evangelical radio stations or putting on gospel music should not be perceived as the outcome of the trajectory of conversion or the starting point. Listening to evangelical radio, CDs, cassette tapes, and MP3s can be seen as the performative assertion of an identity that is much less fixed than often presumed. People use these media to understand, feel, and demonstrate what the difference is between "being in the world" and "being of the world."

The sixth chapter focuses on the place of television and other visual media. For Pentecostal adherents in the favelas, television viewing involves a dynamic of attraction and rejection, related to Pentecostal bodily disciplines and practices. It shows that Pentecostalism and mass media should be defined not only by that which crentes say they watch, but also by that which they say they do not watch (and by their actual viewing habits). Many evangélicos regard telenovelas as diabolical, even when they often do watch them. The attraction to and rejection of images and narratives in telenovelas are related not only to the reading of the message but also to the physical and spiritual experiences of the devil and the Holy Spirit.

The conclusion will take us back to several of the public evangelical performances described in this book to summarize why the evangelical message resonates forcefully with the experiences of favela inhabitants and why they feel attracted to evangelical leaders. Pulling together a thread that runs throughout the book, the conclusion highlights that hypermediated conversion entails spiritual redirection in a life-world saturated by electronic media and characterized by startling inequalities.

The Manichean City
Socio-Spatial Segregation and Pentecostalism

Not long after I had settled in my small apartment in Visionário—a favela on the south side of Rio de Janeiro—I was informed that the renowned Pentecostal pastor Marcos Pereira da Silva of the Assembleia de Deus dos Últimos Dias (ADUD) would hold a service in one of the few public squares of the community.[1] The controversial pastor was widely known for his vigorous style of preaching inside Rio's prisons and at open-air Pentecostal events in favelas, and that night I made sure to be present at the start of the event.[2] For the occasion, church members had erected a huge screen onto which were projected images of the event as it was taking place, alternating with images of an ADUD church service held in an overpopulated prison in the city. The video of the prison showed hundreds of men behind bars listening to a gospel ballad performed by Elaine Martins and shouting in emotional response.

The service in the favela started with a loudly amplified music performance and was followed by the testimony of a well-dressed man. Clutching a microphone in his hand, he loudly spoke of his life before his conversion. He had dealt drugs and belonged to a criminal gang. "In those days I could not have climbed the favela of another comando because its members would surely have killed me. Today Jesus has given me the right to climb any favela and preach the Gospel, because the power of God manifests itself in the life of men. If you believe say *Glória Jesus*," he shouted. The public responded loudly, shouting *Glória Jesus* and hallelujah.

After him, another man climbed the stage to give his testimony. Dressed in suit and tie, he also delivered an emotional speech about his life of crime. At one point he shouted, "Yes, I was walking around with a gun. I was riding in my convertible. I told everybody I was from the Comando Vermelho [criminal gang], but the Comando Vermelho is of the devil. The devil created the Comando Vermelho. He also created the Terceiro Comando [criminal gang]. Was I crazy? Was I dumb? No, I was possessed by the devil. But then Jesus came and the devil lost his power and I was liberated by the glory of Jesus Christ." Approximately three hundred men and women present cheered enthusiastically.

When the second testimony had ended, Elaine Martins sang one of her songs on stage; when she had finished, we reached the apotheosis of the evening. Men and women were invited to come as close as possible to the stage to be delivered of evil by Pastor Marcos and his helpers. As Pastor Marcos preached vociferously, the Holy Spirit would eradicate all demonic presence. The men of the church stepped down from the stage and grabbed people by their heads, praying loudly and firmly. Various people fell down to the ground, touched by the Holy Spirit. The conclusion of the night was reserved for the pastor himself. To demonstrate his authority as powerful mediator of the Spirit, he delivered a young man from a distance of several meters. Simply at the gesture of his hand, the young man fell backward as if hit by powerful blow.

As my short descriptions of the cruzada evangelista and the public service of the ADUD demonstrate, Pentecostalism in Rio de Janeiro acquires its distinctive character in relation to the city's spatial distinctions and the different sociopolitical conditions that characterize its different areas. For preachers, singers, and audience, life in the favelas of the city serves as an important point of reference to signal the magnitude of the spiritual forces at work in the world. Having acquired a near-global reputation as places of criminality and violence, favelas are uniformly understood as exemplary loci of the spiritual battle between God and the devil.

In Brazil and beyond, favelas are known as dangerous areas ruled by criminal factions. Such a depiction can be categorized as one variation on a theme that has been haunting favelas for over a century. The favelas in Rio de Janeiro have been the focus of governments, politicians, and bureaucrats who identify these areas as the locus of problems that spill over to well-to-do areas in the city. Governments have mostly focused on the troubles favela inhabitants have allegedly caused, rather than the hardships they have suffered (see also Perlman 2010).

The advent of the FIFA World Cup of 2014 and the Summer Olympics of 2016 presented another example of such a perspective on the favelas of Rio de Janeiro. In 2008 the state government of Rio de Janeiro launched a number of security measures, among them the installment of so-called Police Pacification Units (Unidades de Polícia Pacificadora, or UPPs) in a number of favelas. As the name Pacification Unit signals, the UPP intervention programs have been developed mainly to regain state control over violence in favelas and principally consist of the installment of police brigades in the favelas at hand. A couple of UPP installments were even preceded by military invasions, indicating the exceptional gravity of the situation.[3]

Interestingly, the government discourse of "pacification" resembles, to a great extent, Pentecostal discourses of peace (*paz*), as both discourses are strongly reliant on the mediatized depictions of criminal gangs as hazardous forces that can and should be overcome. The Pentecostal churches, however, do not occupy favelas by means of spectacular police operations that seek to disarm gang members; rather, they frequently stage cruzadas that present the Holy Spirit as a powerful weapon against violence and insecurity. What to make of such overlaps? How can we understand the enmeshment of representations of urban violence, favela governance, and Pentecostal preaching?

This chapter provides the starting points of my analysis of the intersection of religion, popular media, and urban life and my argument that we can only understand the global spread of Pentecostalism when we see how it merges with the aesthetic and technology of popular media and with the structural life conditions and cultural backgrounds of the people involved. In Brazil, it is first and foremost in favelas where one finds the majority of Pentecostal and evangelical adherents (Cunha 2008). This chapter can do no justice to the many issues related to the genesis and history of favelas or the many factors influencing their development. Nevertheless, it is important to picture the cultural-political environment of Rio's favelas because the transformative spiritual projects that Pentecostal preachers present acquire their depth in relation to favela life and culture. In this chapter, I will give a general account of the favelas in Rio de Janeiro and describe some of the socio-spatial features of the city.

In 2000 it was estimated that 18.7 percent of the population of Rio de Janeiro lived in favelas. In 2010 this percentage had increased to 22 percent. Meanwhile the total population of the city grew from 5.86 million in 2000 to 6.32 million in 2010.[4] In general the people who live in favelas have significantly lower incomes than those living in other urban spaces. On top of that, favela inhabitants generally face social stigmatization, police brutality, deficient health care, and a dearth of decent infrastructure (Perlman 2010).

In this chapter, I will briefly introduce the two favelas where I did fieldwork between 2001 and 2011. This allows me to describe the complexities of law and order in the favelas and demonstrate that many of the favelas in Rio de Janeiro are governed by informal sovereignties (Hansen and Stepputat 2006) such as comandos or milícias. Detailed studies of the power relations in different favelas in Rio de Janeiro demonstrate that the emergence and permanence of local (gang) leaders depend on their personal connections with representatives of state institutions, leading to assemblages of legal and illegal forms of governance.[5] Such complex assemblages of governance produce life-worlds of ambivalence and threat. The success of certain Pentecostal denominations is strongly related to their embeddedness in these life-worlds.

This chapter will also briefly introduce the two Pentecostal denominations that have become very popular among favela residents: the Assembleia de Deus and the Igreja Universal. Though the organizational structure of these two churches differs and their doctrinal positions are not exactly the same, my research took favela life as a starting point of investigation instead of church life. My work has thus been inspired by what has generally become known as the "lived religion" approach (McGuire 2008; Orsi 1999), which highlights the workings of religion in practice.

Although I am very much aware that the two churches at the center of my analysis differ in many aspects, their differences do not feature prominently in this volume. Adherents of the two churches I interviewed during the course of my research in Rio de Janeiro shared several basic ideas about the spiritual battle between God and the devil and the way this battle manifests itself in the surroundings and media they encounter daily. As I try to demonstrate throughout this work, these two Pentecostal churches generally recognize the predicaments of favela residents and offer them meaningful paths in the face of the ambivalences described. The churches present residents with a set of practices and modes of behavior that help them break with lifestyles and predispositions deemed unhealthy and dangerous. Moreover, they generally provide people the means to dissociate themselves from criminal gangs without engaging in direct confrontation with those dangerous groups.

Pentecostalism in Context

As in other contexts where Pentecostalism has bloomed, several scholars who work on religion in Brazil have emphasized the relationship between religious organizations and social deprivation.[6] It is especially in areas of low income that Pentecostal churches have flourished,[7] and the literature on Brazilian Pentecostalism suggests that poverty and violence in the urban areas are important factors in its popularity. In almost all the studies on Brazilian Pentecostalism one can discern the legacy of Max Weber ([1958] 2003), whose emphasis on the entanglement between the Puritan ethic and the development of modern capitalism has greatly inspired scholars to examine the dialectical relation between Brazil's socioeconomic circumstances and Pentecostal movements.[8]

As will become clear in this volume, I generally follow a trend that pictures Pentecostalism as an appealing body of doctrines and practices for people who search for a better life. Throughout this work I foreground relations between Pentecostalism and the desire for health, security, wealth, and success. The spiritual testimonies I collected during my research are rife with success stories that highlight the improvement of life after the acceptance of Jesus as Savior. Moreover, many young male church members I interviewed explained that they joined a Pentecostal congregation because they had witnessed the dangers of involvement with criminal gangs, or with the cultural practices associated with them. Accepting Jesus and joining a congregation helped them dissociate from potentially harmful networks. As a number of scholars have described, in the context of favela life, the public display of belonging to a Pentecostal church is one of the few viable channels for young people to signal that they are not involved with drugs and violence.[9]

Nevertheless, we should be cautious to regard the success of Pentecostalism in light of its own spiritual promises. André Droogers and David Martin, each in his own way, emphasize the ambiguities between Pentecostalism and its social environment. Droogers (1998, 10–24) demonstrates that the models that present Pentecostalism as a positive answer to (1) explosive urbanization, (2) class differences, or (3) failed modernization are all met by powerful counterexamples that complicate neat explanations. Likewise, Martin (2002, 83) argues that Latin American Pentecostalism is characterized by a potent ambiguity in relation to economic ethics, politics, and the family. To this list we might add the ambiguity of violence, as it would be wrong to conclude that Pentecostalism necessarily counters the presence and actions of gangs. The opposition between gangs and members of Pentecostal churches exists on a symbolic level, but there have also surfaced more and more "evangelical bandits" (*bandidos evangélicos*), as Christina Vital da Cunha (2008), Cesar Pinheiro Teixeira (2011), and Edin S. Abumanssur (2015) have shown.

The aim of this work is to explain the attraction of Pentecostalism from the point of view of the inhabitants who live in the favelas of Rio de

Janeiro, without treating the religious practices as conflict-ridden answers to social and individual circumstances. At the individual and the structural level, Pentecostalism offers enabling and constraining practices, and it would therefore be wrong to assume that Pentecostalism presents primarily freedom or emancipation. Pentecostal movements in Rio de Janeiro tend to reproduce some of the anxieties they claim to eradicate. The experience of empowerment is strongly related to specific moral codes and bodily regimes people are expected to follow (see also Goldstein 2003, 223). Members of the Pentecostal churches should ideally refrain from adultery or drinking alcohol, and they are often supposed to stick to a pious or moderate dress code. In addition, adherents frequently demonize popular Afro-Brazilian religious practices and their advocates, suggesting that these form the roots of the violence that haunts popular urban areas (see also Montes 1998). Afro-Brazilian cultural-religious groups, which historically have experienced terrible persecution, thus encounter in Pentecostalism yet another aggressive adversary.[10] Last but not least, locally, people clash with their friends or family members when enthusiastic missionary work is understood as criticism or condemnation.

At a more fundamental level, Pentecostalism presents a body of ideas and practices that are attractive to people who feel that it offers them routes to change their own destiny in the face of limited control. However, to acquire a sense of control over self and environment, people must subject themselves to Pentecostal regimes, which include certain notions of "a self" that is eligible for transformation. Ruth Marshall (2009, 129) explains that the born-again project of conversion "involves a mode of subjectivation, in which the individual is both subjected to this regime and becomes the active subject of the new practices and modes of interpreting the world they involve." Following a similar line of thinking, Jeff Garmany (2010) has argued that it is best when we understand Pentecostal institutions in favelas as part of what Michel Foucault ([1978] 1991) described as governmentality.

Governmentality involves a broadened conceptualization of governance, extending its analysis to include representations of self and society that produce and limit possible action (Foucault 1991).[11] Drawing on Foucault's insights on discipline and knowledge, various authors have investigated how power operates on and through bodies (Butler [1990] 1999) and how power is maintained through the division and control of spaces and people's bodily dispositions within these spaces (Huxley 2008; Mitchell 1988). Power thus operates through institutions, agencies, and spatial "techniques" of domination (maps, censuses, surveillance) but also through self-discipline and self-styling. As people regulate their own behavior and bodily dispositions according to norms and values distributed throughout society, such everyday practices effectively reproduce authority. As we will see, Pentecostal practice in the favelas of Rio de Janeiro indeed should be regarded as a form of governmentality, yet one that is co-structured by other institutions beyond Pentecostal organizations. In chapters 4 through 6 I will describe in more detail how self-styling works and how power and embodiment are related. In the remainder of this chapter, I describe some of the structural conditions of favela life and the socio-spatial segregations that play a significant part in the reproduction of such conditions.

Rio de Janeiro

Throughout history, Rio de Janeiro has been the showcase of the Brazilian nation. After having been the capital of the Brazilian state under the rule of the Portuguese emperor from 1763 to 1808, the Portuguese crown fled Europe and chose Rio de Janeiro as the capital of the Lusitanian monarchy. After Brazilian independence in 1822 it remained the capital of the Brazilian monarchy, and from 1889 to 1960 Rio de Janeiro functioned as the capital of the republic of Brazil. In 1960 the city Brasília became the capital and the federal government was transferred to the new location (Enders 2002).

The metropolitan areas of Rio de Janeiro and São Paulo are the two largest in Brazil, and although their configurations of religion, urban life, and violence display similar characteristics, there is also much that is unique to each city. One of the main differences between the two cities is that many favelas in Rio de Janeiro are built on hilltops within the city, whereas the favelas of São Paulo can be found on its periphery. Three important sets of distinctions form part of the cityscape of the *cariocas*,[12] all of which relate to socio-spatial segregation in the city. The first is the distinction between the different *zonas* (zones) of the city. Zona Sul, the affluent southern zone of the city, is contrasted with the Zona Norte (the northern zone) and the Zona Oeste (the western zone). Most of the neighborhoods in Zona Sul comprise middle-class apartment buildings, while Zona Norte and Zona Oeste largely consist of industrial areas and large lower-class neighborhoods. The city center consists of a mixture of old "colonial" neighborhoods, apartment buildings, and business towers. The second important socio-spatial distinction is that between the municipality of Rio de Janeiro and the Baixada Fluminense—the conglomerate of municipalities (Duque de Caxias, São João de Meriti, etc.) adjacent to the city of Rio de Janeiro. The Baixada, as it is

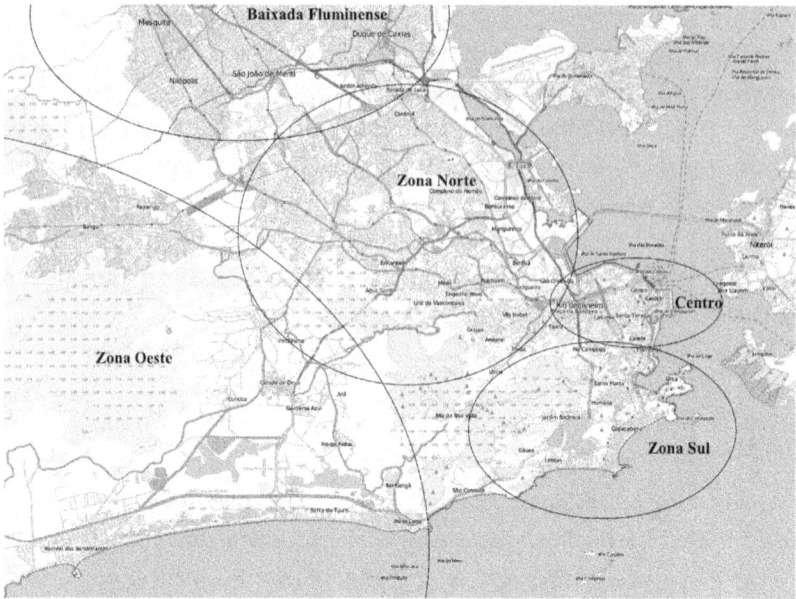

Map of the city of Rio de Janeiro. © OpenStreetMap contributors. Courtesy of
http://www.openstreetmap.org/.

commonly called, is often portrayed as a peripheral, unregulated region of
the city where poverty and violence prevail (Landim 2013). The third important social-geographical distinction is the dichotomy between the *morro*
(hill) and the *asfalto* (asphalt). While almost all of Rio's neighborhoods have
favelas, the favelas of Zona Sul are built on the city's hills and are therefore
commonly referred to as morros.

Inhabitants of the favela Visionário commonly used the distinction
between morro and asfalto to describe the difference between their place
of residence and the surrounding middle-class neighborhoods, and in this
volume I occasionally refer to "the morro" when I write about Visionário.
Some of the favelas *planas* (flat favelas) of the Zona Norte stretch out over
kilometers and from a distance resemble oceans of orange and gray, the
colors of the bricks and cement used to construct the majority of favela
houses. The morro-asfalto dichotomy entails much more than a geographical distinction between different areas in the city. It is also an indicator of
the socioeconomic differences in the city and the ways people narrate these
differences to one another. Such narratives are not devoid of expressions of
fear, disgust, and discrimination. In day-to-day talks of certain middle-class
cariocas, inhabitants of the favelas are regularly described as *marginais*

Figure 1 Several favelas surrounding high-rise buildings in Zona Norte, seen from the Igreja da Penha. Photo: author.

(marginals) or *bandidos* (bandits). This stigmatization of *favelados* (favela inhabitants) is tightly connected to the existence of comandos and milícias but also to historical segregations of class and ethnicity (see also Perlman 2010).

The Favelas of Rio de Janeiro

Throughout modern history favelas have consistently been described as backward places. The genesis of the favelas in Rio de Janeiro and their subsequent categorization as premodern conglomerates are strongly related to the growing population, on the one hand, and the ideas of the ruling classes on civilization, sickness, health, and hygiene, on the other (Enders 2002). Between 1838 and 1920 the population of Rio de Janeiro grew from 137,000 to 1,150,000 (159). From the birth of the republic in 1889 until 1906, the population of the city grew explosively, from 500,000 to 800,000, as a result of migration to the city. The abolition of the slave trade within Brazil in 1888 and the declining sugarcane industry in the north caused an influx of immigrants searching for work.

With all the newcomers, housing became a problem. Owing to the inflow of inhabitants, the city center became a crowded place where, according to

Figure 2 A favela in Zona Norte, Rio de Janeiro. Photo: author.

the elites, sickness and filth reigned. In the old city, many people lived in *cortiços*, large conglomerations of houses and shacks with a single opening to the street. With the advent of the republic in 1888 the *higienistas* convinced the authorities to evacuate the cortiços in Rio de Janeiro, and this likely forced a first wave of inhabitants to climb the hills of the city to build shacks there.

The occupation of the hills in Rio de Janeiro increased during the urban restructuring projects initiated by Mayor Francisco Pereira Passos in 1902. Filled with admiration for what had been done in Paris under Georges-Eugène Haussmann, Pereira Passos and his followers created wide avenues, streets, and parks, but in order to do that they demolished large parts of the center and drove away twenty thousand people from their barracks, cortiços, and pensions (Enders 2002, 214). As a result of the demolition and "restructuring" of the city in the years that followed, many poor inhabitants were driven from the center onto the hillsides, where they constructed shacks out of collected material from demolished buildings (211–27).

The vision of an urban utopia that fueled plans to remodel the city into a European-like metropolis went hand in hand with a "modernist" view on "dangerous classes," "traditional (post-slavery, African) lifestyles," and "backward" habits that stood in the way of this utopian vision and therefore had to be removed from sight. The authorities passed new laws that aimed to improve health and ensure fewer diseases but also forbade all kinds of folk and Afro-Brazilian religious practices that seemed "uncivilized" in the eyes of the elites.

Although the hills in the city were inhabited earlier, many authors place the birth of the first favela in 1897, when soldiers returned from a military campaign in Canudos. Those veterans who could not find a place to live were authorized to build their houses on the Morro da Providência. When they occupied this hill in the city center, they baptized it Morro da Favela. After the baptism, other hill settlements in the city regularly received the name *favela* (Nunes 1976; Perlman 1977; Enders 2002).[13] According to Janice Perlman, *favela* became the generic term for many types of irregular settlements in the 1920s.

According to Guida Nunes (1976), the authorities did not pay much attention to the favelas built on the morros of Rio de Janeiro until 1940. After that, they gradually became identified as a social problem that had to be solved. Continuing migration to the city led to an increasing number of favelas.[14] According to Licia de Prado Valladares (1978), between 1945 and 1965 governmental urban planning strategies oscillated between eliminating the favelas and removing the population to Parques Proletários (social housing projects) and "urbanizing" them—improving their standards to secure better housing and health conditions. Between 1960 and 1970 many favelas were scheduled to be "removed," and this fate did indeed befall many of them. New avenues and urban restructuring programs necessitated the removal of existing favelas yet also freed up room for new ones. Valladares (1978) has also pointed out the relationship between the real estate speculation in the city and the urge to remove the favelas. Some areas in the city became more expensive as a result of the expansion outward and new connections between remote areas. Especially in certain locations in Zona Sul, real estate corporations were eager to build luxurious apartments (Gay 1994), though they did so with limited success.

Fieldwork in Visionário and Roda do Vento

The fieldwork on which this volume rests was mainly done in two favelas in Rio de Janeiro, one located in Zona Sul and one in Zona Norte. The majority of the material in this volume stems from my first period of fieldwork in Visionário between 2001 and 2003. During this time, I lived in the favela for nine months. Living in Visionário gave me unique insight into the day-to-day realities of the people (many of whom became close friends), including the presence and dynamics of media and religion. Between 2003 and 2009, I regularly returned to Rio de Janeiro and to Visionário for short research trips. In 2011 I focused on the favela Roda do Vento, in Zona Norte, to deepen my understanding of the relations among religion, media, and favela life. Though I did not live there as I did in Visionário, during the three months of research I acquired a good sense of the similarities and differences between the two favelas, especially with respect to the issues at hand in this volume. In 2014 and 2016, during my last periods of fieldwork in Rio de Janeiro for this book, I took a somewhat wider perspective and did research in other neighborhoods and favelas in Rio de Janeiro to analyze the presence of Pentecostal churches and events throughout the city.

During the writing of this book, both of the favelas that feature prominently here acquired a UPP. This will probably change some of the dynamics that I discuss in this volume. Nevertheless, it remains to be seen whether the permanent presence of special police forces in the favelas will continue and in what form. Time will tell whether years of severe misconduct of police forces vis-à-vis favela populations can be forgotten and forgiven and a minimal sense of trust in the police restored.

At first sight Visionário appears to be a labyrinth. The favela resembles a beehive of narrow alleys and small stairs leading to houses built close to or on top of one another. Many inhabitants have found creative ways of building their houses of brick and cement against the hillsides, not to mention those who have built their own apartment buildings of four to five levels. In general, the architectural differences between the asfalto and the morro are considerable. The tall buildings, the straight avenues, and the sidewalks of the asfalto contrast with the small self-made houses and narrow maze-like paths of the favela. Visionário borders another favela, located on an adjacent hill, and the two appear to be seamlessly connected. Nevertheless, the two communities are divided by one paved road commonly described as the *estrada* (street). Most people of both favelas look out over the rooftops of many of the buildings of the asfalto down below, and many inhabitants treasure their view enormously.

According to the municipal registry of favelas in Rio de Janeiro, the first inhabitants of Visionário arrived early in the twentieth century, and the first settlements of wooden shacks materialized in the 1930s.[15] The numbers of inhabitants counted or estimated around 1980 range between approximately 10,500 and 13,500. According to several local leaders, the number of inhabitants of the favela during my research was between 17,000 and 20,000.

The borders between the two favelas are almost unobservable, but those between the favelas and the asfalto are clearly demarcated. Moreover, during the time of my research there were a limited number of passageways to and from Visionário: three situated on the estrada, one accessible from a street that passes below the favela and winds down to the asfalto, and one accessible from the street below, comprising a steep flight of stairs. All of these entrances were actively guarded by the police or by members of the criminal gang.

According to the inhabitants, Visionário had transformed significantly during the last decades of the past millennium. While many people lived in wooden barracks up until the 1970s, the number of houses made of brick and cement grew considerably, and little by little the favela acquired running water, rudimentary sewers, and electricity. This does not mean that all infrastructure work is completed or that everything runs smoothly. Nevertheless, many in the favela told me how thrilled they were when they could connect their houses to the water distribution network so they could fill their own *caixa de água* (reservoir) regularly and have running water in their houses.

Many women in the favela work as *empregadas domésticas* (housemaids) for middle-class families in the surrounding neighborhoods, and many men work there in apartment buildings as *porteiros* (doormen). Young people of the favela often find work as employees in the stores or supermarkets on the asfalto, and many people participate in the informal economy at the street level, working as *camelôs* (street vendors), for instance, or at a construction company. Quite a few people have a business in the favela itself, as there are many small grocery stores and bars.

Since the 1980s Visionário has been the terrain of criminal comandos also known as *traficantes* (drug traffickers), who use the favela as a bastion and as a drug distribution center for consumers from the morro and the asfalto. Located on a hill, the favela is a strategic position for these organized gangs to sell cocaine and marijuana to the inhabitants and to people from neighborhoods in Zona Sul. Moreover, given its limited entrances and maze-like architecture, the morro is well defendable against competing criminal gangs and the police.

The presence of the comandos has had an enormous impact on all of the people and social institutions in Visionário. In the mid-1990s there were several periods of armed confrontation between traficantes when different gangs controlled Visionário and the neighboring favela. Several people told me that at the height of the armed conflicts, they had to sleep on the floor or under their beds to reduce the chances of being hit by a *bala perdida* (stray bullet). Ordinary inhabitants were not allowed to pass from one favela to the other. One of the stories several people told me was that one *chefe* (gang leader) was so brutal that he had decapitated one of his opponents and publicly displayed the head as he walked around Visionário.

The hostilities up the hill stopped when one of the gangs conquered the territory of the other and the two neighboring favelas fell under the rule of one comando. Nevertheless, many inhabitants who were born and raised in Visionário claimed that they did not like to go to the other community. They knew far fewer people there, were not familiar with the *meninos* (boys) of the tráfico on the other side, and did not know the way in the labyrinth of alleys. When I lived in Visionário, some of my friends advised me not to walk around in the other favela too often because, according to them, the traficantes there did not know me and would certainly stop and question me. What I understood from these conversations was that people in both communities felt relatively safe in their direct environment among others, because they knew what to pay attention to, which spots to avoid, and when to stay inside.

In contrast to Visionário, Roda do Vento is built on flat terrain. During the time of my research it was estimated to house about fifteen thousand inhabitants. It is a small part of a larger complex of favelas with seemingly few internal borders. Various highways that mark its boundaries surround the complex. The architecture of Roda do Vento is strikingly different from Visionário, as its streets largely follow a grid pattern and there is more space between the different blocks of brick and concrete houses. The complex of which Roda do Vento is a part appears to be a village by itself. It has a number of broad streets with many shops, bars, and restaurants, along with areas that primarily feature more houses and fewer stores.

Not unlike Visionário, Roda do Vento has witnessed many urban changes, especially between 1940 and 1960, when many large-scale construction projects in the vicinity of the complex drew workers and drove people out of other areas nearby. Over the course of this period, different planned housing projects were initiated alongside the spontaneous, bottom-up construction works of inhabitants, resulting in an urban area that displays various forms in eclectic combination.

Despite often being described as one favela, at the time of my research Roda do Vento suffered from severe confrontations between different comandos that occupied different favelas inside the complex. During my fieldwork, friends and contacts often advised me to be very cautious when entering the favela, as certain streets that mark the boundaries between the favelas could be the terrain of gunfights between the comandos.

Anyone who visits Rio de Janeiro will be warned of the dangers, and anyone who lives there is aware of them. The statistics on crime and violence in Rio de Janeiro are terrifying. According to the work of Alba Zaluar (1998), the index of homicides grew alarmingly during the 1980s. The index went up from 23 homicides in a population of 100,000 in 1982 to 63.03 homicides in a population of 100,000 in 1990. In a 2003 study, Luke Dowdney compared the homicides committed with firearms in different urban regions worldwide. The index of 1999 showed that Rio de Janeiro suffered 41.5 homicides by firearms in a population of 100,000, while New York counted 5.6 and Washington, D.C., 10.2 in a population of 100,000 (Dowdney 2003, 96). Both Dowdney and Waiselfisz (2004) confirm that organized crime has greatly affected young people in the urban areas of Brazil. According to UNESCO, the index of homicides among young people (aged fifteen to twenty-four) in Brazil rose from 30 in a population of 100,000 in 1980 to 54.4 in 2002 (Waiselfisz 2004).

In a more detailed study of the specific places where homicide occurs in Rio de Janeiro, Christovam Barcellos and Alba Zaluar (2014) note that in 2009 the overall rate of homicide in Rio de Janeiro was 52 per 100,000 inhabitants, but that these murders occurred especially at the edges of favelas controlled by comandos. Cross-checking the locations of homicide with information about favela occupation by comandos, they noted that inside favelas, homicide rates ranged from 22 to 44 per 100,000 inhabitants, but that one hundred meters away from the borders of favelas homicide rates ranged from 48 to 129 per 100,000 inhabitants (Barcellos and Zaluar 2014, 97). This confirms the general experience that murders occur as a result of confrontations at the edges of favela territory.

The armed violence of Rio de Janeiro is primarily related to the complex territorial struggles between different criminal gangs and between gangs and different kinds of police forces. Rio de Janeiro has three large *facções* (factions) of traficantes, organizations that are structured along hierarchies with ties to other international criminal organizations in Brazil, Bolivia, and Colombia. The factions regularly engage in armed confrontation, attempting to take over one another's territories. The names of the facções are Comando Vermelho (CV), Terceiro Comando (TC), and Amigos dos Amigos (AA). Gang members, regular favela inhabitants, and the press commonly use these names and initials in Rio de Janeiro. It is frequently assumed that the factions are well-structured organizations. However, as Marcus Alvito (2001, 83), has argued, "We can say that in reality, CV and TC, contrary to what their names indicate, do not exist as 'commandos' with a single orga-nization, under central control. What exists, in reality, is only a conjunction of alliances established by the local *chefe* of the tráfico with other *chefes* who on their part have particular allies and enemies, and so on" (see also Leeds 1996, 56).

Though comandos continue to control many areas in the city, in the past few years off-duty police officers, firefighters, and other state agents have begun to form paramilitary groups to "recapture" favelas from the heavily armed traficantes. Initially, it seemed as if these milícias would take on many functions that the state had previously neglected, and some understood their takeover as a positive development. However, it soon became apparent that milícias were extorting local residents and businesses, and that they often used lethal violence against their opponents (Mesquita 2008; Zaluar and Conceição 2007). Milícias became active predominantly in the western part of the city. One of the milícias that became most famous goes by the name Liga da Justiça (or Justice League).

Organized crime grew considerably when cocaine became big business in Rio de Janeiro. During the military regime that took control in 1964 and lasted until 1984, political prisoners and bank robbers were incarcerated together in the prison of Ilha Grande near Rio de Janeiro. Together they formed the Falange Vermelho, a new type of criminal organization with a much more coherent internal structure.[16] In the late 1970s, when cocaine appeared as a lucrative means for trade, the Falange Vermelho, by then called Comando Vermelho, made cocaine traffic its main enterprise. Initially Brazil was used primarily to ship cocaine from Latin America to Europe and the United States. Starting in the 1980s, a domestic market was also supplied.

Although marijuana was sold in the favelas before cocaine, the lucra-tive cocaine business influenced community life to a much greater extent.[17] Favelas became places where large quantities of drugs arrived to be sold to individual consumers.[18] In contrast to cities around the world where the traffic of drugs is concealed from sight, the tráfico in the favelas takes place between the densely built houses and alleys in the favela and is therefore visible to the inhabitants. All the buyer has to do is climb the morro, enter the favela, and go to the spot where the drugs are sold, commonly referred to as the *boca de fumo* (mouth of smoke). These bocas de fumo are generally guarded by armed men who protect the selling points against other gangs that seek to take them over by force.

Most of the people involved in the drug gangs are young men. Depending on their rank in the hierarchy of the *movimento* (the movement), as inhabitants also tend to call the comandos, they can be armed or unarmed. There are those who defend the favelas against attacks (*soldados* or *seguranças*), but many are doing other kinds of work. Some youngsters look out for possible danger (*olheiros*, or lookouts); others transport smaller quantities of drugs both inside and outside the favela (*aviões*, or airplanes). There are young men who manage the drug selling points (*gerentes*, or managers), and there is the boss (*dono*) who is in charge of the local organization.

Apart from the violent confrontations, there are several other consequences of the presence of the comandos in the favelas of Rio de Janeiro. Crime is not limited to drug-related incidents; the trade in weapons has also increased substantially (Leeds 1996). Furthermore, the possession of arms has also made robbery, carjacking, and other kinds of criminal activities in adjacent neighborhoods much more violent.

Local political organizations, such as the *associação de moradores* (residents' association), are pressured to cooperate with a comando or milícia or are told not to interfere with their business. Inhabitants of the favelas are threatened in order to keep them from hindering gang members in their work. In the absence of other institutions that maintain law and order, the comandos rule over the favela inhabitants. Unauthorized violence, robbery, or other crimes committed by inhabitants can be severely punished by the *dono* or local *gerente*, who act as despotic rulers. Living in a favela can therefore be relatively safe as long as one does not obstruct the gangs. Those who willfully participate in the gangs run the risk of falling victim to violence.

Lisete, a sixteen-year-old girl, put it like this: "In the morro only those die who deserve to." While I understood what she meant—that it was less dangerous to live in the favela than often assumed, as long as one avoided relations with traficantes—strictly speaking, this was not true. The effects of the presence of gangs in the favelas are disturbing, as are those of the armed (special) police interventions. During my research I was shocked to discover that among the people who were born and raised in Visionário, there was hardly one family that did not experience the effects of gang-related violence. For example, one of my friends, a young painter, casually showed me the scars of the bullet that went through his shoulder when he passed the boca de fumo as a gunfight broke out.

Extralegal Governance

The favelas of Rio de Janeiro are widely known for the violence that takes place as a result of the struggles between different armed actors that attempt to control urban territories. Especially in the 1990s and the beginning of the millennium, comandos were portrayed as the major threat to urban society. During my research, news programs and newspapers often referred to the gangs that controlled territories in the city as *o poder paralelo* (the parallel power), echoing scientific literature on the subject (Leeds 1996). The term "parallel power" indicates the existence of parallel systems of power that operate in competition with one another. Before elaborating on the accuracy of this concept and my critique of it, let me briefly describe how, in general, comandos exercise the rule of law in many of Rio de Janeiro's favelas.

Comandos that rule favelas maintain several *leis* (laws). These laws are not embedded in a judicial system in which inhabitants acquire clearly defined "rights." However, the analogy is valid to the extent that comandos govern favelas on the basis of a set of loosely defined rules and expectations. The most important rules for the inhabitants are as follows:

(1) One should not interfere in affairs of the traficantes, and they will not interfere in yours. This seems quite impossible in a place where everyone lives so close to one another, but my experience is that avoiding contact works most of the time. A routine of disregard is common to most inhabitants. It is very important to know what one should not pay explicit attention to. Most inhabitants I met knew perfectly well how not to pay attention to the activities of the boys involved in the gangs and to behave as if they were not there. There were some notable exceptions to this common disregard. Community leaders, pastors, and preachers occasionally approached the boys while doing their business. However, they hardly ever opposed their activities directly. The boys involved in the movimento mostly did not talk with the other inhabitants.

(2) One should not speak about what one knows about the traficantes. This is otherwise described as the law of silence *(lei do silêncio)* (Oliveira and Carvalho 1993). In practice this means that one is forbidden to talk with the police. Anyone who speaks with the police might be suspected of being a snitch, and that designation might compromise one's well-being. It might lead to a beating or to expulsion from the favela. Expulsion means that you are ordered to leave the favela and search for another place to live. Staying might lead to another beating and eventually even death.

During the ten months I lived in Visionário I did not see one inhabitant talking to the police officers at their post down the hill. In fact, I learned by looking at the inhabitants that one should ignore the police completely, not pay any attention to their actions, and pretend they are not there. Given the fact that one police post was located on a path right at the entrance of Visionário and police officers often sat outside, one must appreciate the social craft of the favela residents. Inhabitants skillfully ignored the police and the traficantes, behaving as if they did not exist, all the while knowing that the relative peace in the favela was fragile.

(3) Inhabitants have to be protected unless they jeopardize the business of the gangs. In practice this means that gangs act as providers of law and order in many of the favelas in Rio de Janeiro. Criminal behavior of inhabitants vis-à-vis other inhabitants within the favela can be severely punished by the local gang. This leads to the somewhat peculiar situation that one who lives in a favela dominated by a gang does not need to fear much robbery or theft in one's own neighborhood in comparison to the risks of living on the asfalto.

During my research in Rio de Janeiro, I heard different reasons as to why gangs act as sheriffs. It was said that comandos that govern the favelas not only dominate for their own interests, but they also foster good intentions regarding the well-being of the communities they govern. Many bandidos are born and raised in favelas themselves, and looking out for the community at large was described as a responsibility that comes with the "job." This explanation is connected to a common idea among people in Rio de Janeiro that gang leaders also function as local strongmen who take care of the community—for instance, by donating money to organizations in the morros or lending or giving people money in times of need. Some have described this as a "parallel welfare system" (see Leeds 1996). I do not know if this ever was really the case in Visionário. During my research I heard of no such structural help, and in her grand study of favela life in Rio de Janeiro, Janice Perlman (2010) notes that local chapters of the comandos generally rule by instilling fear rather than by providing care.

Another explanation is that comandos seek to secure a minimum degree of legitimacy among the inhabitants to continue their lucrative businesses in these neighborhoods. The majority of the population of the favelas mistrust the police, especially members of the *polícia militar* (military police), because of their involvement with organized crime and because of the extralegal violence they exercise. Some police officers are involved in kidnapping and extortion, and they regularly attempt to gain a portion of the profits from the drug trade by force.[19]

Having to choose between the police and the gangs, it is not uncommon that inhabitants choose the latter. The police treat all inhabitants as possible criminals and show little to no respect to anyone in the favelas.[20] When police officers continue to invade favelas the way they have generally done in the past, it is probable that inhabitants will continue to feel more solidarity with traficantes who leave them be than with police officers who harass and threaten them.[21]

From Parallel Powers to Ghostly Sovereignty

As my own experiences and the literature on comandos, milícias, and police business in Rio de Janeiro suggest, it is conceptually unwise to refer to gang governance as parallel power. As the military operations in favelas preceding the 2014 FIFA World Cup and 2016 Summer Olympics demonstrate, modes of reasoning about the rights of citizen-subjects, security, and justice are strongly related to attempts to "fix" common perceptions of certain urban areas as spaces that escape the state's rule of law. During and after the military operations that preceded the installment of UPPs in favelas in Rio de Janeiro, representatives of the state regularly claimed that the state had reconquered territories dominated by comandos. We should be highly critical of such a description, for it leaves intact a Manichean perspective on the city. As we will see, this perspective might seem to do justice to the violent confrontations, but in fact it helps to reproduce social and spatial segregation.

During fieldwork in Rio in February and March 2014, I was once again struck by the unequal representation and appraisal of state violence in relation to certain areas of the city. As many people have described, a common dichotomy in discourse about favela residents is the distinction between bandido and *trabalhador* (Zaluar 1985). A bandido is the common denomination of someone who is part of a criminal gang. Trabalhador literally translates as "worker," and besides denoting the fact that someone earns his money "honestly," as many people say, it also generally indicates that someone takes care of his family, is lawful, and shows others respect.[22]

In many cases, when police officers willfully or accidentally kill a favela resident, the first question that emerges in popular media is whether the deceased was a bandido or a trabalhador. It is striking how this language, disseminated by news media, remains part of the everyday discourse of favela residents. In the summer of 2014, O Globo, one of the most influential newspapers in Brazil, notified its readers about a young man who was killed by a policeman in a favela in Zona Sul. After the young man was shot, police claimed that he was "involved" with a criminal gang and that they found a gun on him—with which he allegedly fired at law enforcement. In response to these claims, O Globo quoted the widow of the young man, who stated, "It is a lie. He does not have a criminal past; he did not even drink [alcohol]. He was a trabalhador. Loved and known by the community because of his one addiction: Botafogo [a soccer club], his passion for soccer. I want them to prove he was holding that gun."[23] Strikingly, she reproduced a discourse that allows her to claim rights and justice—her man was a worker—and thus her statement could be understood as a powerful demand to be treated equally, as other citizens in other areas in the city, yet it leaves intact a perverse notion that firing at and killing the young man should be regarded differently if indeed he was a bandido.

Research coordinated by Michel Misse from the Federal University of Rio de Janeiro (Misse et al. 2013) shows that according to the official sta-tistics of the state of Rio de Janeiro, between 2001 and 2011, more than ten thousand homicides committed by the police were registered as *autos de resistência*: killings deemed to be in self-defense, for instance, as a result of a gunfight in a favela. According to Misse and his team, this categorization of a type of homicide by state functionaries when dealing with an alleged bandido often means that there will be no investigation into the possibly criminal actions, motivations, or involvement of the victim, effectively turning him or her into someone who can be killed with impunity. Adopting Agamben's (1998) notion of *homo sacer*, Misse and his colleagues thus analyze how the juridical category of auto de resistência in practice enforces the separation of certain classes of the population from the rest, thereby seizing their rights to be protected by the law. Worse, police officers not only think they are justi-fied in killing these alleged bandidos but also feel it is their moral obligation to do so (Misse et al. 2013, 131). Sadly, a repeated saying in certain circles in Rio de Janeiro is *bandido bom é bandido morto* (a good bandit is a dead bandit).

This complex of legalized actions and collective representations has remained in place for quite a long time and perpetuates a tragic dynamic. In her seminal essay "Cocaine and Parallel Polities in the Brazilian Urban Periphery," Elizabeth Leeds (1996) argued that the state of Rio de Janeiro, by way of its two police forces, was involved in the tragic undermining of legiti-mate security in the favelas. According to Leeds, the use of excessive illegal violence against favela inhabitants leads to perpetual distrust of the police and the possibility for other armed actors—drug gangs—to maintain just enough support to make their presence acceptable. Tragically, the presence of armed comandos is presented as legitimizing violent state operations against such gangs, in the name of the restoration of order, often resulting in shootouts between gangs and the police.

While Leeds's essay still stands as an important text, certain conceptualizations she proposes risk reproducing some of the mechanisms she describes. Her notion of parallel powers that emerge in the spaces left empty by protective state structures—often used by other scholars and news media—upholds the idea that the absence and presence of state and other armed actors alternate, while effectively the state is present in its juridical form even though its functionaries may have difficulty accessing the terrains in question. Leeds (1996, 77–78) writes, "The Brazilian state has used the presence of drug groups as an excuse for repressive tactics that, during this period of redemocratization, can be legitimized only if certain activities are defined as aberrant, anti-social, and requiring protection . . . Parallel power structures thus have arisen in a space left empty by the lack of truly protective state structures. In Rio, the state is absent in fundamental ways but remains ready to intervene to take advantage of situations arising out of that vacuum." This quotation lays bare a fundamental problem with regard to the notion of parallel powers. Though, indeed, one might say that the state is de facto not the only organized armed actor governing the city, the nature of the power wielded by the state is of a quite different order than that of the comandos. This difference is often described in terms of that between sovereignty and governmentality (Foucault 1991). Whereas the former is generally described as establishing order over a given territory (often by means of force), the latter is described as a mode of governing its population by means of knowledge and practices beyond (the threat of) force.

The two modes of power are often placed in sequential order—governmentality coming after sovereignty—but it is this ordering that Giorgio Agamben (1998, 2005) resists in his writings. He points out that at the heart of contemporary politics we find sovereign power at work, establishing—by means of the juridical apparatus, among others—the differences between those who are to be protected and those who can be killed with impunity.

In her discussion of the work of Michel Foucault and Giorgio Agamben, Judith Butler (2004) analyzes the interplay of these two modes of power to understand a few things: first, how certain groups or classes of people are portrayed and conceived as highly threatening to the social order, and also how it is possible that killing or injuring these people is constituted as acceptable. According to Butler, this process can only be understood when we recognize that state functionaries are part of the apparatus of governmentality *and* wield sovereign power: "Their decision, the power they wield to 'deem' someone dangerous and constitute them effectively as such, is a sovereign power, a ghostly and forceful resurgence of sovereignty in the midst of governmentality" (59).

In many ways Butler's conceptualization of the interplay between sovereignty and governmentality applies to Rio de Janeiro, where police officers are part of an apparatus that constitutes certain people as denizens, making it possible to kill or injure them in the name of reestablishing order. Conceptualizing comandos and the state as parallel powers and as similar types of violent actors that alternately (or in hybrid form) occupy spaces is unwise, for it masks the ghostly juridical-governmental presence of the state. Moreover, describing these spaces as terrains that are either occupied by one or the other power often legitimates exceptional violence in favelas that are supposedly reconquered by the state, while in effect the state never truly left.

Religion in Visionário and Roda do Vento

As I briefly sketched, Pentecostal churches have presented themselves as powerful answers to favela hardship in relation to other religious practices that are often reconceptualized as sources of misery and misfortune. Instead of giving the reader an overview of all the different religious traditions and denominations that are popular in Rio de Janeiro, I will briefly describe the institutions I encountered in the two favelas where I worked, so as to give the reader a sense of the religious terrain and to make clear that Pentecostalism is by no means the only religious movement. One should keep in mind that collaborations between different religious organizations extend beyond particular favelas and in fact form elaborate urban circuits of members, practitioners, preachers, and musicians who move throughout the city.

At the time of my research in Visionário there was one Roman Catholic parish in service, one Baptist church, four congregations of the Assembleia de Deus, and one of the Deus é Amor. The Roman Catholic parish, located on top of the morro, had been there since the 1960s. In the late 1970s a group of inhabitants active in the Catholic Church, the Grupo de Trabalho da Igreja, rebuilt the church and erected one of the first large edifices of bricks and concrete instead of wood. The construction of the church and the crèche attached to it marked the beginning of the transformation of the entire area from wood into brick, as the inhabitants felt more secure about investing in

43

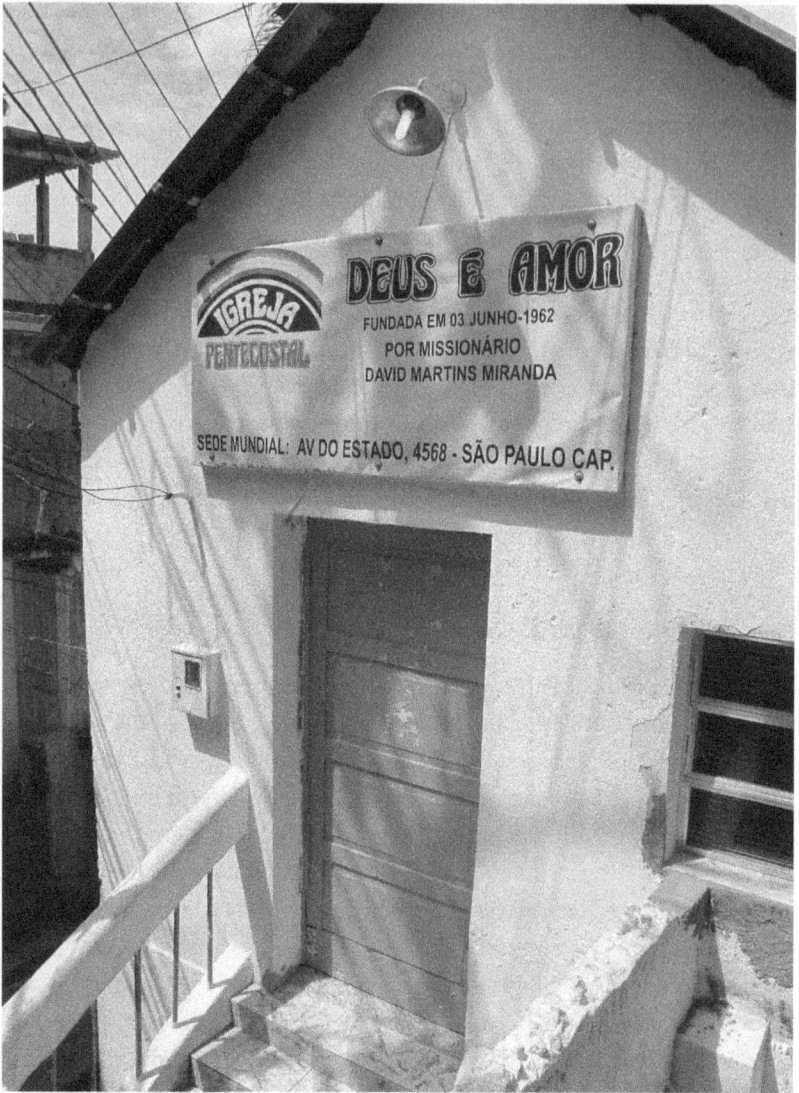

Figure 3 A Deus é Amor Pentecostal church in a Zona Sul favela. Photo: author.

their houses.[24] Though many people I encountered identified themselves as Catholic, the parish did not hold mass regularly.

The non-Catholic churches in Visionário were all smaller than that of the parish but regularly attracted many inhabitants. Of the Pentecostal churches in the favela, the congregations of the Assembleia de Deus appeared to have the highest number of participants. The Assembleia de Deus, founded in 1911, is often portrayed as an "old," somewhat conservative Pentecostal denomination, supposedly less willing to adapt to many of the features of the late-modern consumption society of Brazil. However, the Assembleia de Deus is the Pentecostal denomination that has the most members among all Pentecostal denominations in Brazil, and the church has grown much in the past decades. Confirming this image, my interviews with leaders of the Assembleia de Deus in the favela showed that many of the local Assembleia de Deus congregations were created between 1985 and the present. Two of the congregations of Assembleia de Deus were part of a wider network of churches that belonged to a large Assembleia de Deus church located on the asfalto, not very far from Visionário. The two other churches of the Assembleia de Deus belonged to other networks.

Movements between congregations and denominations are quite common. Apart from the people who told me they had attended one congregation before they switched to another, I also found that the pastors of two of the congregations of the Assembleia de Deus had begun their careers in the largest Assembleia de Deus in the favela. They left this congregation and started their own, taking some members along with them. These attempts to build new churches and to expand existing networks show that some pastors might well be described as religious entrepreneurs who seek to create and enlarge churches by attracting a clientele.

Apart from the Pentecostal churches located in the morro itself, there were many larger Pentecostal churches near the morro that also drew people from the favela. Most popular were the congregations of the Igreja Universal on the asfalto, within walking distance of the morro. In general, the church-planting strategy of the Igreja Universal stands in contrast to that of the Assembleia de Deus, as the former seeks to build mega-churches at points in the city that are easily reachable by public transport and highly visible in the cityscape (Gomes 2009). The strategy of the latter is to create modest temples in the residential areas of its followers, using materials similar to those used by the inhabitants (see also Fajardo 2015). Walking down from Visionário I invariably met some of the uniformed *obreiros*[25] of the Igreja Universal on their way to church; the majority of the people who attended the Igreja Universal seemed to live in the favelas nearby, as I regularly witnessed people returning to the favela after a church service.[26]

In Visionário there was only one non-Pentecostal Protestant congregation, a Baptist church. On a number of evangelical occasions, Pentecostal leaders presented people from the Baptist church as fellow evangélicos. However, in my discussions with the members of the Baptist church, they underlined the distinctions between them and the people of the Pentecostal churches. In particular, the presence of the devil in Pentecostal doctrine and practice was considered at odds with their beliefs.

With regard to the Afro-Brazilian religious practices of Candomblé and Umbanda, it is striking that, although the practice of Candomblé in Visionário was mentioned many times during my research, it was barely present publicly, and I hardly witnessed its practice. When it was mentioned, it was mostly in the negative sense and referred to as *macumba*, which for the evangélicos also often entailed the practice of Umbanda, another strand of Afro-Brazilian religion centered on spirit possession.[27] Within these religious traditions macumba is often associated with black magic, but in Rio de Janeiro macumba was originally the name given to the local variant of what later generally became known as Candomblé (Prandi 1996). Evangélicos in Visionário generally used the term *macumba* when they talked about Afro-Brazilian religious practices. According to the inhabitants, there had always been a *terreiro* (shrine) of macumba in the favela until the last *mãe de santo*[28] died three years before my research began. The fact that since then no new *terreiro de Candomblé* was established in the morro, or at least not a public one, is significant. It indicates the place these practices have attained in Visionário in relation to other religious institutes and other social processes. Many people from Pentecostal churches said to me that they had "won the battle" and successfully evangelized the favela so that no new mãe de santo came after the last one died. The disappearance of the terreiro fits in well with this evangelization narrative and the conversion testimonies of many people in Visionário. Many people from Pentecostal churches explained to me that they had practiced macumba in the past, "before they had learned that there is only one real God," after which macumba became something purely diabolical for them.

On the one hand, the disappearance of the terreiro runs more or less parallel to the growing popularity of Pentecostalism in the favelas of Rio de Janeiro, public exorcisms performed by Pentecostal pastors, and the mass mediatization of the demon hunt by the Igreja Universal. On the other hand, when I asked people why I did not encounter Candomblé practices, some said people were performing these secretly. This evokes images of the past, when Candomblé was forbidden but practiced nonetheless. Furthermore, the mediatization of some of the practices identified as macumba by the Igreja Universal paradoxically reproduces knowledge of these practices to a wide audience (see also Montes 1998) and indicates that it is still very popular among cariocas. In other words, I tried to remain critical of the victorious words of the evangélicos when they claimed it had "disappeared."

My research in Roda do Vento centered on one congregation of the Assembleia de Deus, but throughout the whole complex, of which Roda do Vento is part, there are many other religious institutions that are meaningful to residents. The complex features several larger congregations of the Assembleia de Deus, a congregation of the Baptist church, several Roman Catholic parishes, and a temple of the Igreja Universal, to name but a few.

While most *cultos* (services) are held in churches, many Pentecostal cultos, *vigílias* (nightly devotions), *orações* (prayers), and other types of meetings take place in people's houses or in the public squares of favelas. Some of these meetings are directly related to a particular denomination, but others are organized independently or in collaboration with people from other denominations. This is not to say that the Pentecostal church buildings are not considered important places of worship. Most inhabitants recognize them as powerful institutions, whether they like them or not. However, Pentecostal and other Christian practices continuously transgress these concrete church buildings and their denominational boundaries.

Apart from the popular religious institutions, many people performed different kinds of religious practices that I do not describe here. Among them are those practices related to *espiritismo*, according to the teachings of Allan Kardec. This kind of espiritismo is based on the notion of reincarnation and often works with persons who function as mediums who transmit messages from the spirits. *Kardecismo*, as these practices are also often called, is very popular in Brazil. Besides espiritismo, there are those practices that are not easy to grasp, simply because they were not represented by one or another institution or because they escape systematic labeling. For many people, religious signs and symbols that cut across institutional boundaries are points of reference of religious practices outside the institutional context. The Bible, statues of saints, portraits and drawings of Jesus, the crucifix, biblical images and texts, reproductions of waterfalls, necklaces and armbands—all these spiritual goods that can mediate between the human and the divine circulate in the favelas outside the institutional contexts in which they generally appear.

Insurgent Believers

After having discussed some of the mechanisms at work in the reproduction of socio-spatial segregation in the city, the words of the member of the

Assembleia de Deus dos Últimos Dias, reproduced at the beginning of this chapter, hopefully acquire more depth. When the man exclaimed that Jesus had given him the right to climb any favela now that he had converted from gang member to believer, he not only alluded to the fact that comandos were less likely to kill him but he also claimed a new identity beyond the stigmas reproduced by society at large. In response to the widespread stigma that the majority of favela residents are criminals, evangelical residents often state that they are pious believers who behave according to strict moral codes. One of the reasons why Pentecostalism has become popular in the favelas of Rio de Janeiro is that identification as a crente is one of the few classifications available to signal that one is not involved with crime. The terms *crentes* and *evangélicos*—both regularly employed to describe members of Pentecostal churches—have gradually been added to the term *trabalhador* to signal that someone has no relations whatsoever with the comandos or with criminality.

As I would like to suggest, Pentecostal practice thus provides a variant of what James Holston (2008) has described as "insurgent citizenship." As Holston eloquently argues, Brazil is characterized by "differentiated citizenship," a citizenship regime defined by the systematic unequal distribution of substantive rights. While Holston recognizes favela residents as people who resist this differentiated citizenship by means of reappropriations of the law and by means of rights claims, he does not mention explicitly the power of religious ideologies. In fact, Holston concludes, "If, in the past, the oppressed found expression in millenarian religious movements, today they have a secular voice and it speaks in rights talk" (309).

Here I think Holston incorrectly describes insurgent movements as secular. In the past decades, Pentecostal leaders and members in the favelas have presented strong demands to be treated equally with the well-to-do Brazilians on the asfalto because they are living strict moral lives and are not involved with crime. According to the majority, in fact, they are among the few who can counter injustice, corruption, and mischief at all levels of society because they are faithful believers who have God on their side. As Ari Pedro Oro (2003, 58) states, "The consequences of this discourse are that for the *iurdianos* [members of the IURD] to vote is not only a civil exercise. It is also conceived as a quasi-religious act. It is a gesture of exorcism of the demon encountered in politics. It is to deliver it so that politics can be performed by 'people who fear Lord Jesus.'"

During my research in Visionário the majority of the people who worked together in the local council of leaders were Pentecostal pastors. Despite the fact that we should not take discursive oppositions between evangélicos and bandidos for a fact (see Cunha 2008), pastors are often presented as legitimate representatives of favela residents because they appear to be morally upright. In chapters 3 and 4 we will return to the representations and practices of Marcelo Crivella of the Igreja Universal to see how mass mediated religious ideology and practice are presented as a powerful counterforce against misery and violence.

Conclusion

This chapter has provided a first sketch of the geography of Pentecostalism in Rio de Janeiro. Pentecostal doctrines present clear-cut distinctions between good and bad. For these and other reasons, I think Jeff Garmany (2010) is correct when he proposes to see religion—and Pentecostalism in particular—as an example of governmentality in operation in favelas. Pentecostal preachers and members attain a certain *status aparte* in the favelas, and self-styling and self-discipline are very important features of their recognition as "different" people (see chapter 4).

Nevertheless, the governmentality of Pentecostalism in many ways relies on representations and techniques of domination that are reproduced by other agents and institutions inside and outside the favelas (see also Machado 2013). The recurrent description of favelas as dangerous places riddled with comandos is part of a general representation of favelas by news media and the state, and this representation plays a large role in legitimating excessive police violence. Moreover, the self-styling that Pentecostal adherents advocate acquires its meaning and expression vis-à-vis the many popular cultural practices that are present in the favela—as I will show in more detail in the following chapters. I thus think that scholars leave unanswered how we should understand the governmentality of Pentecostalism in relation to the wide array of popular media present in favelas. Many of the people I interviewed during my research in Rio de Janeiro personally experienced the hardships of favela life on a daily basis, but they also made many references to mass mediated images and narratives of crime, violence, spiritual evil, and immoral behavior to explain why it was necessary to accept Jesus Christ as Savior.

What I often recorded during interviews were intricate webs of narratives that mixed personal accounts of life experiences with references to news programs, public crime stories, radio broadcasts, telenovelas, and so forth. Moreover, as briefly demonstrated above, Pentecostal preachers gratefully "remediated" (Bolter and Grusin 1999) narratives about the city to strengthen their sermons and testimonies. When we recognize that a grand part of the "world" that people dwell in consists of what Don Slater and Jo Tacchi (2004, 2) call a "communicative ecology"—"the complete range of communication media and information flows"—we are pressed to include in our descriptions the "big" and "small" media (Spitulnik 2001) that are part of the fabric of favela life (see also Swatowiski 2009).

50   When we want to understand what the "new modes of interpreting the world" (Marshall 2009, 129) entail and why it is attractive to subject oneself to a Pentecostal regime that presents new practices in the world, we should include these mediated representations and experiences. As I will show in the forthcoming chapters, the world that presents itself to favela inhabitants is not only made up of face-to-face encounters but—among other things— also consists of amplified music and mediated images of evil.

Sonic Struggles
Sound, Religion, and Space in the Favelas

The first nights in my small apartment in Visionário, five floors up in the brick and concrete house of José, I could hardly sleep at all. It was very hot and humid, but what kept me awake mostly those nights were the loud music and the noises emanating from different places in the morro. I had moved to the favela earlier in the week, and on the first Friday evening I saw and heard the many different celebrations that mark the beginning of the weekend. The different churches of the Assembleia de Deus, whose services had all started between eight and ten, had their doors open and I could hear their music and songs clearly. The little shop on the estrada had been playing *pagode*[1] music since the afternoon, while the bars nearby were playing mostly *forró*.[2] That Friday night I could hear the sounds of dance music all night long. Tired as I was that Saturday, I was also quite thrilled: it appeared to me that life in the morro never stopped for one moment and that people celebrated the end of the workweek together.

I was soon disabused of that sense of togetherness. The different music and sounds not only came from different groups, but people from these groups often demonstrated their distinct social positions through the music they played. Forró was commonly thought to belong to the *nordesti-nos*—immigrants from the northeastern region of Brazil who had recently migrated—and pagode to the "authentic" inhabitants of the morro. *Funk*[3] belonged to the youth and was—according to many evangelicals—associated with the comando, while gospel belonged to the crentes. Most people from the Pentecostal churches were very keen to stay away from the little bars where the pagode or forró music was playing, let alone dance to that or other kinds of music in public. Conversely, the open doors of the nearby

Assembleia de Deus did not signify the great love of gospel music among a large proportion of the non-Pentecostal inhabitants.

During my research in the years after my relocation, I learned that boundaries between groups are drawn quite sharply at times and that one of the ways to accomplish this was along the lines of musical preference. This was even the case with people from different Pentecostal churches. Many who attended the Igreja Universal, for example, said they preferred to play music from their own gospel-singing pastors than from pastors of other churches,[4] and the music that was coming from little shops or houses in the morro often signified the religious preference of one of their residents— though certainly not all of them. In other words, while the inhabitants of the favela initially had appeared to me to be a homogeneous group, in fact they formed a heterogeneous collection of people who identified with different social and religious categories.

In this chapter I argue that sound and music are essential to the constitution of identities in the favelas of Rio de Janeiro and to the struggles to produce spaces in which different forms of subjectivity can develop. In the density of the favelas, different collectives try to exercise a politics of presence through the sounds they produce. I will introduce several of these collectives and institutions by way of the sound and music they produce and describe their presence in the soundscape of the morro.

This chapter should begin to clarify why gospel music is very important for favela residents who attend Pentecostal churches. As more and more people point to the significance of music for Pentecostal movements around the globe, this chapter clears the ground for an understanding of how exactly this music does its work in relation to space and culture.[5] When we approach religions as cultural flows that make possible both "crossing and dwelling," as Thomas Tweed has argued (2006), we begin to understand that religion and space are intrinsically related, yet this leaves unanswered how this works in urban settings such as favelas, where religions interact with one another and with other cultural flows.

According to Robert Orsi (1999, 54), one of the most influential scholars on religion and urban life,

> Religious practice and imagination . . . continually rework urban land-
> scapes that are themselves forever in upheaval. Religious practices
> have served as media for creating and sustaining bonds among people
> scattered across the city and between people in the city and others
> beyond its borders, and for constituting a meaningful sense of space

on intersecting neighborhood, urban, national, and global levels. Religious cartographies disclose the coordinates of alternative worlds for practitioners, remaking the meanings of ordinary places and signaling the locations of extraordinary ones, establishing connections between the spaces of the city and other spaces, real and imaginary, between humans and invisible sacred companions of all sorts.

Taking Orsi's writings on religion in the city as inspiration, I argue that electronic media are part of contemporary urban landscapes, as the urban theorists Ash Amin and Nigel Thrift have also stated. According to Amin and Thrift (2002, 78), we should understand the city as a mediated social environment and as "a set of constantly evolving systems or networks, machinic assemblages which intermix categories like the biological, technical, social, economic and so on."

An analysis of the soundscape of favelas highlights the fact that Pentecostal sounds and music—transmitted, amplified, and remediated—are not received and understood independently from other music styles or other social groups, but in close relation to them. In general, Pentecostal adherents pitch their "godly" sound and music against the "worldly" sounds of their neighbors and try to transmit the Holy Spirit to the other inhabitants in order to convert them to their faith. Understanding how favela residents are enveloped by sounds and how they interact with them, which I endeavor to accomplish in this chapter, leads us to a better understanding of the hypermediated conversion I describe in chapter 4. Chapter 5 will deal more intensely with the intricate relation between religion and sound and could be read in tandem with this chapter, which explores the relation between sound, space, and identity in the favelas of Rio de Janeiro and attempts to lead the reader into a sonic imagination of the favela environment, so that she or he can begin to understand what is at stake for the favela inhabitants when they engage with one or the other kind of music, and particularly what is at stake for inhabitants attracted to Pentecostalism.

Sound, Place, and the Politics of Presence

There are several reasons to describe favelas by means of their soundscapes (Schäfer 1994), even though such a description can never live up to the synchronicity and sensuousness of the sounds themselves. Many people in the favelas of Rio de Janeiro make sense of who, what, and where by recognizing the sounds they hear and knowing what they represent. For example, one of the repeated questions inhabitants of Visionário asked me when I first met them was whether I had heard gunshots and whether I was scared. After some time I began to understand the question as an introduction to the place. Living in a favela in Rio de Janeiro means being confronted with the sound of shootings now and then, understanding the background, and coping with the dangers involved. These are important experiences that inhabitants share (see also Cavalcanti 2008).

Occasionally, I heard gunshots and witnessed emotional reactions. I saw, for example, how one of my friends immediately began to search for her grandchildren who were playing somewhere in the favela. She ran outside to find them, shouting out their names, calling them to come home quickly. On another occasion, a mother told me that the worst thing that could happen to her was hearing the sound of gunshots up the morro while being down on the asfalto, knowing that her children were playing somewhere in the alleys.

Recognizing the sound of gunshots is not that easy. Sometimes I thought I heard gunshots, but when I asked other people they would assure me that what I had heard were fireworks. Fireworks were often used by olheiros to alarm other gang members that police officers were entering particular parts of the morro. The sound of fireworks also alarmed the other inhabitants of activity somewhere in the vicinity and told them it was wise to be cautious.

One of the ardent supporters of a sonic approach to space is Steven Feld, who argues that it is through sound that people experience and know a particular place. Therefore, according to Feld (1996, 97), we should devote our attention to "acoustemology," "an exploration of sonic sensibilities, specifically of the ways in which sound is central to making sense, to knowing, to experiential truth . . . Acoustemology means that as a sensual space-time, the experience of place potentially can always be grounded in an acoustic dimension." Sounds are particularly important to place-making: "Sound, hearing, and voice mark a special bodily nexus for sensation and emotion because of their coordination of brain, nervous system, head, ear, chest muscles, respiration, and breathing." Though emotion may be predicated on discourse, sound should not be uncoupled from the discursive practice: "Emotions may be created in discourse, but this social creation is contingent on performance, which is always emergent through embodied voices."[6]

Clearly, as Feld also indicates, the description of the soundscape of the morro should not be seen as replacing a description of the cityscape, but rather as complementing it. My attention to the ear in this chapter is meant to accompany the eye, not to substitute for it. Attention to the soundscape of favelas is important because of the material specificities of this urban landscape. The morro comprises small houses built on top of one another, narrow alleys, and small flights of concrete stairs. The houses are poorly insulated and often inhabited by many people. Social life in the favelas of Rio de Janeiro is ineluctably characterized by proximity, and this has several consequences for the formation and consolidation of social groups at particular moments in time. Social life in favelas could well be characterized by the tension between propinquity and the need for dissociation. Inescapably, people live close to one another, are related, or know one another's families well. People are often dependent on the solidarity of neighbors. Despite this, people take great care with whom they are involved or seen in public. In Visionário, for example, inhabitants regularly passed moral judgments on one another through gossip, rumor, and slander, and to many people it mattered a great deal with what groups they could be identified.

Sound is an important instrument of identification of social categories, especially in a place characterized by proximity. People are easily confronted with the sounds of others. Though by no means can the significance of sound be taken at face value, the particular boundary-crossing capabilities of sound do indicate its unique capability to designate and identify the presence of certain groups and activities in the cityscape of the favela. Especially in relation to musical preferences, I witnessed clearly the relation between group formation and sound. As I experienced during my residence in the favela, self-identification was often framed along the lines of musical preferences. People described one another as *sambista*, *pagodeiro*, and *funkeiro*, depending on their preference and affiliation. Likewise, crentes and nordestinos were often recognized by the music they played and consumed.

Identifications in terms of these music styles were enforced because different groups purposefully used amplified music to exercise a politics of presence in the favela, especially the criminal gangs and the evangélicos. Such efforts highlight the fact that sound is applied to reorganize people's relation to space and place (see also Bull 2004) and remind us that the soundscape is a site of power and conflict, as Jacques Attali (1985) and Alain Corbin (2000) have forcefully argued. This is especially relevant for the favelas of Rio de Janeiro because much of the remediation of sound is not confined to the private space of the home. The architecture of favelas hardly allows for neat divisions between urban (public) spaces and domestic (private) spaces because of the limited acoustic insulation. Moreover, the amplified sounds of events that take place in the open spaces of the favelas regularly travel throughout the neighborhood. As people from different groups generally amplify their own music during these events, they temporarily control the entire soundscape. Such a seizure of the soundscape demonstrates how electroacoustic technology can be used to privatize public space in an urban context like that of a favela, and it shows how groups attempt to claim political space in the density of the morro. Before going into the details of the different groups and their music, the following section discusses the relations between music, style, ethics, and identity.

Music and Style

Music is important in the context of the favelas of Rio de Janeiro not merely because it is ubiquitous but also because of the tight relations between music, identification, and moral codes. As Idelber Avelar and Christopher Dunn (2011) emphasize, Brazilian popular music and notions of citizenship exhibit particularly strong connections, since it is often by means of music that communities are experienced and collective feelings of rights and violations are expressed. In relation to religious life in the favelas, music often features as one of the most important elements, yet music can also display and make palpable the boundaries between different religious and political communities. Inhabitants of Visionário and Roda do Vento who love to make or play Christian evangelical music generally identify and live accordingly to the lifestyles prescribed by evangelical churches and often demonize the lifestyles of those who adore funk or pagode. How should we understand these pertinent relations between music, morality, and identity?

Music is a special type of sound, which exhibits a particular structure as well as special structuring capabilities. "Music is a means of understanding peoples and behavior and as such is a valuable tool in the analysis of culture and society," as Alan Merriam (1964, 13) stated some time ago. Nevertheless, what music might mean to people has to be analyzed in the context of their engagement with it. As the ethnomusicologist John Blacking (1987, 34–35) has argued, "Musical performance is only able to communicate to the participants because they have learned to make links between different kinds of knowledge and experience. . . . But no music has power in itself. Music has no consequences for social action unless it can be related to a coherent set of ideas about self and other bodily feelings."[7]

Understanding the meaning of music thus asks us to explore the shifting relations between music, notions of self, and contexts, each of which exerts its own kind of influence over the others. As Charles Keil and Steven Feld (1994, 84) state about listening to music, "Each listening is not just the juxtaposition of a musical object and a listener. It is a juxtaposition—in fact an entangling—of a dialectical object and a situated interlocutor. 'Dialectical object' reflects the fact that a sound object or event can only be engaged through recognition of a simultaneous musical and extramusical reality: the experience is mental and material, individual and social, formal and expressive."[8] As Keil and Feld suggest, style is crucial in connecting musical to extramusical reality. Preferences for certain musical styles often appear at the heart of identity politics and the creation and maintenance of boundaries between groups.[9] In general, style can be defined as "the forming form" (Maffesoli 1996, 5) or, as Keil and Feld (1994, 202) argue, "a deeply satisfying distillation of the way a very well integrated human group likes to do things." Keil and Feld write that "the presence of style indicates a strong community, an intense sociability that has been given shape through time, an assertion of control over collective feelings so powerful that any expressive innovator in the community will necessarily put his or her content in that shaping continuum and no other."

The fact that people can experience a particular style as deeply authentic reminds us that sound and music share the ability to touch us profoundly (see also Connor 2004).[10] Sound can evoke a sense of social boundaries that are not merely symbolic but also physical. Dissatisfied with the visualist language on knowledge and learning, Daniel Putman (1985, 60) argued that touch, rather than sight, gives us insight into the specific way musical experience teaches us something: "The way that music refers to something is the same way that touch refers to something—immediate, nonconceptual, frequently imprecise, often emotionally powerful, definitively informative. Two lovers who are sensitive to each other can learn something about each other's disposition simply by touching. The phraseology for reference is best stated by the phrase, 'expressive of.' Experience in life teaches us that tactile sensations are expressive of certain meanings." Reflecting a similar understanding of music as (aesthetic) experience, Simon Frith (1996, 109) has argued that we can only understand the strong link between music and identity when we highlight the capacity of music to create and construct experience and in the process influence our relation to the world and ourselves: "Music, like identity, is both performance and story, describes the social in the individual and the individual in the social, the mind in the body and the body in the mind; identity, like music, is a matter of both ethics and aesthetics." Listening to music both reflects and constitutes identity. It resonates with a sense of self and of others.

Such a notion of music sheds light on the question of why music is often experienced as such a powerful expression of group identity. Playing music constitutes identity both for oneself and for the other in a direct, immediate, and emotional manner, not least because it connects notions of the good life (ethics) to notions of transcendence (aesthetics).

A characterization of music listening as a momentous solidification of collectives and selves on the verge of dissolving fits well with authors who argue against essentialism and who stress that social groups are formed performatively.[11] Over time and depending on contexts, inhabitants of the favelas of my research identified with different styles of music and adjusted their bodily comportment to the socially sanctioned movements that accompany listening. As we will see below and in chapter 5, this is strongly perceivable in relation to (narratives about) conversion, when certain styles of dancing are heavily criticized and certain ecstatic bodily movements are described and experienced as desirable. While in many instances the inhabitants of the favelas treated music-related identities as essentially different, it is clear that the formation of these groups, mediated by electroacoustic technology, involve contextual identity performances that imply multiple parties in a field of power relations.[12] Being seen as someone who adores one or another kind of music can have consequences such as exclusion from certain church rituals, for instance. Before explaining this in more detail throughout this book, let me describe some of the sounds and groups under consideration.

Forró, Community, and Migration

Loud forró music regularly emanates from the bars or shops at the entrances of the morro, highlighting the origins of their owners or clientele. Forró is a popular type of music and dance from northeastern Brazil. In the morro the sound of forró was mostly associated with nordestinos, migrants from the Northeast who had traveled to Rio de Janeiro since the 1970s and 1980s. Forró is an important element in the symbolic community of migrants from northeastern Brazil and provides people with a shared sense of origin. In Rio de Janeiro it plays a prominent part in the São Cristóvão fair, which since 1945 has offered northeastern goods and music and has traditionally been attended by northeastern migrants. The popular version of the origin of the name *forró* insists that it was derived from the English words "for all," written on the doors of the dancing clubs that were opened during railroad construction in the Northeast at the beginning of the twentieth century.

The forró that can be heard day and night in the morro echoes the flow of immigration from the Northeast to the morros of Rio de Janeiro. This region of Brazil is extremely poor, and its recent history is characterized by authoritarian landowners, drought, hunger, and disease (Scheper-Hughes 1992, 31).

Not surprisingly, the northeastern region of Brazil had the highest number of interregional emigrants between 1960 and 1990. In that period, 8.1 million people left the region, and most moved to São Paulo and Rio de Janeiro, states that witnessed rapid industrialization since the 1950s and thus offered better job prospects (Brito and Carvalho 2006). This emigration wave was part of a broader process of urbanization, as 42.6 million people moved from the countryside to the metropolitan areas of Brazil between 1960 and 1990.

Forró also tells of the often forgotten discrimination among people of different descent and color in the context of the morros of Rio de Janeiro. In Visionário, narratives of origin and descent intermingle with popular views on the northeastern migrants to provide explanations for poverty, inequality, and insecurity. During my research, several people claimed that the majority of people from one side of the favela were born and raised in the favela while most people from another part were nordestinos. Many inhabitants of Visionário considered the recent migrants from the Northeast a separate and unified group, even though the people came from many different places and regions. In my conversations with people, they often talked about "those paraíbas" in degrading terms.[13] The terms nordestinos or paraíbas were often used to lump together a heterogeneous group of immigrants who worked hard to pay for their rented apartments in the favela. Some of the people born in Visionário felt discriminated against by immigrants from the Northeast. One of my contacts in Visionário claimed that some nordestinos discriminated against the "autochthonous" population based on their skin color: "There are some that don't like people who have our color," she said as she pointed to her dark skin.

Despite such claims of autochthony on the basis of descent and color, inhabitants of the morro cannot be neatly categorized into groups that occupy certain spaces. Discrimination and conflict signify that descent and color are important elements in the discourses on identity rather than the fixed characteristics of cleanly separable groups. Nevertheless, notwithstanding my efforts to deconstruct the natural inclination of the archetype nordestino to listen to forró, the people I knew who had recently migrated from the Northeast did in fact love to play forró and experienced the music as "theirs," compared to the samba or pagode, which were felt to be distinctively carioca.

The Sound of Samba and Pagode

On many occasions I woke up early on a Sunday morning because someone was still drumming the pandeiro, the Brazilian tambourine used in samba and pagode music. Obviously he or she could not get enough of it after the long Saturday night festivities at the *quadra de escola de samba* (samba school dance hall). Live music was played mostly in the weekends, but there would often be rehearsals during the week. Besides live music, people played samba music on their stereo during celebrations, parties, or simply for their own enjoyment.

Practically every morro in Rio de Janeiro has an *escola de samba* (samba school) (Zaluar 1985). The samba schools of Rio de Janeiro are powerful institutions that have become synonymous with an image of what Brazil is, both inside and outside the country. Especially in Rio de Janeiro, where the famous annual *desfile* (parade) in the *sambódromo* takes place during carnival, escolas like Beija-Flor, Portela, or Mangueira have become big organizations that manage to generate plenty of money to finance their extravagant and expensive parades. Their names are known worldwide, and many tourists, officials, and celebrities come to Rio de Janeiro each year to witness and partake in the parades in the sambódromo.

Samba is commonly represented both inside and outside Brazil as the "authentic" Brazilian music style that originated and flourished in the favelas. Most chroniclers place the origin of samba around the start of the twentieth century, with the 1917 recording of the musical piece "Pelo Telefone" (By the telephone)—composed by Ernesto dos Santos (Donga) and Mauro de Almeida—representing a watershed. Many accounts of the birth of the samba as the national music style par excellence claim that until the 1930s it was repressed as an undesirable Afro-Brazilian expression, until the government could no longer deny its popular appeal. However, according to Hermano Vianna (1999), the notion of samba's authenticity was itself invented and cultivated. Vianna attempts to free the history of samba from the misconception that this so-called authentic music style was repressed until it suddenly became the most celebrated Brazilian music style, and in so doing he introduces a more complex and hybrid idea of popular culture. Vianna does not deny the repression of elements of popular culture, but he argues that repression coexisted with other types of social interaction occasionally contrary to repression.

In the past, many schools were dependent on the infamous bankers of the gambling game *jogo do bicho* who financially supported them. Later, the samba of Rio de Janeiro became a million-dollar business, and the biggest schools developed into enterprises firmly entrenched in the popular entertainment industry (Santos 1998). Not all escolas de samba have grown so big. There are several competitions on different days during carnival. The big, famous schools compete in the *grupo especial*, but there is also *grupo A*, *grupo B*, and so forth, in which the smaller escolas compete. Members of the smaller escolas all hope to be promoted to the grupo especial one day. The dance hall where the members of the escola de samba of Visionário practice is generally known as the *quadra* (square), and besides samba school rehearsals it is used for festivities, baile funk parties, pagode performances, and other gatherings, such as Protestant/Pentecostal services and community events.

During my research I lived very close to the quadra, directly opposite a local Assembleia de Deus. The "square" is in fact more of a hall that can be closed if necessary. Especially in the months leading up to the carnival, the people of the escola de samba practiced regularly for the desfile in the sambódromo. Before and during carnival, these rehearsals (*ensaios*) were held on the asfalto and in large clubs so that, in practice, there were several big events in which the escola demonstrated its qualities. Many people from the morro participated in the samba school, and many more experienced it as a genuine representation of their community to the world "outside."

The samba schools have been and still are important sociopolitical institutions of the morros in Rio de Janeiro, although here as well the traffic in drugs has changed their relationship with the communities significantly (Santos 1998). Alba Zaluar (1985) notes that the *blocos de carnaval* (carnival bands) often competed with the associações de moradores of Cidade de Deus for the representation of the favela to the state and the society at large. The important position of the school in Visionário was exemplified by the members of the escola de samba, who attained public status and were considered part of the local governance of the morro (*liderança*). One director—who represented the escola de samba in the association of samba schools of Rio de Janeiro[14]—was also an esteemed member of the *conselho de liderança* (council of leaders of the favela). The sociopolitical status of the escola de samba members ultimately depended on the musicians and composers and the quality of their performances. If inhabitants had not loved their samba songs and recognized the pleasure they gave them, such a status would have been hard to achieve. Many favela residents dressed up, danced, courted, and sang during the festivities, and it was their participation that made the school important.

Given this love of samba, the amplified sound of the samba coming from the quadra was apprehended positively by many inhabitants of the morro. Strikingly, not all inhabitants identified with the sound. Precisely because it is associated with Afro-Brazilian history and tradition, samba has become one of the popular cultural expressions often demonized by the Pentecostal churches in Brazil. Following this demonization, the genre itself became an expression of a lifestyle deemed inappropriate by many evangelical inhabitants of the favela. Evangélicos who lived in the morro preferred to play their own gospel music, as I will describe below.

Besides the school rehearsals, there were many other festivities at the quadra. On the weekends there were often pagode and baile funk parties, which attracted inhabitants from the entire favela. Historically, pagode was the name of the festivities that slaves held in the slave houses (*senzalas*). In Rio de Janeiro in the 1970s, people in the morros gave the name pagode to the festivities that involved eating, drinking, and samba. From there, pagode also became a type of music that quickly gained popularity. Pagodes were often held in the quadra, but they could also involve a smaller band that played at the small bars in the morro.

The Sound of Baile Funk

Besides the sounds of samba and pagode, other sounds echoed through the night and took control of the soundscape. Funk definitively won every contest in terms of loudness. Funk—also known as carioca funk—is a Brazilian form of electronic dance music that became enormously popular at the public parties in Rio's favelas in the 1990s. Carioca funk derives its name from the funk parties (bailes funk) that originally featured music similar to North American funk and later incorporated music influenced by Miami bass, a North American hip-hop/dance style developed in the 1980s and 1990s.

The popular funk music, perhaps best described as dance music with "fat" beats, was played so loudly during bailes in the morro that no one could hide from it. Mostly on Fridays, the trucks of the "Big Mix," an organizer of baile funk parties, would arrive to set up the equipment. Two walls of approximately eight by four meters of professional loudspeakers were unloaded and placed in one of the favela's open spaces. Around midnight the first sounds would thunder through the community. The electric sound effects enhanced the experience of being taken over by a force from another dimension. When I asked the older inhabitants how they felt about the sounds, many of them just sighed and replied, "Estamos acostumados" (We are accustomed to it).

In general, people showed diverse reactions to the parties. Some complained, damned, or accepted, while others simply enjoyed them. Most of the inhabitants did not seem to think they could stop or tame the baile funk parties. The fact that these bailes were organized and supported by the local comando was most probably the biggest reason people felt the need to accept them. The baile funk parties in Visionário are typified as *baile de comunidade* (community baile) in contrast to *baile de corredor* (gallery baile), at which gangs meet each other in semi-organized fights (Cecchetto 1998). Though I agree with Livio Sansone (2001, 143), who warns us about "an a priori direct link between rage, revolt, violence, gangs and funk," the bailes de comunidade in Visionário were generally "protected" against invasions by armed traficantes of the Comando Vermelho; furthermore, many inhabitants associated the bailes with the tráfico. In particular, the sound of one particular form of carioca funk—*funk proibidão* (forbidden funk)—is closely connected to Rio's comandos, and it was this type of funk that often echoed through the nights in the favela.

Though bailes were often portrayed as favela events, the baile funk parties were also loudly audible in the neighborhoods surrounding the favela. As such they transcended not only the micro-areas within the favela but also the geographical distinction between the morro and the asfalto. One friend told me that inhabitants of the asfalto had pressured the municipal governments to end the parties' burden and, as a result, the police had forbidden the bailes in the past. He also told me that during my research the president of the associação de moradores of the favela was called up by traficantes in the middle of the night and pressed to convince the police that a baile they had shut down should continue. This anecdote demonstrates the qualities of sound to traverse spaces that are otherwise often seen and treated as isolated and contained.

In the favela the bailes were held either in the quadra do Visionário or another quadra close by. The festivities were not confined to these spaces, however, which would have been physically impossible, given the size and structure of the morro. Around the squares, in the alleys leading to them, people were chatting, drinking, smoking, and making out. From what I have seen it was mostly adolescents taking part in the festivities. Nevertheless, I have also frequently seen young children and older inhabitants going to the bailes. On the "dance floor" people were dancing, courting, or simply checking out the scenery and looking at one another. The loud music made it hard to speak, but that was not what most people had come for.

For me the parties were a thrilling experience. During the festivities armed men mounted the dance floor and moved through the crowd with their firearms in full view. Songs that praised the power of the Comando Vermelho enforced the feeling that the armed men were parading. These songs that accompanied their entrance were met with cheers, and people sang along with the funk lyrics. In general, the lyrics expressed the status of bandidos, life in the favelas of Rio de Janeiro, and the power of the traficantes. Take, for example, these lyrics, which come from a tape of funk recordings I copied from Carla, a teenage girl in the favela:

Agora é chapa quente	The heat is on
eu vou no bonde	I am part of the gang
ja tô bolado tô maluco tô chapado	I am loaded, I am crazy, I am stoned
o maluco vem neste bonde	The crazy man is part of this gang
guerreiros estão voltando	The warriors are returning
ser bandido é facil	To be a bandit is easy
dificil é ser do Comando	What is difficult is to be in the Comando

These lyrics celebrate the warrior status of the traficantes of the Comando Vermelho. Many of the funk lyrics are a reflection of the violent living conditions experienced by the young people who are involved in the tráfico in the favelas and a demonstration of the territorial power of the tráfico. Take for example the lyrics below, which were a parody of a very popular song performed by the Brazilian singer/celebrity Ivete Sangalo. The original text read as follows:

Avisou, avisou, avisou	They have warned [3x]
Que vai rolar a festa	The party will begin
Vai rolar	It will begin
O povo do gueto	The people of the ghetto
Mandou avisar	They have called for a warning

Instead of an upcoming party, the tráfico warns of the war that it is about to commence. I heard this version often during the bailes in Visionário, and also on other occasions, such as when people played the tapes at home. The song starts with the sound of shots from an automatic rifle. The following texts are sung:

É uniao todos que mandam estavam lá	It is union, everyone who rules was there
É Comando é Comando [Vermelho]	It is Comando, it is Comando [Vermelho]
Não podemos estranhar	We cannot estrange ourselves

O pt do Vidigal, da Jacaré, da Mangueira	It is the *pt* from Vidigal, of Jacaré, of Mangueira
[et cetera][15]	[et cetera]
Esse bonde traz amor e fé	This gang brings love and faith
Avisou, avisou, avisou	They have warned [3x]
Que vai rolar a guerra	War will come
O bonde do B mandou avisar	The gang of B has called for a warning

Carla, the girl who let me copy the tape of baile funk tracks, laughingly warned me that if customs found the tapes on me at the border I would be sentenced and imprisoned. She sang along with these lyrics at home and frequently attended the bailes with her girlfriends. On many Friday nights she would spend hours preparing to go to a baile in the morro. She was the one who took me to my first baile. Her mother, Maria, was worried that she was dating (*namorando*) a bandido and repeatedly told her in front of her brothers and sisters (and me) that she would give her the beating of her life if she caught her with a bandido.

Of her seven daughters, three had dated bandidos in the past, and she knew what kind of trouble it could bring. A gang of traficantes had expelled her niece—the daughter of her oldest sister—from the morro. The niece had a relationship with a bandido, but when the young man had fallen out with the other gang members they considered her a liability and a threat. The traficantes told her never to come to the morro again, unless given permission for an exceptional visit. During my stay I met the niece twice in the house of the family. On both occasions she had ignored the warning and ascended the morro without permission. Her sister warned her not to stay too long, knowing the kind of trouble it could bring. Heedless of such warnings, Carla was not intimidated by her mother and went to the bailes anyway.

The bailes were very popular among the young people in the morro. Most of them had little to no money to go to a *boate* (disco) on the asfalto. When I asked if they minded the fact that armed boys were parading around, most people replied that for them it was simply the way it was: "We are accustomed to it," they would say. Also, we must remember that many people enjoyed these bailes very much. Young male friends of mine cleaned their Nike tennis shoes, put on their hippest clothes, and set out to watch the girls dancing. The girls, who were generally scantily clad in tank tops—showing their bellies—and hot pants, likewise were looking at the boys. Inside, or rather on the dance floor, the "fat" beats were truly intoxicating, and I had no trouble understanding the persuasive power this music exerted on people.

As Adriana Caravalho Lopes (2011, 89) describes aptly, carioca funk involves much more than mere hedonism. It is a conjunction of practices, styles, and channels that allow for the articulation of the thoughts and feelings of favela inhabitants who are often misrepresented by other hegemonic channels, such as those supported by media conglomerates and state institutions. When the funk proibidão lyrics speak of war and armed combat, it is also because many favela inhabitants have suffered or witnessed excessive police violence and feel that all favelados are criminalized by society at large.

Nevertheless, the funk proibidão lyrics also demonstrate how baile funk can be used to communicate that a morro is in the hands of a comando. While living in Visionário I perceived that the loud music could be heard well beyond the confines of the morro, thus signaling to all relevant parties that the Comando Vermelho was in charge. As Paul Sneed (2007) has described most insightfully, funk proibidão is part of an ideological arena in which competing powers—gangs and state forces—attempt to convince residents of the legitimacy of their rule. Funk lyrics remind favela residents that traffickers control the means of violence in the favela, but traffickers also attempt to convey that they are loyal to the favela community.

Besides entertainment and expression of ruling power, the parties also implied business. On many Friday nights the police were suspiciously absent from the vicinity of the squares where the bailes were held, and many people suspected they were paid to stay away from these events. Since I lived so close to the quadra, I could witness what was going on around it quite well. The public consumption of marijuana and cocaine was considerably more visible on those nights than during a night of pagode or samba.

Even though many young people said they were "accustomed" to the rifles and guns, my evangelical friends hardly went to the bailes in the favela, and some warned me of the dangers involved. Roberto, a young man who had recently converted to a local Assembleia de Deus, told me he had been in a baile at the quadra once when the police came and started shooting. He claimed that several people continued dancing while the police were shooting at the traficantes and vice versa. Rafaela, another friend, tried to prevent me from going to a baile. Her best friend had been shot when she was in the line of fire, and the father of one of her children had been killed near a baile during a confrontation between traficantes and the police. Though the warnings were sincere, both of my friends were ambivalent with regard to church life and the dangers of the bailes. A couple of months after her warning, Rafaela was dancing at the bailes as she had done in the past, and so was Roberto.

The Sound of Pentecostalism

On most nights of the week, from my little apartment I could hear the loud, amplified voice of Pastor Francisco during the cultos. In the first weeks when I heard him shouting "Satanás" (Satan) with enormous enthusiasm, I was surprised and impressed by the tone of aggression and often looked out the window to see if perhaps there was a conflict happening. Later, I got used to the screams and the shouting coming from the churches during the cultos. From my window I could see the Assembleia de Deus where Pastor Francisco worked. It was built strategically at the corner of the main road (estrada) and the alley that enters a more dense part of the morro, opposite the quadra de escola de samba. Because of its central location the church was very visible and extremely audible to many people living in that part of the morro. Everyone who walked up on the estrada passed the church. On the opposite side of the road there were several *biroshkas* (little shops) where people bought small groceries throughout the day. The *combi* (van) that brought people up the morro stopped right in front of it.

Just like the other Pentecostal churches in the morro, the doors of the Assembleia de Deus at the estrada stayed open during the cultos, exemplifying their outreach to the nonconverted inhabitants or other visitors. Besides a strategic location, the amplified sounds are also essential to the outreach of the churches of the Assembleia de Deus in the morro. In one of my interviews, one of the elder congregants, Linda (a woman of sixty years), remembered what it was like when the church had been established, approximately forty years ago:

> I was not a crente, I was of the escola de samba, a sambista [her daughter laughs loudly]. . . . When we passed the church on our way to the samba practice, Jão, the doorman of the church, stood in the threshold and said to us, "Jesus loves you and calls for you," and invited us to come in. I replied, "Jão, one of these days I will enter and see this shouting of yours." The Pentecostals in these days were "Glória, Glória" [imitates the sound of high-pitched screaming people], that noise, it was louder than today. It was a kind of shouting so different from us Catholics, us Catholics [she starts whispering] we would sit in church, in that silence, that reverence, even when we prayed. In the Pentecostal church it was "Senhor Jesus, my Father, bless, do this. . . ." So it was that noise, everyone praying out loud, we in the morro had never seen before. So I

said, "Jão, one of these days I will enter and see what this shouting inside is about." He replied, "Come and see." We had this concept that when these crentes began to shout, that screaming, the praying, everything, the baptism in the Holy Spirit, us who were not crente, we said, "That is when the men are grabbing the women" [her daughter laughs], that is why they are screaming. . . . One day, I said, "I will go in and you [her friends] have to remain outside and wait for me. If they start to grab me or if I see the men grab the women, I will call you and you will come and we will get him off."

As we read, the emotional shouting and praying formed part of the attraction for Linda to enter the church. Interestingly, Linda describes herself as a sambista before her conversion to the Assembleia de Deus and associates Catholicism with silence. Her transformation from sambista to crente demonstrates the importance of music in the formation of identities. As with the other churches of the Assembleia de Deus in the morro, the music and praying were loudly amplified so that participants inside were firmly surrounded by the wall of sound.[16] Nevertheless, the amplification of sound carried the Pentecostal presence well beyond the church walls.

The Pentecostal presence in the soundscape of the morro prompts us to evaluate the relationship between religion and territoriality in the age of electronic mass media. Following Danièle Hervieu-Léger (2002), modernity has brought a significant shift in the relationship between religion and territoriality. Although Hervieu-Léger recognizes a built-in tension in the territorialization of religion—its embeddedness in local communities and its claims to universal significance—the "dismantling of traditional bonds of belief and belonging to a local community," reinforced by the "intensive moving around of individuals and the explosion of various means of worldwide communication—is leading to the emergence, through novel forms of sociability, of new configurations of this tension" between the deterritorialization and reterritorialization of religion (103).

Three characteristics of the modern relation between religion and territoriality that Hervieu-Léger mentions help us understand the situation in the morro: (1) the particularity of denominational pluralism; (2) the religious and ideological competition for presence in space; and (3) the mobilization of modern communication technologies (104).[17] In a situation of denominational pluralism, different religious institutions attempt to sacralize space in order to attract and retain believers, though none of them is able to claim a territory exclusively. In the morro this is exemplified by the multiplicity of

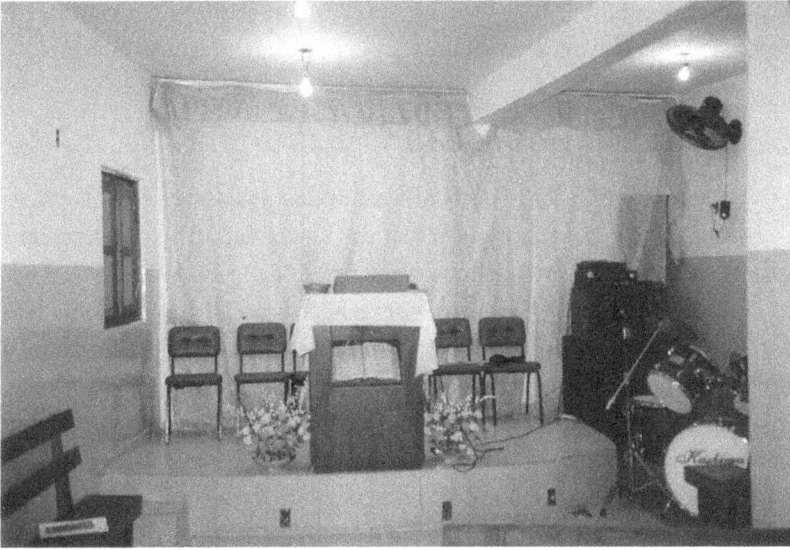

Figure 4 The inside of a small Assembleia de Deus church in Visionário. Photo: author.

different church buildings of different religions and denominations. While the amplified religious sounds mostly emanate from the churches of the Assembleia de Deus, on Sundays they have to compete with the bells of the Roman Catholic parish, for example.

Nevertheless, one might add to the insights of Hervieu-Léger that the described pluralism is not strictly "religious" but also ideological and political, and that it depends very much on the listener and the context of how the public presence of a certain group is coded and evaluated. The struggle for space in the morro is exemplified by struggles over the soundscape between sambistas, funkeiros, and crentes, all of whom use modern communication technologies to make themselves audible. In other words, the struggle over the organization of life in the favelas and their inhabitants is played out in both the landscape and the soundscape. Sound not only reflects (symbolizes) power, it also constitutes power. In the favelas of Rio de Janeiro, territorial struggles involve multiple types of institutions that use communication technologies in their politics of presence. This is exemplified by the competition between the bells of the Catholic parish and the amplified prayers, but perhaps even more so by the competition the gospel music and the sound of pagode and funk music.

Before exploring how adherents of Pentecostal churches experience and deal with this pluralism and how the majority categorize music and make sense of the soundscape in which they dwell, let me clarify how identification and space could be understood in relation to the architecture of favelas.

Local Territories and Trans-Local Sounds

In Visionário and in Roda de Vento, amplified sounds mediate between the homogeneity and heterogeneity of the inhabitants. This heterogeneity is partly related to territorial divisions inside the favelas. While both are often described as unified territories, inhabitants usually distinguish different smaller areas, which have their own names. This is not uncommon in the favelas in Rio de Janeiro. In much of the literature on these favelas, scholars stress the tensions between the internal and external boundaries of the favelas. Though on the outside the favelas are often represented as one bounded space, on the inside there are many very important divisions. Marcos Alvito (2001, 73) describes the favela Acari in terms of a continuum of micro-areas to supra-local institutions. Likewise, Alba Zaluar (1985, 175), who did research in the favela Cidade de Deus in Rio de Janeiro, writes, "The representation of locality is one of the most important in the ideology of the poor urban [subject] in this city. And this locality has territorial divisions and sub-divisions, and the more there are of these, the more there have to be organizations that unite, mobilize and create the identity of the local people."

Locality is, among other dynamics, defined by the relations among inhabitants. As both authors acknowledge, the proximity between the inhabitants of favelas calls for an understanding of the importance of "neighborliness" (*vizinhança*). Neighbors who occupy the same little space (*pedaço*) in the morro often form solidarity networks that strengthen their sense of territory. In Visionário I often witnessed the interdependence of and care for neighbors. People would share food or lend one another certain appliances and thus maintain a minimum of internal solidarity.

Yet, concurrently, inhabitants identified with supra-territorial institutions that spoke in the name of larger collectives in the morro—for example, the associação de moradores, the escola de samba, the Igreja Universal, or the Comando Vermelho. In some cases this was not considered problematic, since they could be integrated in a nested hierarchy. People in the morro could easily identify themselves with certain local and supra-local identities, such as when they simultaneously present themselves as *morador* (inhabitant) and carioca. However, in many instances there was great tension between different identities and solidarities. Take for example the case of my friend Maria, who always maintained good relations with her neighbor and was often invited to join in the festivities when there was a *churrasco* (barbecue). Yet when her neighbor had converted to the Assembleia de Deus and invited her friends for a barbecue, Maria did not want to set one foot across the threshold of her neighbor's house. She felt the people of the church looked down on her as unfaithful and criticized her behavior. When her son married in a local church of the Assembleia de Deus, she stood in the porch and refused to enter for the same reason: "I don't want all those people looking at me and gossiping about me, no," she said to me. Similarly, people who attended Pentecostal churches often expressed a tension with non-converted neighbors or with non-evangelical institutions, and few of them would be seen inside the escola de samba. This example demonstrates that the neighborhood is not the sole determinant of identity in the morro, nor is neighborliness the sole determinant of sociability. Inhabitants also identify with certain institutions in the morro—for instance, the churches, the escolas de samba, or the tráfico—and they have to cope with the presence of other-minded people around them.

A description of the favela as a site of both local and trans-local sources of identification is in accordance with Alvito's (1998; 2001) description of the favela as a space that is constantly invaded by supra-local institutions and supra-local structures. Alvito introduces the terms "locality" and "supra-local institutions" for the favela to distance himself from those who take "community" as the objective unit of analysis. "Community," according to Alvito (2001, 52), presupposes a boundedness that is in fact not present. While I concur with Alvito's description of the favela as a locality characterized by a multitude of territories (the micro), his description of supra-local institutions has its disadvantages. Alvito's conceptualization of locality is based on a definition from Anthony Leeds (see Alvito 2001, 52), who defines locality mostly in terms of visual characteristics. As such, Alvito's analytical framework of the different networks in which the inhabitants participate favors a geographical understanding of the favela, with a strong visual and spatial bias. The micro level is defined mostly in terms of space and territory, and the macro level as structures that are linked to that space, such as the state, the media, or the churches. Institutions, like the churches or the state, are described as hovering above locality. In my opinion, such a description downplays the importance of sounds in the movement between institutions and micro-areas. Notwithstanding Alvito's apt criticism of the presumption that favelas are bounded communities, I think these institutions are better described as trans-local to highlight the fact that localities are in fact produced in close relation to (global) media flows (Appadurai 1996).[18]

Many sounds of the morro represent and constitute groups that form part of larger imagined (and experienced) collectivities that transcend the limits of the morro. Both the local churches of the Assembleia de Deus and the local comando are part of networks and institutions that connect different neighborhoods to one another. While the sounds of these groups mark their places in the favela and reproduce a sense of belonging for particular groups, the sounds are often transmitted from other places, or came from computers, discs, or cassettes that were produced somewhere else.[19] People who turn up the volume of their radio and amplify gospel music broadcast from somewhere else partake in a rhizomatic (Deleuze and Guattari 1987) chain of remediations that connect people in different places to one another (often simultaneously).[20] In the case of the morros, such remediations exemplify one particular form of the reterritorialization of religion. Furthermore, since the amplified sounds transcend the limits of particular micro-areas, they momentarily overcome territorial divisions while enforcing religious and ideological boundaries within the favela or between the favela and its adjacent neighborhoods.

Since this book is about the constitution of Pentecostal subjectivities amid the plethora of lifestyles that characterize favela life, let me now turn more specifically to adherents of Pentecostal churches and begin to describe their categorization of sound and music in relation to their sonic environment.

Música do Mundo Versus Música Evangélica

Besides the numerous doctrines and practices, music is a very important aspect of Brazilian Pentecostalism; in fact, most church services start with music. The hymns (*louvores*)[21] are accompanied by music that may range from a recorded tape or a single synthesizer to a large band of semiprofessional musicians. Gospel music has become an important segment of the Brazilian music industry. It is no longer necessary to go to an evangelical shop to purchase gospel records, because they are on sale in large record stores all over the country. The Igreja Universal has had its own record label, Line Records, since 1991, and record labels that are not attached to one denomination but primarily produce gospel music (e.g., MK Publicitá) have expanded substantially in the last few decades. As a result of the popularity of Christian music, since 2010 major record companies such as Sony Music and Som Livre (Rede Globo) have begun to contract Brazilian gospel singers.[22]

Figure 5 A small evangelical shop with gospel music. Photo: author.

Music is also an important aspect of Pentecostalism in Visionário. Most members of the Assembleia de Deus carry a small book called the *Harpa Christã*, which contains texts of hymns that are sung at the beginning of each culto. Generally speaking, Brazilian gospel music is influenced by North American gospel and pop music. The popular songs are often low-tempo ballads that express great emotion. When I started my research in 2001, people listened to the songs of popular Pentecostal artists such as Kleber Lucas, Marquinhos Gomes, and Cassiane, but during my last research period in 2016 the popular artists were Regis Danese, Aline Barros, and the group Diante do Trono (to name but a few).

Many young men who attended churches of the Assembleia de Deus in the favelas where I did research played an instrument and wanted to take lessons, eager to be a member of the church band of musicians. Electric guitar, bass, synthesizer, and drums were the most popular instruments among the young men. Women were often asked to sing, either solo or in a choir.

My own entrance into church communities was greatly aided by my modest ability to play drums. During one of my first encounters with Pastor Abrahão of an Assembleia de Deus a bit higher up the hill in Visionário, he showed me the musical instruments belonging to the church. When I saw the drum kit standing at the back, I asked him if I could play a little. He picked up his electric guitar and we jammed for a while. He was quite enthusiastic and told me I should participate in one of the cultos. At the next culto I attended he asked me to play with him. Up until then his seven-year-old son had been playing in the cultos, but he had much to learn, according to his father. After that first time, I was allowed to play regularly at the cultos of his and another church of the Assembleia de Deus in Visionário.

In the Assembleia de Deus located near the main street I was not allowed to play drums during the services. Apart from the fact that they had their own skilled drummer, the pastor (and members) objected to the fact that I had not accepted Jesus as my Savior and was not baptized. In the other churches the pastors and members were less strict and generally saw my interest as a step toward my conversion.

The fact that they would not let me play the drums in the Assembleia de Deus must be understood against the background of the strict (discursive) separation between *música do mundo* (music of the world) and *música evangélica* (evangelical music) that many people in evangelical churches try to safeguard. By and large, people criticized popular Brazilian music on the basis of its lyrics. People were wont to say that if the lyrics contained non-biblical, blasphemous, or heretical content, the songs should not be listened to, let alone played. It was, for example, clear to many people that you should not listen to ordinary funk music voluntarily because it was bound up with moral transgressions and violence.

Playing the drums gave me the benefit of participating in a unique manner: the members appreciated my work, and I could sit beside the pulpit and observe the participants during the culto, but most important, I experienced the importance of music in the cultos. Not unlike in other Brazilian religions, it is the music that inspires people and sets in motion the emotional participation that leads to the reception of the Holy Spirit, demonstrated by people who start shaking, dancing, and speaking in tongues. Many a time I witnessed how the interaction between musicians and other members would lead to an exalted state of being. The repetition of chords and lyrics, and the increased tempo and volume, would set the tone and environment for the Word of God to be preached with the right fervor to move people in the church. When the pastor began preaching in the emotional style that characterizes most Pentecostal sermons, people would reply with "Hallelujah" or "Jesus." When musical performances and sermons reinforced one another, the culto would *pegar fogo* (catch fire), they said.

My experiences and descriptions of the church services add to the work of Peter Althouse and Michael Wilkinson (2015), who argue that we should take seriously the role of music in the production of emotional energy that helps produce strong ties between people in religious worship activities. Basing their theoretical considerations on the work of Chris Shilling (2005), among others, Althouse and Wilkinson posit that collective ecstatic experiences in musical activity have lasting effects on the participants' embodied state of mind, which, in the case of the participants in their study, translated to strong feelings of godly love. Signs of high emotional engagement always marked the services in the churches of the Assembleia de Deus in which I participated. People cried, yelled, sang, clapped, or went into states of trance, and there is no question that music was the essential conduit for the perceived manifestation of the Holy Spirit in these churches.

Nevertheless, I also found that the willingness of people to hand themselves over to this power of church music was firmly related to their categorizations of different styles of music and the boundaries between them. The people who attended Pentecostal churches strongly disapproved of the baile funk parties, not least because (according to them) the lyrics of the music contained *palavrão*—foul language—about sex, drugs, and violence. For most of them going to a baile funk was generally associated with the *caminho errado*—literally, the "wrong path" that leads one astray from God. This does not necessarily mean people never went before or after their conversion. Many of the young people who later converted to either Assembleia de Deus or Igreja Universal had been to the bailes, including Pastor Abrahão.[23] Yet the first time I went to check out a baile at the quadra de Visionário, I went directly against the advice of one of my friends of the Assembleia de Deus. She warned me that if I attended the baile funk, people of the church would begin to doubt my spiritual state of mind and would no longer let me participate in the cultos without an explanation. Some people who had accepted Jesus stopped going to church after a while and, among other things, started attending bailes again. Others never entirely gave up the bailes in the first place.[24]

Like the funk parties, the pagodes and samba parties were spoken of with contempt by many of the people attending Pentecostal churches. Many people would not like to have been seen near such a party. Overall, people who went to the pagode in the favelas loved to party, dance, sing, and drink. Often the festivities would go on for hours into the night, and more than once I woke up at five or six in the morning with the sound of people outside still singing and drumming or clapping after the band had gone home. Many in the evangelical churches disapproved of such a lifestyle and advised me not to attend the pagodes. Early one Sunday morning I was descending to get my bread at the biroshka on the estrada when I encountered a local pagode musician with his *cavaquinho*[25] in his hands. He was smiling euphorically and shouted loudly to me, "Gringo, I am going to my second pagode!" I smiled at him while he passed an *obreiro* (assistant) of the Igreja Universal who was ascending the morro. I knew both of them, and when the young man had shouted I nodded at the obreiro, who had obviously also heard it. He shook his head wearily and said, "Only the Lord of the Light," to express both his contempt and his hope for a spiritual transformation.

The relation between the strong experiences of transcendence experienced while listening to music in the churches on the one hand, and the strong disapproval and rejection of certain other styles of music on the other, is aptly described by Chris Shilling (2005, 145), who highlights these two aspects of music in relation to the body and society in terms of music's dual capacity to engender experiences of transcendence and social objectification (or immanence).

The opposition between evangélicos and funkeiros or pagodeiros that plays itself out in the daily life of the favelas should be seen as attempts to demarcate clear lines between moral and immoral behavior from the perspective of the people who attend Pentecostal churches. The opposition to certain popular Brazilian practices is a recurring phenomenon in evangelical circles. In the media of the Assembleia de Deus and the Igreja Universal, the lifestyle of the pagodeiros is presented as irreconcilable with that of an evangélico. In these media, samba and pagode were almost invariably associated with the forbidden fruits of carnal pleasure. One of the most famous sambistas of Rio de Janeiro, Bezerra da Silva, composed many songs about the *malandros* (crooks) and bandidos of the morros. His style was named *sambandido* because in his music he sang about the violent life in the morros of Rio de Janeiro (see also Lorenz 2011). After many years of practicing Candomblé, Bezerra da Silva joined the Igreja Universal in 2001. His conversion was broadly publicized to demonstrate the power of Pentecostalism.[26] Understandably, the conversion of Bezerra da Silva was portrayed as a victory for the Lord. On the cover of the evangelical magazine *Enfoque*, accompanying a photo of his portrait, was printed the text "Bezerra da Silva with thirst for the Bible." The article in the magazine stated, "Bezerra makes clear that although he has lived among sambistas, he was never a lover of the night. He also did not like to drink or to use drugs."

Despite these discursive oppositions, the distinctions between all these groups are constantly negotiated. As Sansone (2001, 150) writes on the basis of his research among young people in a favela in 1991, "No stable youth sub-cultures form around the consumption of a single type of music, as we know them from the Anglo-Saxon literature. Rather there is a circumstantial use of music as divider and, occasionally, ethnic marker in particular moments. The informants show what one might call a cash-and-carry attitude toward musical genres and youth styles; they know how to move very well across different styles and genres." While I agree with Sansone, the successful attempts to demonize lifestyles associated with pagode and funk by members of the Pentecostal churches—especially by the older members—make certain movements between styles and genres easier than others. In other words, the constraints on certain behavior exercised by the evangelical communities in favelas make it easier to incorporate certain styles than others, and the subsequent question to be asked is, what are the cultural and religious ideologies and practices that support certain changes and impede others?

Unquestionably, it is becoming increasingly difficult to separate evangelical music based on the musical style and genre alone. Though in theory Brazilian gospel music may include a wide variety of (global) music styles, in practice, discussions about the divine status of certain music recordings and performances revolved around differences among styles. For example, whereas nowadays one may often hear gospel music with Afro-Brazilian samba rhythms, for a long time Pentecostal adherents agreed that gospel music styles could range from slow ballads (*baladas românticas*) to up-tempo rock and pop songs but should not include Afro-Brazilian styles of music. Many Pentecostal adherents considered these typical Brazilian styles to be pagan or demonic. Nowadays, most Afro-Brazilian styles have been accepted in evangelical circles as legitimate forms of gospel music, just as hard rock gospel and hip-hop gospel have also become more accepted in Brazil.

To understand how certain adoptions are made acceptable, it is important to remember the insightful work of Jay Howard and John Streck (1999, 13), who have analyzed the incorporation of popular music styles in contemporary Christian music (CCM) in the United States. According to Howard and Streck, genres should not be conceived as static forms but rather as temporary expressions of an ongoing process that involves negotiations among artists, producers, critics, and audiences and that is ultimately about the reproduction of community. In the same vein as CCM, Brazilian gospel can also be conceived as a "splintered" art world, "characterized by distinct and occasionally competing rationales for the forms that are created." However, understanding the transformations of the boundaries of Brazilian gospel requires an understanding of the ways in which Brazilian musical styles are connected to Brazilian social life. Therefore, before returning to the complexities of cultural and religious change in the forthcoming chapters, let me first describe the presence of evangelical sounds in the morro.

Transmitting the Holy Spirit

The use of electroacoustic technologies radically altered the spatialization of religion in the favelas of Rio de Janeiro. For example, when I went to buy bread or visit people in Visionário I could often hear the voice of Edir Macedo, the leader of the Igreja Universal, emanating from radios in local biroshkas owned by evangélicos. The biroshka owners who amplified gospel music and evangelical prayer occupy an important position in the public space of the favelas. For obvious reasons, they are often located where many people pass by, and consequently many people perceive the evangelical presence. In the case of the favela Acari, Christina Cunha (2002) had noted an increase in the number of local shops and biroshkas owned by evangélicos. Cunha argues that with the growth of evangelical places of worship after a police occupation of Acari in 1997, there was also a significant increase in evangelical owners of shops and biroshkas. This increase in churches and shops led to what she called "the evangelical occupation of space" in the favela:

> The social space is permeated with their ever-growing presence. There are many "crentes" who circulate in the streets and alleys with their distinctive clothes and their Bibles in their hands. They are easily identified in public by their clothing (above all the believers of the conservative churches such as the Assembleia de Deus) and they move around in groups. They hold their feasts and cultos throughout the day and invite their neighbors to participate, not sparing them or passersby from the religious proselytism so characteristic for believers of this religion, pronounced loud and clear. Some of these encounters rely on speakers, microphones and musical instruments like the guitar and tambourine to encourage the *cânticos*. Concluding, the evangélicos have infiltrated distinct spheres of "life" in Acari and in this context, the "occupation" of physical and social space is just one of the many facets of this phenomenon. (92)

This vivid description of the evangelical occupation of space in Acari is very similar to the situation in the favelas of my research. Yet while Cunha recognizes that evangélicos claim public space in the favela through their physical presence and the sounds they produce, she does not link the growing presence of evangélicos and their shops to the increased mass mediatization of sounds, transmitted from shops, houses, and churches. Nor does she investigate the particular Pentecostal experiences of the relationship between sound and space.

In the case of many of my informants in the morro, when talking about music transmitted by singing, radio, or CDs, the analogy of the movement of sound and the movement of the Holy Spirit became especially apparent. Take for example what the locally famous gospel singer/musician Alberto told me during an interview:

A: What matters to me is the Holy Spirit. The Holy Spirit for me, I love it. I love it when God talks with us and the Holy Spirit is transmitted to the people. For me, this is what the Holy Spirit is. I feel the Holy Spirit in my life and I can transmit the Holy Spirit to the people who are listening. It is my heart's wish. I don't want it just for me, I want the people to feel the good things that I feel.

M: Are you saying that the Holy Spirit uses music?

A: Music, that is it. *Louvor* is the instrument—in the church we call it *louvor*—sing and everybody sings. Louvor is something that flows, so when people *louva* the Lord Jesus the Holy Spirit comes automatically, you feel that joy and you transmit that to other people. And the people become glorified, become sane, and even people who are ill, physically ill, spiritually ill, feel cured through the louvor, people are cured through the louvor. For example, those who are on the verge of doing something stupid, who want to commit suicide, who want to leave their family, who want to leave everything behind or do bad things. Normally when those people listen to louvor that is dedicated to Lord Jesus, that louvor makes them feel different, the opposite of what they felt. Those people open their heart and let it flow, and nothing bad happens.

Not only does he attribute spiritual power to music dedicated to Jesus, the imagination and experience of the Holy Spirit that reaches people through space by means of louvor also allows the idea of the spiritual occupation of space by means of gospel music. People can become mediators of the Holy Spirit through the louvor they produce and amplify.

This capacity to reach people with the help of evangelical mass media is perhaps best described by the tactics of Gilberto, one of my friends who at the time of my first research period attended the Assembleia de Deus. Apart from his never-ending invitations to visit a culto of his church, his enjoyment of very loud gospel music, and his plans to revive the local gospel radio program, he showed me another evangelization scheme he claimed to exercise frequently. While passing by the shops at the foot of the morro, he dragged me into a record shop where he asked for a specific gospel CD. When they had found one he wanted, he asked if he could hear it played in the shop in order to decide whether he wanted to buy it. When they had replaced the background music in the shop with his gospel CD, he pretended to be unsure about his purchase and asked the girls behind the counter to increase the volume. When they did so, he stayed to listen only briefly until the attention of the personnel shifted to another customer, after which he dragged me outside. As we left the shop behind us I could hear the sound of gospel music coming from the shop. It was loud enough to be audible from a hundred meters down the street, and I immediately understood how he attempted to reach the people who were shopping. "Louvor muda o coração, Martins" (Louvor changes the heart, Martijn), he said while he smiled at me.

Conclusion

The appeal of Pentecostalism cannot be understood exclusively on the basis of its doctrines and practices. People are attracted to its message in relation to the environment of the favelas where forró, samba, pagode, and funk echo day and night. The cacophony of sounds and music reflects the power struggles in the morro and the position Pentecostalism occupies in it. Language, music, and noise are important tools in the (trans)formation of identity and the creation and maintenance of boundaries between groups. It is primarily through sounds that people exercise a politics of presence in the landscape of the morro. Sound and music not only reflect the presence of different groups but are essential to the constitution of group identities.

Pentecostal music acquires its meaning against the background of the music that is defined as "worldly" instead of "godly." Furthermore, the religious meaning and experience of louvor that defines gospel music as a vehicle of the Holy Spirit marks the specific power of Pentecostal sound in the soundscape of the morro. A focus on the soundscape of the morro also highlights the fact that electronic media are woven in the fabric of its social life. Almost all the sounds one hears in the morro are technically mediated in one way or another, and these sounds demonstrate that identity is not produced either locally or supra-locally, but rather in relation to one another (i.e., trans-locally).

This chapter has attempted to break with a prevailing tradition to foreground visual descriptions of place not only because I want to make a theoretical point about ocular-centrism in academic scholarship, but primarily because the reproduction of Pentecostal subjectivity in the favelas is strongly related to the sonic environment. To be able to explain in more detail how Pentecostal adherents envision a break with cultural practices—which I describe as hypermediated conversion in chapter 4—it is important to give the reader a sense of how these cultural practices touch the favela residents. Before returning in more detail to the ways that Pentecostal residents deal with sound in chapter 5, the following chapter offers an analysis of the reproduction of the Pentecostal worldview in relation to mass mediated images and narratives concerning the threats of lethal violence in the favelas of Rio de Janeiro.

Mass Mediating Spiritual Battles

Pentecostalism and the Daily News

The open-air deliverance in Visionário, described in the introduction of this book, featured a number of men who presented their emotional testimonies publicly. The former traficante shared his past life of crime and violence with his audience in order to persuade the listeners to accept Christ as their Savior. During the open-air service, the church members showed images of an overpopulated prison in Rio de Janeiro to emphasize the possible consequences of becoming part of a comando or milícia. The public event up the morro ended with the deliverance of several men and women who had gathered in the public square. In this ritual performance the Pentecostal church portrayed itself as the liberator of the evil of the favela and of Brazilian society at large.

The link between religion and violence is commonly approached in two ways. The first links the two by focusing on the upsurge of armed conflict, terrorism, or genocide under the banner of religion; the second links the two by focusing on the possible smoothing out of conflict through religious doctrine and practice (Appleby 2000). In several Latin American contributions to studies on Pentecostalism, it has been argued that the Pentecostal doctrines and practices offer spiritual interventions in harsh social conditions (again, see the introduction of this volume). Leonildo Campos, for example, argues that the neo-Pentecostal rituals of the Igreja Universal are so popular because they offer people tools to deal with their social conditions. The Pentecostal rituals and practices of the Igreja Universal have a strong "magical" character that people employ to conceptualize and combat the dangers and risks of daily life:

The rites, practices, and vision of the world in the Igreja Universal, prompt us to think that the relations between magic and religion are often much better defined by continuity and complementarity than by exclusion. Possibly, in this Igreja, the visibility of the magical and the tension between the two poles are more readily perceptible because its target audience consists of people in extreme situations. Those individuals experience the uncertainties of urban life intensely, in the framework of a capitalist economy under reconstruction, coupled with a disarticulation process of modes of living provoked by the coming of a "postmodern" style. All this provides opportunities for the use of rituals that reduce the uncertainties and restore in the individuals the belief that the world can be manipulated and is not arbitrary. (Campos 1997, 42)

Although I broadly agree with Campos that the Igreja Universal offers people rituals, routines, and practices that seek to "reduce the uncertainties and restore in the individuals the belief that the world can be manipulated and is not arbitrary," the cruzadas I described in the preceding chapters suggest that Pentecostal churches also emphasize the violent conditions of daily life up the morros of Rio de Janeiro in order to present themselves as a powerful counterforce.

In this chapter I will argue that we should be mindful not to portray Pentecostal practices as merely soothing. While Pentecostal churches generally depict themselves as institutions that deliver the cariocas from evil, they actively invoke images and narratives that must ineluctably confirm the violent nature of Brazilian society in order to present themselves as powerful institutions that counter it. The apparent paradox is that Pentecostal practices and discourses can thus never fully attain a sense of peace, an end of uncertainty, because the promise of ending violence by means of massive evangelization in the city is dialectically related to the representation of the city as an evil place.[1]

A second argument that runs through this chapter—and the entire book— aims to persuade the reader that we can only fully understand the seduction and truthfulness of the Pentecostal representations when we analyze the Pentecostal media in close relation to other media. Following the indications of pastors and fellow church members, people search for confirmation of biblical truths in newspapers and television. As I will demonstrate in this chapter, these media tend to confirm what people see and hear around them in the morro, producing what Schwartz (1995, 316) calls a "reality effect."[2]

To put these points across I will discuss several of the representations the Igreja Universal and the Assembleia de Deus employ to enforce a Pentecostal imagination of the batalha espiritual, the metaphysical battle between God and the devil. A discussion of these representations will clarify how these churches attempt to weave together different visual tropes to represent Brazilian society as inherently violent. In particular, the representations in the *Folha Universal* demonstrate that the Igreja Universal presents violent events in Brazilian society as diabolical evil, which can only be stopped through the mediations of Pentecostal pastors (Montes 1998; Birman 2006). Moreover, the example of this newspaper also demonstrates the publication's intertextual character. As we will see in chapter 4, where I will discuss a magazine of the Assembleia de Deus, the *Mensageiro da Paz* (Peace messenger), other Pentecostal media offer similar representations of crime and violence, and at the local level followers of the two churches present markedly similar re-narrations of mass mediatized violence. I have chosen to emphasize the *Folha Universal* in this chapter because I encountered the newspaper in the homes of many favela inhabitants who congregated at different Pentecostal churches and because the evangelical newspaper arguably presented an innovative bridging of genres, as we will see below.

My attempt at unraveling images and narratives of violence represented in the *Folha Universal* are in line with a method of intertextual analysis put forward by Norman Fairclough (1995, 61), who writes, "Intertextual analysis aims to unravel the various genres and discourses—often, in creative discourse practice, a highly complex mixture—which are articulated together in the text." The Igreja Universal has been able to put forward its compelling Pentecostal interpretation of Brazilian society because its message is intertextually framed against the background of spectacular urban violence (Birman 2006).

Urban violence is one of the popular media topics in Brazil. Not only is it emblazoned daily in the newspapers and television news broadcasts, but it also often features on infotainment television and in popular Brazilian magazines (Flausino 2003). The Brazilian news media conspire to construct an image of society that is fundamentally divided between "the good" and "the bad." While in all these media the spectacular images of violence are highlighted, an analysis of the origins of violence is less prominent. This leaves ample room for the Pentecostal churches to seize the images and narratives of urban violence and to transform the dichotomy of "the good" versus "the bad" into the Pentecostal dualism of "God" versus "the devil."

The incorporation of mass mediatized violence in the media of the Igreja Universal and other Pentecostal churches creates a powerful Pentecostal narrative that people employ to narrate their own experiences with violence in Rio de Janeiro. This also holds for the inhabitants of the favelas. Even though comparatively they are the citizens who generally face more armed violence than the well-to-do people who live in other neighborhoods—on the asfalto—this does not mean their understanding of the city and their own environment comes into being by means of unmediated experience. As I briefly pointed out in the introduction, it is better to follow William Mazzarella's (2004, 353) insight that "local worlds are necessarily already the outcome of more or less stable, more or less local social technologies of mediation."

Spectacular Violence and the City

Violent conflicts over territories in favelas between comandos, police forces, and milícias are part of the everyday broadcasts and print media of Rio de Janeiro. They feature daily in the headlines of newspapers and in talk among inhabitants of the city. Though news media and investigative reports provide important information about collective well-being, crime news is also part of politicized fields of representations (see Jewkes 2004). Crime and violence form part of a market of images and narratives that news media appropriate discursively for commercial use. Moreover, in order to capture audiences, news media frequently seek to affect viewers emotionally through dramatization and spectacularization of daily urban conflicts. This means that we cannot take crime news for facts. It also means we should be aware that crime news has a life of its own (see also Hayward 2010); it co-constitutes shared evaluations of city life and categorizations of urban populations and territories.

While reporting on violence is arguably one of the functions of news media in modern democracies such as Brazil, many authors feel that Brazilian mass media play an important role in the production of what the Brazilian anthropologist Luiz Eduardo Soares (1995) has called the "culture of fear" (cultura do medo). In her groundbreaking study on crime and urban segregation, Teresa Caldeira (2000) analyzed the paradoxical role of the narrations of urban violence in São Paulo. According to Caldeira, the talk of violence, intended to control and counteract it, also generates violence itself, thus unintentionally contributing to a cycle of violence. Although my understanding of Rio de Janeiro is much influenced by her analysis, I think the mass mediation of urban violence cannot be grasped in terms of narration alone. We should also consider images and sounds that together produce imaginations of the city. As became apparent during my fieldwork among favela inhabitants in Rio de Janeiro, television programs, music lyrics, and other media contribute in different ways to the imagined presence of mundane and transcendent forces that make the city a terrain of violent struggle. One might think of the funk proibidão lyrics I described in the preceding chapter or of the Pentecostal testimonies, to name some examples.

Following Arjun Appadurai (1996, 31), I treat imagination as social practice and as "a form of negotiation between sites of agency . . . and globally defined fields of possibility." My understanding of imagination, moreover, is influenced by work on the "technologies of imagination" by David Sneath, Martin Holbraad, and Morten Axel Pedersen (2009), who argue that different technologies open up space for imagination without predetermining the phenomena they help to bring about. Their emphasis on the technologies of imagination connect well to the writings of media scholar Jesus Martín-Barbero (2002, 27), who has argued that in Latin America media have become "part of the basic fabric of urbanity."

As I argue in this chapter, mass media play an important part in the imagination of urban violence, allowing for archetypical urban characters in a field of violent confrontations. Since the mid-1990s, when forces of the Brazilian military took hold of a number of morros during Operação Rio, television programs and newspapers have reproduced images of the city as existing in a "state of war" (Leite 1997). As Marcelo Lopes de Souza (2008) has argued more recently, continuing representations of Brazilian cities in terms of a *guerra civil* (civil war) in fact increase the militarization of certain public spaces and push political projects that are in favor of repressive state measures against people who live in favelas. According to Souza, for these reasons, the Brazilian megacity could best be conceptualized as a *fobópole* (city of fear).

Though media representations in and of Rio de Janeiro present different narratives as to who or what threatens the city at particular moments (e.g., comandos, milícias, the police), one of the driving dichotomies remains the distinction between urban "heroes" and "villains" (see also Coimbra 2001, 36). Such a driving dichotomy allows for dramatic narratives of struggle, violence, and justice that lend themselves well to religious and spiritual appropriations. One of the media that shows well the overlaps between religious ideology and journalism is the weekly newspaper of the Igreja Universal: the *Folha Universal*.

Pentecostal Adaption of the News

Before the penetration of Internet and social media in the favelas of Rio de Janeiro, the printed version of *Folha Universal* was one of the most prominent media the Igreja Universal used to inform its members, to attract new followers, and to manifest itself as a credible political institution in a mass democracy. The weekly newspaper is principally distributed in the churches of the Igreja Universal, but one can also access a digital version of the newspaper on the church's website.[3] Volunteers of the church also hand out the newspaper on the streets and in the favelas to attract new members.

Interestingly, the headlines and large color photos of the newspaper's front page often feature the same subjects as those of the major daily newspapers in Brazil. At first sight one may not immediately recognize the newspaper as part of an evangelical megachurch. This may strike certain people as problematic since it blurs the commonly accepted normative boundaries between religion and politics. In Western state formations, religion has often been described as a private matter that should not enter the public domain (Casanova 1994), unless in a particular rational manner (Hoover 1998). One of the consequences of this normative distinction is an apparent tension between the professional ethics of journalism and religious faith. In the United States, for example, the ideal of objective newsgathering is commonly considered antithetical to the subjective expression of religious faith (Gormly 1999, 27; Schmalzbauer 2002, 166).

However, as John Schmalzbauer convincingly argues, religious discourse and journalism cannot be separated easily. For example, evangelical and Catholic journalists employ different strategies to overcome the apparent opposition. Journalists translate their religious convictions into professional discourse through what Schmalzbauer (2002, 168) calls "multivocal bridging languages," which combine vocabularies drawn from both journalism and religious groups.[4] According to Schmalzbauer, multivocality means that texts may have multiple meanings, "capable of eliciting more than one interpretation" (171).

The evangelical editors of the *Folha Universal* employ a similar strategy of multivocal bridging. As Luís Mauro Sá Martino (2002, 316) suggested, the Igreja Universal generally uses the *Folha Universal* to "codify the news in order to integrate it into a larger narrative." This larger narrative is structured by the notion of the cosmic spiritual battle between God and the devil, and in practice it can be woven through many of the news stories reproduced daily. One could think of natural disasters, armed conflict, or other types of violence, for example. According to Sá Martino, this larger religious-political narrative aims to convince readers that sociopolitical action in this world is part of a divine plan in which Pentecostal leaders (politicians) and followers may participate.

One of the questions concerns how this works in practice. How do people come to regard events in the world as confirmations and examples of a Pentecostal worldview? Following the approaches of Schmalzbauer, Sá Martino, and many others, we should understand news media as important contributors to the social construction of reality (Berger and Luckmann 1966) and thus as important sites that produce and confirm our notions of the world. Yet, in contrast to the original description by Berger and Luckmann (39), who describe religion as a distinct province of meaning, the Pentecostal narrative of the *Folha Universal* is so appealing because it does not present "religion" as something beyond everyday life. On the contrary, Pentecostal adherents are constantly invited to think of "ordinary" events in Pentecostal terms.[5]

But how does this work specifically in relation to news media? The concept of genre may shed light on the manner in which the Igreja Universal is able to portray the spiritual battle between God and the devil in its newspaper. Though genres are open-ended by definition—and therefore can contain intertextual images and narratives—they must display a certain coherence in form and content over time to be meaningful to both producers and consumers (McQuail 1994, 263). The news genre has several particular characteristics that distinguish it from other genres. The moral-political reading of news reports is largely dependent on "neutrality" and "facticity." To produce "facticity" news reports must display consistency in form and content—for example, they must display a recognizable order in the events that happened recently, and this must be presented as facts rather than as stories open to interpretation. In the case of the newspaper, the layout of the front page is also very important. The headlines on the front page present the news deemed most important that day, framed in such a way that the reader is presented with the core issue immediately, often accompanied by a photo that features the object under scrutiny.

Not only are the subjects on the front page of the *Folha Universal* similar to other newspapers in Rio de Janeiro, but in general the size and paper of the journals are also much alike, as is the layout of the front page. All front pages address socioeconomic problems in Brazil: the great gap between rich and poor, the high unemployment, the violence in urban areas, and so forth. Apart from these common front-page topics, the greater part of the *Folha Universal* presents information that is evangelical in content: testimonies of people who have joined the Igreja Universal and have witnessed their lives change for the better, words of instruction from pastors, photos of churches filled with faithful followers, and the like. Given this distinction, one might think that journalism and evangelism are neatly separated in the journal. A closer reading, however, unequivocally reveals that the news items on the front page are placed in a particular relation to Pentecostal doctrine further on in the newspaper.

While I think Sá Martino rightly argues that the *Folha Universal* plays an important role in the social construction of reality, both he and Schmalzbauer do not say much about the role images and photos play in such a construction. This is striking because news media put great emphasis on visual material and because a number of influential religious scholars have emphasized the importance of looking at the formation of religious subjectivity (Meyer 2006; Morgan 1998).

Photographs are not mere illustrations of the headlines and texts. Rather, they "factualize" the news, as Susan Sontag (2003) has reminded us. Most people only experience news events as "real" after having seen the images that portray them. Given the consistency of the newspaper form, the Igreja Universal can employ the news genre to present its evangelical messages as "factual." Therefore, in the *Folha Universal* news is often portrayed as factual on the front page, after which the reader is directed to another page that employs "the news" to factualize an evangelical message.

Photos that portray perpetrators, victims, and symbols of violence in Rio de Janeiro are essential to this process. Photos in newspapers commonly read in Rio de Janeiro confirm the reality of a violent society, and photos and images take up a central position in the *Folha Universal*. To regard them merely as illustrations of the text would be to miss the point. Since images are in essence multivocal—they have no fixed or definite meaning—they facilitate the convergence between the social reality presented in the *Folha Universal* and the social reality presented in other media. One could say they are bridging signs par excellence.

Let me give a small example. The headline of the *Folha Universal* of June 16, 2002, read, "Brazil is the most violent in its use of firearms." The small article beside the photo that shows a rifle and ammunition explains that Brazil is on top of the list of sixty-nine countries that experience the most crime and is in the top five countries where homicide is committed by use of firearms. A smaller photo of a collection of weapons with a police sign placed behind it accompanies the photo of the rifle. Such a display of weapons is part of the common visual representation of a successful police operation in which such items were confiscated from criminals. Similar photos appear in all kinds of newspapers and television programs in the city every day. In conjunction with the photo of the rifle, this photo suggests that firearms are indeed used in homicide.

Nevertheless, the photos in themselves are not sufficient to construct a Pentecostal perspective on the world, and the text itself also does not

appear to be explicitly Pentecostal. So how are readers persuaded to think of this news in Pentecostal terms? At the end of the small article in the *Folha Universal*, readers are directed to read page 1B of the same newspaper. Here, more data on violence has been added, including a list of firearms that have been encountered in the hands of the infamous comandos of Rio de Janeiro. At the bottom of the page, in a separate article, a pastor of the church explains that even though there are various circumstances related to violence—addiction to drugs and alcohol, social inequality, unemployment, adultery—the fight against violence should commence at the level of the family and the church. According to the pastor, "Human beings have in them goodness and badness, and if the child learns the path of goodness, of faith in God, of justice and of truth, teachings that should be inculcated by the parents and are preached in the churches, certainly we would have a world of peace. That is why we are going to ask God to free us of evil. May God bless everyone."[6] The words of the pastor place the journalistic accounts of the preceding pages in the *Folha Universal* in a Pentecostal perspective. The pastor claims that the violence must be interpreted in the light of the spiritual battle between God and evil and that to counter the violence in Brazil, one should study the Bible and have faith in God.

As we will see, the described dialectic between the factualizing power of news media and the Pentecostalization of news media plays itself out in other Pentecostal representations, and it can also occur outside of media when people interpret and express certain news events in Pentecostal terms. In the context of the favelas of my research, the representation of urban violence was one of the most explicit domains of this dialectic, as we will see below.

Moral Dichotomies

The image of Rio de Janeiro as one of the most violent cities in the world is primarily related to the violent encounters between comandos, police officers, and milícias in and around the favelas. For obvious reasons, among the most important political issues are those that concern *segurança pública* (public safety). As journalists are happy to remind the governors, recurring armed conflicts that cause casualties in and around favelas exemplify the incapacity of the state government to gain a monopoly on violence. The creation of UPPs can be seen as an attempt to counter such accusations.

The proliferation of news on violence has other consequences, however. The constant production of news about chaotic violence, robberies, and assaults strengthens (and structures) the existing fear of violence among the population. As Alba Zaluar (1998, 246) stated about violence some time ago:

> It has become part of the day-to-day conversations in the home, in the street, in the school, in the commercial establishments, in the newspapers, on the radios, on all the channels of the television, in the judicial inquiries and processes, everywhere one wants to discuss what happened or could happen. It has incorporated itself both in the informal practices, pertaining to the field of tacit agreements of day-to-day life, which are not made explicit in any code but are fully accepted by people in their social interaction, acquiring an invisibility of that which is "natural" or habitual, and in the sphere of the institutions created to defend the law.

Several Brazilian authors have argued that the Brazilian mass media play an important role in the production of a local "culture of fear."[7] As Elizabeth Rondelli (1994) argues, violence and crime form part of a market of images and narratives that *telejornais* (television news broadcasts) appropriate discursively for commercial use. According to Rondelli, "It is difficult to deny that there is a repressed and voyeuristic curiosity among the public for violent episodes" (98). Telejornais offer viewers dramatization and spectacularization, thereby disassociating crimes from the socioeconomic and historical circumstances in which they are committed. These programs attempt to organize reality according to clear-cut definitions: "In the case of violence, the media do not only define, but also organize the world from the perspective of the moral dichotomy of good and bad, designate their attributes, name their practitioners, determine punishments."

Many Brazilian newspapers—including "serious" newspapers—feature spectacular representations of violence common to the telejornais. Publications such as *O Globo* or *Folha de S. Paulo* also regularly indulge in spectacular accounts of violent events. Sandra Jovchelovitch (2000, 98) has argued that in these journals and magazines "the Brazilian streets" are represented as a violent, chaotic domain ruled by criminals and drug traffickers. Her analysis comprised five Brazilian journals in 1992, including the popular weekly magazines *Veja* and *IstoÉ*, and deals primarily with the symbolic construction of public spaces in Brazil. Cecilia Coimbra analyzed five newspapers, including *O Globo*, before, during, and after the military interventions in the favelas of Rio de Janeiro in 1994. Steering the same course as Rondelli, Coimbra (2001, 36) argues that the language of Brazilian newspapers is largely organized based on the dichotomy of "the good" and "the bad." While both authors point to the spectacularization of the news, they barely touch on the importance of the photos and images that portray perpetrators and victims of violence. This is remarkable given the fact that these images literally give faces to the dichotomy and generally feature prominently in newspapers, websites, and television programs.

During my first phase of fieldwork in Rio de Janeiro, several violent events haunted the city's newspapers for weeks.[8] In this section I analyze two cases that produced icons of mass mediated violence in Rio de Janeiro as a result of their repeated presence in all kinds of media, including Pentecostal channels. One of them concerned the murder of Tim Lopes, a *Globo* journalist, who was killed, quartered, and burned by traficantes when he tried to film drug deals with a hidden camera on June 2, 2002. The other concerned the murder of local drug lords by their rival, Fernando Beira-Mar, inside Rio de Janeiro's maximum-security prison, Bangu 1 (see also Gay 2010; 2015). Both events reproduced several personae as symbols of urban violence. In particular, the repeated reproduction of the faces of the protagonists—perpetrators and victims—on the front pages of the newspapers, in magazines, and on television established them as the icons of urban violence.

Tim Lopes had been missing for more than a week before the police were convinced he had been murdered. Besides the earlier reports on his disappearance, the headline of *O Globo* on June 10, 2002, read, "Tráfico sentenced, tortured, and executed Tim Lopes." In the weeks and months thereafter, Tim Lopes became the martyr of comando-related violence in Rio de Janeiro. His name and face reappeared again and again in association with news reports concerning his violent death: in relation to memorials organized as protest against the violence;[9] after the DNA identification of his bones (found in an illegal burial site in a favela);[10] after his burial; and after the capture of the alleged killer, "Elias Maluco" (Mad Elias), 109 days after his death. One photo of Tim Lopes in particular was used repeatedly for several months. This photo was carried on the banners of demonstrations and displayed during his funeral wake; for that reason, it became the iconic representation of the fight against comando-related violence in Rio de Janeiro.

Around the same time, another man's representation became an icon of the violence committed by the drug gangs. On September 11, 2002, Fernando Beira-Mar, the alleged head of the Comando Vermelho, instigated a rebellion inside the maximum secured prison Bangu 1 and brutally killed the leaders of another comando also imprisoned there. The *Jornal do Brasil* of September 12 opened with the headline "Tráfico terrorizes Rio . . . Beira-Mar commands rebellion and deaths in Bangu 1," accompanied by a photo of a sign with the letters "CV" on it, hanging from the prison wall. *O Globo* presented a similar photo with the headline, "Beira-Mar takes command of the parallel power and terrorizes Rio." By his actions, Fernando Beira-Mar not only confirmed his domination over the Comando Vermelho, he also consequently acquired the status of media celebrity.

In many broadcasts and newspapers in September 2002, Beira-Mar was presented as the symbol of the tyranny of the comandos and the inability of the state to counter the actions of criminal organizations. On the cover of *Veja* on September 18, 2002, Beira-Mar is portrayed, unshaven, against a red background that arguably enforces his evil appearance (see figure 6). The caption beneath the photo states "He mocks the law" and "Fernando Beira-Mar is the proof that the Brazilian state does not even succeed in keeping a criminal isolated inside a prison." While it remains unlikely that Beira-Mar in fact terrorized the whole city, he appeared in all types of media channels again and again and became the symbol of comando-related killings.

In the weeks following the news broadcasts, headlines, and articles about these two cases, the protagonists frequently appeared in evangelical media, and inhabitants of the morro regularly referred to the cases in daily talks. As I will explain in the following section, editors of the *Folha Universal* incorporated the common representations of "evil perpetrators" and "innocent victims" in their representations of a society characterized by a spiritual battle.

Incorporating Spectacular Violence

In the same month that all the headlines discussed the murder of Tim Lopes and the alleged power of the comandos, the *Folha Universal* presented a series of headlines on the topic of urban violence. During the first week of June it opened with the headline "Tráfico exploits seven thousand underaged in Rio." This was accompanied by a photo of three handcuffed youngsters with their faces against a wall. In the third week of June, the *Folha Universal* opened with the headline "Brazil is the most violent in its use of firearms"

Figure 6 Beira Mar on the cover of *Veja*, September 18, 2002. Published by Editora Abril. Photo courtesy of ANP/Reuters.

alongside a photo of a rifle and other weapons. During the fourth week of June, the *Folha Universal* featured the headline "Middle class is violent as well," and below that, "The relationship between the richest and poorest neighborhoods is not confined to their proximity." In the text accompanying the headline, Pastor Jerónimo Alves explains that violence can be attributed to "the lack of knowledge of the Word of God." As is the case in other issues of the *Folha Universal*, the reader is directed to page 1B, where the pastor states the following:

> The cruel assassination of Tim Lopes leaves us with a sad and shocking reality: violence has taken over the large urban centers . . . we know it is not culture, employment, or housing that will transform the life of a people imprisoned by a super-human force, what will counter this pattern is the power that comes from God. . . . The lack of knowledge of the Word of God, which lets us meet Christ and leads us to a full, worthy life, has brought our nation to this harsh reality. "Blissful is the nation whose God is the Lord" is what the Bible says in Psalms 33:12.

With this message the Igreja Universal apparently seeks to explain violence as a reflection of a spiritual—rather than a sociocultural—struggle and, simultaneously, attempts to counter the idea that people in the favelas are solely responsible for crime and violence. Nevertheless, in order to substantialize and factualize the spiritual battle between God and the devil, the Igreja Universal incorporates powerful media symbols: the victim—"Tim Lopes"—and the perpetrator—"the traficante." In a separate article, another pastor of the Igreja Universal explains that since there is not one single social factor that explains or counters violence, it is clear that only God can save the nation. Importantly, as we will see in more detail below, the Igreja Universal presents its own Pentecostal politicians as mediators between the spiritual and worldly realm and as people who can save the nation from the perils that threaten it.

An example of the way comando-related violence is incorporated in the political project of the Igreja Universal comes from the first *Folha Universal* of 2003.[11] This edition offers the reader a "Retrospectiva 2002," a look back at the events of the prior year, including a montage[12] of photos of (in)famous celebrities of that year. The montage presents both victims and perpetrators who were involved in violent confrontations and violent crimes, among them Tim Lopes, Osama bin Laden (and George W. Bush), and the daughter of the Von Richthofen family, who killed her own parents with the help of her boyfriend and his brother. All these celebrities represent violent stories that were discussed repeatedly in all Brazilian news media in the year 2002.[13] The text alongside the montage asks, "Mundo vive o final dos tempos?" (Is the world living the end of time?), a question echoed in the article below the montage: "Could it be that the apocalyptic beasts have been released? Only the faith in our Lord Jesus can liberate humanity from so much evil."[14] In addition, gang leader Fernando Beira-Mar is described as "the bandit who held the people hostage in the arms of the parallel power."

The format and content of the montage proved to be a popular way of creating a retrospective of the year. The cover of the *IstoÉ* of December 25, 2002, featured a similar montage of photos of the main characters of 2002: George W. Bush, Saddam Hussein, and Fernando Beira-Mar.[15] The striking difference between the montage in the *Folha Universal* and the montage on the cover of the *IstoÉ* is the central character of the montage. In the *IstoÉ*, Ronaldo, the star soccer player who had led the Brazilian national team to victory in the world championship that year, and Lula, the elected president, are featured. The montage of the *Folha Universal*, on the other hand, features a Pentecostal hero. The middle of this montage presents a large photo of Pastor Marcelo Crivella of the Igreja Universal making the victory sign. This juxtaposition of images and texts highlights the way the Igreja Universal aims to present itself as a powerful force opposing violence in Brazilian society.

As I will describe in more detail at the end of this chapter, pastors of the Igreja Universal ran for political positions, and in different media they are presented as powerful mediators who can combat the violence taking place on both spiritual and worldly levels. Their capacity to wield power is projected onto an intertextual background of dramatized violence produced by the Brazilian media in its totality. Before explaining how the political and religious capacities of celebrity pastors mirror and enforce one another, let me say a bit more about other news media in relation to Pentecostalism, after which I will present some examples of the ways inhabitants of Visionário talked about the news media and news events and how they related the representations of society in these media to their own daily environment.

Watching the News

Television occupied a central position in most of the small living rooms I visited in the favelas over the years (see chapter 6 for more information on the role of television). Though many people read the headlines on the newspapers that were pinned to kiosks in the streets on the asfalto, I encountered no such kiosks in the favelas. Many people in Visionário watched daily news programs (*notícias*) and reality programs that showed crimes, police operations, and other urban events. Two popular programs in the category "reality programs" at the time of my research were *Brasil Urgente* (Urgent Brazil), offered by the network Band, and *Cidade Alerta* (Watchful city), offered by the network Record.[16] Both programs offered live and recorded images of shootings, accidents, car chases, and similar events. The journalists who hosted these programs repeatedly presented dramatized accounts of the urban violence. Markedly, the network SBT had featured a similar program, called *Aqui Agora* (Here and now), in the 1990s, highlighting the abundance of "real" crime and violent television on the open channels of Brazilian television.

While I discuss television-watching practices in depth in chapter 6, it is important to acknowledge that the spiritual battle against the devil also concerns the selection of which mass media should and should not be watched and heard. In practice, this means that many members of Pentecostal churches expressed their worries about certain television programs and types of music. Many claimed there were certain restrictions on viewing non-Christian programs, which were considered "of the world." Often, these programs showed nudity, sex, or sinful behavior according to Pentecostal doctrines. Though these prescriptions circulated among most of the evangélicos in the favelas I encountered, it certainly does not mean none of these people ever watched the programs they condemned. Yet in their discussions of these programs they expressed certain restrictions on viewing and listening that amounted to self-disciplining practices concerning the mass media. Contrary to the programs considered suspect, such as telenovelas, notícias were never mentioned as dangerous in any way (see also Bakker 2007). In my conversations and interviews with Pentecostal adherents, notícias were presented as natural representations of "the world" and harmless in terms of Pentecostal/moral content. They were not discussed as programs made by particular networks, as was the case with, for example, the telenovelas of TV Globo, nor were they made part of discussions about their religious validity in relation to the Bible. They were certainly not discussed as cultural constructs filmed and edited by people who make choices about how to present certain events on the bases of conventions of style and format.

People who attended the Igreja Universal often complained about the immoral content of Globo television programs, but criticism of Rede Record rarely passed their lips. Edir Macedo, leader of the Igreja Universal, owns Rede Record, but this does not mean the network offers only Pentecostal programs. TV Record broadcasts all types of programs, ranging from notícias and sports to telenovelas and movies. These programs show little or no relation to the Igreja Universal, apart from the program *Gospel Line*, which features gospel singers from the Igreja Universal record label. Programs of the Igreja Universal are broadcast in the early morning, the afternoon, and late at night. Its programs, such as *Ponto de Luz*, generally follow the format of a talk show in which a pastor addresses the spiritual problems of his guests, followed by recorded testimonies of others (see chapter 6 for more on this program). These evangelical shows advertise the Igreja Universal as a church that offers spiritual help for many different individual problems (e.g., insomnia, stress, fear, and anxiety), which are portrayed as signs of demonic possession. To get rid of them, people are advised to come to the Igreja Universal, where they can be delivered of their oppression through exorcism (*descarrego*).

The other programs on Rede Record showed little or no sign of this evangelical endeavor. *Cidade Alerta*, which brings live and recorded news of crime, violence, and accidents, was one of the few non-evangelical programs on Rede Record in which an explicit evangelical message appeared. During *Cidade Alerta*, images of police interventions and armed encounters in favelas were regularly interrupted by comments from Marcelo Crivella or another pastor of the Igreja Universal. These pastors responded directly to the violent images with an *oração* (prayer) in which they asked God to bless the people and protect them—us spectators—from harm. What becomes obvious is that the message of spiritual and worldly peace efficiently projected against the background of the mass mediated violence in Rio de Janeiro does not feature only in the montage of the *Folha Universal*, but also in television programs of TV Record.

Interpreting Violence

During the period I lived in the morro, I learned that the worldviews people presented to me in conversations and interviews resembled the intertextual montages that the Igreja Universal printed in the *Folha Universal* and broadcast on *Cidade Alerta*. Evangelical inhabitants often referred to images that had been broadcast on the news to substantiate their feelings of anxiety and to confirm biblical truths. Take for example the words of Carla, an eighteen-year-old girl: "The things that are happening in the world, people starving, those towers that fell, the wars, various glimpses that one has of evil, all because God is returning. . . . That day when Fernando Beira-Mar ordered all the stores to close, a heap of stores and various bars closed. There were people who went to church in despair thinking that Jesus was about to return because God is about to return. They asked, the pastor said it. They called to ask if God was returning. The pastor said he did not know; no one knows the moment when God will return." In her statement, Carla refers to an episode not long before my talk with her, when, on September 30, 2002, Fernando Beira-Mar allegedly "ordered" all the shops in Rio de Janeiro to close as a demonstration of his power. According to the information spread, shop owners would face severe consequences if they did not obey. A reconstruction of the chain of events showed that early in the morning, a couple of men belonging to the Comando Vermelho had spread the rumor that all the shops that stayed open would be attacked. Then, after the first shops stayed closed in Tijuca, a neighborhood that witnessed much gang conflict at the time, media coverage of this fact ensured that the "order" spread rapidly all over the city, setting off a chain reaction of shops that closed their doors. Many shops, schools, and other institutions located near morros known to be commanded by the CV closed their doors. Few shops were eventually attacked, but mass mediatized threats had done most of the work; the day after, the newspapers and news broadcasts confirmed what they had magnified themselves, that the whole city had been "paralyzed by fear." On October 1, 2002, the headline of the newspaper *O Dia* read, "Medo" (Fear) alongside photos of closed shops, and the headline of *O Globo* read, "Rio refém do medo" (Rio hostage of fear) with similar photos. The mediatized event demonstrates the intricate relationships among violence, media, and struggles over sovereignty, but—as the words of Carla show—it also became part of a local Pentecostal narrative that leans heavily on the Book of Revelation, which predicts that a time of great turmoil will precede the Second Coming of Christ.

Carla and I discussed the question of whether Beira-Mar's actions signaled Christ's Second Coming. According to Carla, many members of the Igreja Universal went to ask their pastor whether Beira-Mar's actions indeed heralded the Apocalypse after that day of unrest. Interestingly, as Carla's statement also exemplifies, leaders of the Igreja Universal maintain a seemingly paradoxical stance with regard to news events and such apocalyptic predictions.

On the one hand, the church reproduces the imagination of an apocalyptic society based on mass mediatized images and narratives, often derived from local and global news broadcasts. Yet, on the other hand, it claims to have no definite knowledge of when such a time will commence. In terms of the appeal of their message and their success, this can be regarded as a very productive paradox. It allows the church to frame societal catastrophe and tragedy in biblical terms with a linear progression toward an envisioned end, while simultaneously keeping this particular cosmological phase of turmoil in suspense and informing interested listeners that it would be better to accept Jesus today rather than tomorrow.

Carla was not the only one who laced together different media events to confirm an image and sensation of the world ruled by diabolical evil. Take for example the words of Roberto, a young man who also attended the Igreja Universal at the time: "Like the bispo said to us: the world is not what it used to be. Meaning, who is ruling the world: God or the devil? It is the devil, you understand, the majority of the news [notícias] is his, the bad news, understand? Lately there has only been death, death, death, understand, in the whole world: the guy who blew up the towers, countries entering into war with one another, here a prisoner killed other prisoners. You think that is coming from God? One feels evil stamped in one's flesh twenty-four hours a day." Strikingly, Roberto referred to the events of 9/11 and the subsequent military actions of the United States, which had been dominating news broadcasts for years. Moreover, Roberto's reference to the prison killings does not appear to be a coincidence. My interview with him took place not long after Fernando Beira-Mar killed several of his adversaries in Bangu 1. The evil that Roberto feels stamped in his flesh twenty-four hours a day, in other words, appears to be mass mediatized evil. This is important because it gives us insight into the functioning of images as powerful bodily confirmations of certain understandings of the world. In chapter 6 I offer a more detailed analysis of religion, television watching, and bodily sensation, and I demonstrate the relation between Pentecostalism and what Christopher Pinney (2001, 158) calls "corpothetics": "the sensory embrace of images, the bodily engagement that most people . . . have with artworks." For the moment, it is hopefully enough to point to the fact that Roberto's words show us in more detail how a social-religious construction of reality is supported by news broadcasts that were not explicitly or intentionally produced as "religious" media content but nevertheless become part of the cultural body of Brazilian Pentecostalism.

The particular way Pentecostal adherents incorporate news images and stories in their own understanding of daily life is exemplified by the local reception of a dramatized story of a surgeon from São Paulo in January 2003. On a Monday that month, I was visiting my friend João in the morro. We went to drink a cup of coffee at a little canteen run by Dona Denise. She had lived in Visionário all her life and was well respected by many people. She was also a member of the Igreja Universal, and I loved to chat with her in her cafeteria. This time the television was on, showing the program *Hora da Verdade* (Moment of truth) on Rede Band. The program, an infotainment talk show, repeated over and over again the details of a horrible story about an infamous plastic surgeon named Farah Jorge. Farah lived in São Paulo and had confessed that he killed his ex-girlfriend, after which he had cut her into many pieces, which were later found in suitcases in the trunk of his car. The news about this violent crime had been in all the other newspapers that week and was featured in various telejornais and other television programs. Marcia Goldschmidt, the host, exclaimed dramatically, "That someone could do such a horrible thing, why . . . ?" We—Dona Denise, João, and I—were all captivated by the images of the surgeon, who seemed like a "normal guy," while the story of the brutal death was told again and again by Marcia. The televised crime story was told without any context; therefore, the motives of the perpetrator were incomprehensible, leaving us hardly any other option than to conclude it was likely "madness" or "illness." Dona Denise reacted to the program with a sigh and a gesture that implied confirmation of what she already knew: "What a devilish thing." Then she turned to me and said, "You have to be careful, my son, the enemy is there waiting, but the angels of the Lord are circling around me." Then she began to recount a trip to Rio Sul, a large shopping mall in Rio de Janeiro. During her lunch at the mall she had asked someone to put out his cigarette while in the food court, and the man had reacted very aggressively toward her. In his reaction, Dona Denise saw the devil, who tried to make her lose her balance. However, he did not succeed, because she had God on her side and did not have to be afraid: "The devil is waiting to bite, but I have put all our lives in the hands of Lord Jesus." Immediately after that she told the story of a pastor of the Igreja Universal who was killed by nineteen gunshots three days before. Pastor Valdeci Paiva de Jesus had been elected state deputy in the elections of 2002 and was about to take his seat when he was killed. The police suspected it was a political crime because he had received threatening phone calls warning him not to take the seat. Dona Denise continued, "He was almost a *deputado* but the devil wanted to stop him from becoming one. He will not succeed, shoot this bispo and there will come another one, we still have bispo Crivella, bispo Rodrigues. There will always be another one."

Dona Denise not only reveals what she regards as the causes of the crimes committed, but she also links this kind of societal evil to threats experienced in her own life and to the crimes committed against pastors of her church. Moreover, in her words, one may also hear the echo of the idea of systematic persecution of the Igreja Universal. Since their fights with Rede Globo in the early 1990s, the church and its members regularly describe institutions and people who attack the church as puppets of the devil trying to cast obstacles on its path to glory. Leaders of the church have strategically presented critiques of their message and methods as signs that they are being persecuted much like Jesus was (Mafra 2002). Dona Denise connects the mediatized story of the plastic surgeon to her own experiences and to the murder of the pastor, and she structures all of these according to a Pentecostal framework of *guerra santa* (holy war).

This Pentecostal framework is repeated systematically in the media of the Igreja Universal and in their church services; the following example shows how pastors play an instructing role during church services that seek to direct people to interpret news according to this framework. On February 23, 2003, almost one month after we sat in Dona Denise's canteen, I participated in a service of the Igreja Universal on a Sunday night. The service was themed *busca do Espírito Santo* (search for the Holy Spirit) and was attended by approximately one hundred people, many of whom lived in Visionário. At the end of the service, the leading pastor took a *Folha Universal* that was about to be distributed and read out loud its headline: "Surgeon slices up and removes the skin of his ex-mistress." The front page of the *Folha Universal* featured a large picture of the man's face with more text: "The banality of the violence committed shocks the population more every time." While the pastor brandished the paper, he spoke forcefully into the microphone: "He removed the skin of the woman, that is horrible, do you believe that is a human thing to do? I do not believe it is. I believe that is a satanic thing. Even when you hate someone you are not capable of doing that, who believes it is a demon, *igreja*?"[17] Many people enthusiastically lifted their hands in confirmation.

After the service, I made sure I got my hands on this *Folha Universal*. The article on the front page described what the man had done to the woman and elaborated on the abundance of horrific events presented in news media: "Assassinations with the uttermost cruelty are filling the pages of the journals and the screens of the television so frequently that, unfortunately, they no longer surprise us. . . . In the wave of inexplicable violence that leaves even psychologists, anthropologists, and sociologists confused, Brazil has witnessed repeated scenes of barbarism that have become part of the nation's day-to-day existence." Whereas the article rhetorically questioned the origins of this "inexplicable violence"—supported by the subheading that read, "Evil or madness?"—the remainder of the *Folha Universal* was dedicated to providing an explanation. Subsequent pages of the *Folha Universal* in question were filled with references to many of the violent crimes that featured in established daily newspapers such as the *Folha de S. Paulo* in the weeks before. Strikingly, all the violent crimes mentioned had in common incomprehensible motives: a baby thrown against a vehicle, a woman who killed her nephew "in a macabre ritual," and so forth. The presentation of violent crimes with incomprehensible motives supports the Pentecostal notion of the sadistic nature of the devil and the necessity to collectively summon the powers of the Holy Spirit to stop him and to bring peace. For example, Pastor Jerónimo Alves responded to the presented collection of crimes in an article in the *Folha Universal* in the following manner: "In the journals the notícias are unbelievable: father kills son, son kills grandparents and some of the police, the authorities, many of them are corrupt and do not give to society the support that it needs so much. . . . People need to find the Lord Jesus so he may assuage the human rage, which, if not confined, might lead to the extermination of the species. We, bispos and pastors of the IURD, pray to the Lord Jesus so that He may bring peace among men. 'Blessed are the peacemakers, for they shall be called children of God' [Matthew 5:9]. God bless you." This last example demonstrates how pastors in church services and in church media conspire to institute a particular reading of news broadcasts and journals. Dona Denise's interpretation of the mediatized event shows us how people recount events according to the Pentecostal framework these pastors repeatedly offer their audiences.

Here it is important to return to the thoughts of Leonildo Campos, presented at the beginning of the chapter, and emphasize that the Igreja Universal not only offers an explanation for the seemingly incomprehensible evil and suffering in Brazilian society, but it also offers a host of ritual practices that seek to undo, prevent, and heal such tragedy. Moreover, the Pentecostal framework that provides an explanation of societal conflict and a response to it also provides an important foundation for the political projects of the Igreja Universal and other Pentecostal churches.

A Singing Pastor-Politician

Pastors play an important part in the political aspirations of the Igreja Universal. In 2002 Marcello Crivella, nephew of the founder of the Igreja Universal, Edir Macedo, was elected senator for the state of Rio de Janeiro (and mayor of Rio de Janeiro in 2016). His success is partly the result of the hierarchical bureaucratic structure of the Igreja Universal and the steady influx of money and rally work from its members.[18] However, equally important to his success is his mass mediated image. In his work on televangelism in the United States, Quentin Schultze (1991, 92) argues that charismatic TV preachers represent the latest version of personality cults that have always been part of Christianity.[19] According to Schultze, television has created the possibility of channeling religious charisma in such a way that people become "religious authorities" in a small amount of time. Such authority also lends itself well to the political endeavors of church leaders.

In line with this chain of thought, Michael Warner (1992) argues that bodily representations of political candidates have become indispensable to the mass identification that is required for political success. As public figures, political candidates have become mass media "icons," not unlike other celebrities. While Warner speaks mostly of "the West," Geert Banck's (1998, 29–30) work on personalism and body politics in Brazil demonstrates that the mass mediated image of the Brazilian politician is firmly embedded in the country's political process:

> The photographer's lens, by making the fluidity of a meeting independent of place and time, magnifies and casts into solid images the centrality of personal relations in Brazilian political culture. The photographer and camcorder operator have thus strategic backstage roles in the rituals of public meetings. They are, however, not merely a technical presence. They are, be it at another level, as much part of the political domain as the politicians themselves. In a political culture like the Brazilian, with its code of personalism constantly weaving itself into the public representation of institutional politics, they are the strategic decoders and "amplifiers." They produce, select, multiply and distribute the iconography of power, mostly in accordance with or commissioned by politicians.

The political endeavors of the Igreja Universal have been greatly facilitated by the church's appropriation of visual mass media. Since certain pastors of the Igreja Universal appear repeatedly in the mass media of the church, their images have been widely publicized. Before and during state and federal elections, adherents of the Igreja Universal put up images of their campaigning pastors throughout the morro, for example.

In general, the public image of the pastors of the Igreja Universal is carefully managed. When they appear in church, in photos, or on television they are always neatly dressed. As Eric Kramer (2005, 13) has argued, pastors of the Igreja Universal can be seen as "living icons."[20] Their shirts, suits, ties, and expensive-looking accessories aim to display the success of their prosperity gospel. As such, "their outer appearance expresses their own inner victory and spiritual blessing." In particular, those pastors who regularly appear on television and in magazines have become mass mediated icons of the Igreja Universal.[21]

Among the pastors of the church, Marcelo Crivella occupies an extraordinary position. Apart from being a pastor, he is presented as an engineer, gospel singer, architect of social projects, and politician. Given his multiple talents and positions, Patricia Birman (2006) identifies him as "the perfect pastor" who simultaneously embodies social, political, and financial success. As the "perfect example" of a man of faith, he represents the success people can achieve, provided they regularly attend the church. Since Crivella often featured in talks of members of the church who lived in the morro, I briefly want to return to his representation in this last section of the chapter.

Arguably the position of Crivella's image in the middle of the montage I discussed above is considered legitimate because people believe he is capable of creating a better society. As I argue, this is the case because he is represented as a powerful mediator who can combat the violence taking place on both spiritual and worldly levels. While the representation of Crivella differs depending on the medium and genre, his multiple worldly and spiritual capacities are united in his image nonetheless. His image has thus become a very important bridging sign that unites his political and religious identities without explicitly violating the normative boundary between them. Even though his spiritual and social-political works are represented separately, echoes of his other identities resonate in each separate representation of him.

Marcelo Crivella is most often presented as a political leader. Various representations of Crivella on his website show him neatly dressed in a shirt and tie or in a shirt with his sleeves rolled up.[22] Strikingly, his website does not show any images of Crivella during a church service. While Crivella often appeared in the media during campaigning periods, he was rarely portrayed performing his function as pastor. This may seem remarkable considering the fact that part of his political success appears to be directly related to his high position in the Igreja Universal, where he also functions as a powerful mediator of the Holy Spirit (which I will show in more detail in the opening section of chapter 4).

Presumably the omission of his spiritual role in the Igreja Universal can be attributed to the ideological and juridical separation between state and religion in Brazil and to the desire to attract voters who do not attend Pentecostal churches. The church in general and Crivella in particular have been recurrently accused of using religion for political ends by other political candidates in Brazil, and in their political campaigns and pamphlets they have been careful to avoid adding fuel to such accusations. Nevertheless, images have the capacity to function as bridging signs between religious and political representations precisely because they are polyvalent. Crivella's

105

spiritual role as pastor in the Igreja Universal is not visualized on his website, but his image may convey his powerful ability to mediate the power of the Holy Spirit nevertheless. This is possible, in part, because other photos of Crivella have circulated in other domains.

Crivella's identity as a gospel singer is enforced by the reproduction of his image on his CDs and advertisements of his music in Igreja Universal media. In many of the church's magazines, for instance, photos of Crivella's album *Coração a Coração* (Heart to heart) are printed, featuring his image prominently. Resonating with his perceived capacity to exorcise evil spirits and to mediate the powers of the Holy Spirit through music—both of which we will see more of in chapters 4 and 5—Crivella's image on political pamphlets arguably carries more meaning for evangelical adherents than do his capacities as a political leader.

Conclusion

During my fieldwork it became apparent that the evangélicos who live in the favelas where I did research often conceptualized in Pentecostal terms the risk of becoming a victim of crime and violence. They generally described crime and violence as the worldly manifestation of the spiritual battle between God and the devil. As I have shown by means of the narratives of the favela residents, spectacular media events that concern violent encounters between comando leaders and victims are woven through their descriptions of the urban environment. These narratives generally serve to confirm the reality of the spiritual battle taking place in the world. This circular confirmation of the state of the world—what is seen on news media confirms what is seen and experienced in the favela, and vice versa—is best understood with the help of Noël Carroll's notion of "perceptual realism." According to Carroll (1998, 139), "Realistic imagery . . . is said to carry a certain rhetorical force, namely it leaves the impression that what it depicts is the case. Perceptual realism tends to convince viewers, in some sense, of the veracity of what they are seeing." Regarding this dynamic through the lens of Pentecostalism gives us more insight into the effect of news media on the reproduction of a Pentecostal worldview, and it helps us understand that adherents of Pentecostal churches seek a confirmation of the spiritual battle in media and in daily life simultaneously. According to Karla Poewe (1989, 7), Charismatic Christianity "regards the whole universe and the whole of history [be it personal, natural, or cosmic] as consisting of signs. These signs are available to explore the meaning of life in a concretely meaningful way.

In other words, these signs are metonymic. They are the current manifestations of the creative activity of the Creator. In a high-tech world, not only the television or computer monitor but also the human being are manifestations of signs or manifest themselves through signs."

What I have tried to demonstrate in this chapter is that Pentecostal churches do not necessarily reduce the uncertainties and anxieties of people, nor do they seem to want to do so entirely. Having demonstrated the entanglement of media and daily life in the reproduction of the Pentecostal worldview, we come to the question of how this relates to religious practices on the ground.

In the following chapter I will demonstrate in more detail how Pentecostalism presents itself as a powerful counterforce to the dangers perceived, and we will see that Pentecostal doctrines and practices present particular performative models that help conceptualize and sometimes overcome the perils of daily life.

"Deliver This Favela"

Space, Violence, and Hypermediated Conversion

One afternoon during my research in Visionário, I heard that Marcelo Crivella of the Igreja Universal was coming to the favela to give an oração.[1] I was eager to photograph this event on one of the few public squares of the morro, not least because Crivella was launching his campaign for senator of the state of Rio de Janeiro. My evangelical landlady told me that he was coming to film the "development" projects in progress in the favela. The square where the oração would take place is a significant space not only because many public events, including bailes funk, were held there but also because—at the time—the square marked the boundary of comando territory. In the alley leading to the square, young boys of the comando generally oversaw and checked who entered their part of the favela.

While I was waiting with my camera in hand, Marcelo Crivella arrived at the square with a large following. Among them was a cameraman, a couple of young obreiros of the Igreja Universal who lived in the morro, two pastors of local churches of the Assembleia de Deus (Pastor Denilson and Pastor Abrahão), and Rogério, president of the associações de moradores. Rogério was also a self-confessed evangélico and one of the leaders of an Assembleia de Deus in Visionário. Upon their arrival, children and adolescents who had been waiting were arranged in front of the camera. Rogério had gathered the children of a community crèche, adolescents of a state-subsidized community project, and some other residents to perform in a couple of short video clips meant to demonstrate Crivella's care for the underprivileged people of Rio de Janeiro. Silence was requested and the recording began. Crivella commenced with an oração for the people of the community. He closed his eyes and spoke out loud to the Lord, asking Him to bless the young children and to grant the inhabitants of the morro a prosperous life. After the oração, Rogério was also given an opportunity to speak. He thanked the Lord for the fact that there was no more violence in the communities and that with His help there would be only progress for all.

After the orações Crivella invited the people present to receive a healing and a *libertação* (deliverance). He put his hands on the sides of their heads and charged the evil demons (*encostos*) to abandon the person.[2] The first public exorcisms were filmed by the cameraman in Crivella's retinue as well as by a cameraman Rogério had brought along. Yet, at a certain moment, Rogério pointed to a barrack building overlooking the square and down came several bare-chested young men, who formed a row in front of Crivella, neatly waiting to be "delivered of evil." Suddenly both cameras were put on standby; though I wanted to raise my arms in order to take a photo, I noticed two things that made me change my mind. The first was the abrupt lack of interest everyone seemed to feign and the second was a tattoo with the letters "CV" on the shoulder of one of the boys. Just in time I understood that "CV" stood for Comando Vermelho and that taking photos of these young men was not the wisest thing to do. I had heard from many inhabitants that the boys and men of the comando were not fond of being photographed because the police could use the photos for identification. I lowered my camera and observed what happened.

Crivella grabbed the first of the boys in line tightly by the head, seemingly struggled with the unleashed powers, and forcefully called out "Sai!" (Leave!) several times. During this ritual, the two pastors of the Assembleia de Deus stood behind Crivella with their hands raised in the direction of the pastor and the boy. As I understood it, they were directing the positive spiritual energy of the Holy Spirit to aid the process of deliverance. After Crivella had performed the same ritual practice on all three boys, their faces showed signs of relief and they disappeared back to the barrack building from which they came. Crivella shook some hands, left the favela, and everyone went on their way.

What should be made of this public performance that united several religious figures by means of a common Pentecostal language and practice? What does the exorcism of young men in a public square, located at the border of gang territory, tell us about the attraction of Pentecostalism for the inhabitants of the morro? How is it possible that Crivella was assigned the role of powerful exorcist?

This chapter could be seen as a bridge between the first three chapters (which attempt to convey Pentecostal ideas and practices in relation to spatial segregation, the mediated soundscape of the favelas, and the visual representations of violence) and the last two chapters (which discuss in more detail the relations between religious conversion, electronic media, and practices of listening and watching). In the first three chapters I have tried to give the reader a sense of the "communicative ecology" (Slater and Tacchi 2004) that forms part of the environment of people who live in the favelas of Rio de Janeiro. At this point it is possible to analyze in more detail how Pentecostalism becomes embedded in this mediated life-world and how it interacts and merges with other popular cultural practices. Repeating the order of the first three chapters, the last three chapters of this book also focus on space, sound, and vision, yet they focus much more specifically on the ways people in the favelas of Rio de Janeiro come to understand Pentecostal practices, rituals, and worldviews as credible and powerful responses to the hardships of favela life.

In general, one of the important strategies Pentecostal churches apply to attract adherents is to classify, incorporate, and purify many "worldly" phenomena that surround people. Evangelical churches attempt to strengthen a sense of the divine order by classifying and incorporating popular cultural practices, symbols, media, and spaces. The rationale of this strategy is two-fold: incorporating popular, worldly phenomena aims to attract people by means of established popular practices, and it demonstrates the power of a specific church, pastor, or adherent to confront and overcome the demonic elements that are attached to such practices.

Crucial to this strategy is the selection of domains eligible for purification. Enveloped by favela life, saturated with television, radio, Internet, and amplified sounds, church leaders and members press one another to identify the places, practices, objects, images, and sounds that possess malevolent spiritual powers and evaluate how to grasp or deflect them. Before focusing on radio and music in chapter 5 and television and images in chapter 6, in this chapter I will focus on the relation between the ideas and practices about spiritual purification that are related to space and territory. As we have seen in the preceding chapters, experiences of urban space are heavily influenced by the augmented presence of the comandos. Not only do residents of the favelas experience the effects of the drug business when walking through their own neighborhood, but they also see it and hear about it on news broadcasts and infotainment shows.

By means of their media, their church services, and their daily conversations, adherents of the Assembleia de Deus and the Igreja Universal offer discourses and practices that serve as a response to the presence of the

Figure 7 Young congregant of an Assembleia de Deus church after his baptism. Photo: author.

armed comandos. People of the Assembleia de Deus and the Igreja Universal discursively distinguish Pentecostalism from crime, violence, and the tráfico. Yet they do not actively oppose the comandos. Rather, they offer rituals that seek to enforce holy protection and a path that promises redemption for all those who accept Jesus as their Savior, including the traficantes.

The discourse of peace and redemption—as I call it here—is firmly related to several cleansing practices, which remind us of the work of Mary Douglas ([1966] 2002). Many Pentecostal groups attempt to rid the space of the favela of its diabolical forces by means of collective prayer and the physical/spiritual occupation of spaces in the favelas. The attraction of the discourses and practices of peace and redemption rests on the Pentecostal model of the subject, on deliverance rituals, and on (mediatized) conversion narratives.

In small and big Pentecostal media, conversion stories are narrated and re-narrated. Often these stories recount the radical break from a sinful life, often after an encounter with God and the expulsion of demons. Testimonies of former traffickers support the imagination of a gradual disappearance of violence in the favelas as a result of the mass conversion of criminals who are delivered of their demons and give up their life of crime. This does not mean, however, that the conversion narratives I recorded were exclusively related to crime, drugs, and violence. The majority of the evangelicals I interviewed had not been directly involved with the tráfico. Nevertheless, the presence of the comandos in the favelas of Rio de Janeiro influences many domains of social life, and the violence affects many inhabitants. Subsequently, many evangélicos referred to the drug trade, drug abuse, and violence to exemplify the work of the devil and subsequently described their own safety and well-being in terms of holy protection. In addition, people understand the examples of traficantes who convert as confirmation of the Lord's power to bring peace where all other measures fail.

The Batalha Espiritual

Many of the people in Visionário and Roda de Vento maintained a pragmatic relation to religious institutions and the boundaries between them. Numerous people I interviewed switched from one religious affiliation to another, or said they did not have "a church" but infrequently attended different congregations inside or outside the favela. Nevertheless, adherents of the Pentecostal churches tended to present themselves as distinct from other inhabitants, and in many cases religious boundaries between people were drawn sharply in relation to conversion from a Catholic or Afro-Brazilian religious background to a Protestant or Pentecostal church.

Conversion is based on the common Pentecostal distinction between the realm of God, the realm of the devil, and the imagined batalha espiritual between them. The batalha espiritual is of central importance in many of the Pentecostal doctrines and practices in the favelas. In most of the sermons of the Igreja Universal and the Assembleia de Deus, pastors preached about the dangers of falling victim to the devil's machinations and the necessity of acting according to Pentecostal doctrines. The pastors of the Assembleia de Deus especially called for rigorous distinctions between *as coisas de Deus* and *as coisas do mundo*, things of God and things of the world. "Things" of the world were generally associated with the devil if they were described as sinful in the Bible or if they posed a threat to what people in considered a Christian life.

The *Bíblia de Estudo Pentecostal* (glossing Rom. 8:5–14), mostly used by people who attended the Assembleia de Deus, says the following, for example:

> Paul describes two classes of people: those who live according to the flesh and those who live according to the Spirit. (1) To live "according to the flesh" ("flesh" here means the sinful element of human nature) is to desire and to satisfy the contaminated desires of the sinful human nature; to derive pleasure from them and to

occupy oneself with them. That is not only fornication, adultery, hate, selfish ambition, outbursts of anger, et cetera (see Gal. 5:19–21) but also obscenity, addiction to pornography or drugs, mental and emotional pleasure from sex scenes, plays, books, video, and so on. (2) To live "according to the Spirit" is searching for the orientation and the competency of the Holy Spirit and to submit ourselves to them and to concentrate our attention on the things of God. It is constantly to be conscious that we are in the presence of God and in Him we trust that He will guide us and grant us the grace we long for so that His will is realized in us through us.[3]

In practice, things of the world were often presented as analogous to things of the flesh, and things of God as analogous to things of the Spirit. Hence, things of the world are often associated with carnal pleasures and sinful desires. According to most adherents, the consequence of indulging these desires is that the Holy Spirit cannot reside in a person and therefore that person will be spiritually dead. Abstaining from these desires means that the Holy Spirit can reside in that person and that person can experience eternal life.

Following the work of Edir Macedo (1999), leader of the Igreja Universal, a similar distinction between living in the world and being of the world stands at the basis of the doctrines of the Igreja Universal. Nevertheless, with regard to clothing styles and codes of conduct, the Igreja Universal generally dictates a less puritan style than the Assembleia de Deus; women can wear makeup, dress in jeans, and use beauty products without being scorned.

As we have also seen in chapter 2, religious and social boundaries in the favelas of my research were often drawn along the lines of cultural practices understood as sinful or plainly dangerous in the eyes of the crentes. Most crentes understood samba and funk to be sinful because of the social behavior that was generally associated with them. Drinking, swearing, adultery, and drug abuse were commonly understood as diabolical habits that were part of the life of funkeiros and sambistas. Not surprisingly, most pastors preached that adherents had to abstain from the many practices common to the daily life in the morro. In contrast to these practices, evangélicos attempted to regulate daily behavior according to Pentecostal doctrines and habits. Transformation in modes of conduct and dress and a regular participation in church life were commonly understood as inward and outward signs of the transition from "being of the world" to being a crente.[4]

The adherents of the Assembleia de Deus in particular dressed piously and avoided close contact with non-evangelical neighbors. The term *crente tem que ser diferente* (the believer has to be different)—which people of the Assembleia de Deus often use—lucidly shows how the adherents attempted to separate themselves from the "people of the world" in the dense social environment of the favelas. Pastors of the Assembleia de Deus in the morro often pointed out that there could be no exceptions to restraint at any time. In the words of one pastor, "I have to teach you how you should behave and please God. The crente has to be transparent, serve God at all times. Be different. We are different. With Him it is all or nothing."

Most adherents of the Igreja Universal I interviewed explained the distinctions between things of God and things of the world in the same terms. When I asked Sandro, a young aspirant obreiro, how I could understand the difference between him and the others of the world, he answered, "I am [*estou*] in the world but I am not [*não sou*] of the world, I am in the world but I do not live the way the world lives, I do not commit sin. I am among the sinners, but I am not one of them." When I asked him what the most difficult sins to avoid were, he answered, "To me there are no big or small sins, to obey or not obey that is it, but there are sins that are difficult to repudiate, for men to stop having many women . . . for young people it is very difficult to have only one girlfriend, not to have sexual relations before marriage."

Among the adherents of the Pentecostal churches, sinful practices were often described as the results of the manipulations of the devil, who is always ready to "steal, kill, and destroy" whenever the chance occurs. Surely, people themselves are generally seen as responsible for identifying the nature of such practices in light of Christian ethics and are supposed to act accordingly, but it is the devil who tries to persuade and seduce men and women to do otherwise. In many instances, such diabolical schemes were explained with examples from life in the favelas. During an interview I asked Emerson, a young man who participated in the *grupo jovem* (youth group) of the Igreja Universal, whether, and where, he saw manifestations of the devil. He answered,

> I see plenty, even in here [in the favela] you see death, you see young people who are violated by their own parents, sometimes when you see a young girl who is pregnant and you ask who the father is, she says it is her own father. You see much inequality, a mother killing her children, young people who become prostitutes. In our group we have four people who were prostitutes. Today one of them came with a box of clothes and she said, "These were the clothes that I wore and I never want to put on my body again." This kind of *short*

[hot pants], you know. You see many bad things, youngsters who end up in drugs. Fathers who end up in alcoholism.

As the words of Emerson exemplify, inhabitants often explained the distinction between the domain of the devil and the domain of God—and the spiritual battle between the two—by means of examples from their own social environment, and this environment is heavily influenced by the struggles over sovereignty and armed conflicts.

Crentes and Traficantes

As I argue throughout this book, the presence of the comandos greatly enforces the message of the Pentecostal churches in the favelas. It is a powerful force behind the self-disciplining efforts of the adherents of the churches and tightly connected to the symbolic divide between the realm of God and that of the devil. In many of my talks with affiliates of Pentecostal churches, people would point to the consequences of committing sins by referring to the violence associated with the tráfico. Almost all of my evangelical contacts explained the necessity of living life according to biblical conventions by referring to the proximity of the evil that surrounded them (see also Mafra 1998).[5] The presence of armed traficantes sauntering through the favelas or sitting at the boca de fumo smoking marijuana was often cited as the proof of the existence of the devil and a very clear sign of the necessity of Jesus in the lives of all the people involved. Likewise, occurrences related to the tráfico were often interpreted as manifestations of the spiritual battle. During one interview in the house of a member of the Igreja Universal, for example, I heard several gunshots next door. The man, who was explaining the message and practices of the Igreja Universal, tried to continue without stopping when the gun went off, although we had both clearly heard the shots. When I tentatively asked him what the noise was, he explained it was his neighbor firing a gun. Then he said, "We are accustomed; it is the devil who tries to hinder the speaking of the word of God. If one is predisposed to speak the word of God, one has to endure the battle."

In general, the adherents of the Pentecostal churches interpreted the involvement of the young boys and girls in organized crime within their religious frame of reference, which clearly condemns criminal behavior. Nevertheless, even though they were inclined to describe behavior in dualistic terms—right or wrong, Christian or non-Christian—the behavior of armed traficantes was generally interpreted in light of a Pentecostal worldview, which portrayed a reality in which God and the devil were pulling the strings. Therefore, traficantes were also often regarded as victims of the devil.

Members of the Igreja Universal and members of the congregations of the Assembleia de Deus in the morro frequently evangelize in their neighborhoods and try to persuade the inhabitants to come to their church services at night. Walking through the favelas, searching for people to invite, they regularly passed a boca de fumo or a group of traficantes, and some of my Pentecostal friends proudly told me that they were not afraid to talk to the boys of the comando and tell them of the power of God to change their lives. My friends generally believed they had nothing to fear from the traficantes because the Holy Spirit protected them against evil.[6] Rather, they said, they were instruments in the hand of God to combat this evil. The fact that some boys indeed give up their comando life and become crentes greatly supports this conviction. Not surprisingly, the stories and testimonies of converted traficantes are excitedly shared among the crentes. To give an example of such a story, I will describe the testimony of Pastor Denilson, born and raised in Visionário.

A Grenade from God

At a certain moment during my fieldwork, someone told me that Pastor Denilson, head of an Assembleia de Deus congregation, had been involved in the tráfico in the past and had suffered a terrible accident, after which he converted. Furthermore, I heard that the accident, an explosion of some kind, had taken place in the house of Maria, the woman I visited every day and with whom I had established a solid friendship. It was hard to believe she had never told me anything about it, so the next day I immediately went to Maria to tell her what I heard. Maria laughed cynically and told me that an explosion had indeed taken place, right in her bedroom. When I asked her why they had never told me, Maria replied, "Because you never asked." I jokingly replied that I generally did not visit people in the favela to ask, "Has *senhora* by chance had a bomb explosion here?" They laughed and told me that Denilson—not yet a pastor then—had thrown himself on top of a grenade that was about to explode in the bedroom. He had been torn to pieces, which was why he had become a pastor. Gilberto, Maria's youngest son, explained that at the time, one of his sisters had had an affair with a young man who was the local comando chief, and she, Denilson, and the chief were in the bedroom together that day. According to Gilberto, the chief had sniffed a bit too much cocaine and had pulled the pin out of the grenade as a kind of trick, without realizing the danger. Denilson had tried to save them by throwing himself on top of the grenade. Maria said there was blood all over the place, and Gilberto showed where I could still see the splinters of the grenade on the ceiling of the bedroom. Then he enthusiastically said I should interview Denilson because his testimony was great. Apparently, Denilson's brother was a *macumbeiro* who had tried to attack him with a knife to draw his blood to offer to the spirits. He had almost died in the explosion, which was another sign of the power of God to save those who turn to Him. Maria said that after the explosion her daughter changed her life totally and dissociated herself from the men involved with the comando: "Virou de vinho a água" (She turned from wine into water), she said.

The next week I interviewed Pastor Denilson, whom I had visited many times and with whom I had established quite a good rapport. He told me that, as a child, he had been in the church but had left it as an adolescent. The local chief was a childhood friend, and after Denilson had left the church he and his friend were both involved (*envolvido*) in crime and drugs. His friend had been at a *centro de espírito* (Afro-Brazilian temple) in order to *fechar o corpo*,[7] and he had been in a ritual fast lasting seven days. That day the chief was in Maria's house and Denilson came to bring him some food. There he had found his friend with the grenade in his hand. He pulled the pin, threw the grenade, and tried to leave the room. That was when the grenade went off: "I think that was a plan of God, it was so that He could come close to me and speak that He had permitted this accident to happen. I could pass in the shadow of death but that in His name I could be glorified. From then on I went through the process . . . I went to the hospital and almost died. It was terrible. I made a promise that if He would get me out, I would return to the church and stay strong." Denilson thought it was a miracle—the hand of God. A similar accident had occurred in a neighboring favela, where an entire barrack building, including its owner, had been blown to pieces. I asked him why he thought his friend had pulled the pin. Denilson replied, "He was possessed by an evil entity [*entidade*], because he had been in this ritual, locked up inside without food, using only drugs. It was the devil. In his case the devil's spirit entered and took over, because he was sitting there and suddenly he pulled the pin. In reality, the devil wanted to take me, because I was a promise. The devil did not want to take him because he would lose a lot. He wanted to take me, but the Lord showed me mercy and gave me another opportunity." He also told me that when he decided to return to the church and he accepted Jesus, he was strengthened in his faith. Upon his return, some comando members wanted to kill him because the chief had been disgraced and therefore Denilson should be eliminated. While his friend was indeed killed by rival traficantes, Denilson believed that God did not let him die because he had already returned to the church. Strikingly, Denilson also provided a spiritual explanation of the causes of the comando members' violent behavior: "Traficantes are always involved in macumba, because they are searching for protection and ask for consultations about how they should engage in certain matters. They call these spirits *entidades* [entities], while in reality they are demons."

As becomes apparent in this excerpt from Denilson's testimony, his escape from certain death is considered powerful proof of God's interference. The testimony also offers an example of the belief that violence is caused by the devil taking hold of certain individuals. This belief is further enforced by the idea that Afro-Brazilian religions such as Candomblé and Umbanda are in fact diabolical. In this Pentecostal frame of reference, violence is often understood as emanating from people who practice such faiths (see also Montes 1998, 136; Alvito 2001, 209–18). Yet, because Pentecostalism generally offers individuals the possibility of redemption and a *novo nascimento* (new birth), such individuals are in some ways respected as possible subjects for salvation.

Sanctuary

Denilson's testimony gives us a better understanding of the public exorcism of the traficantes I described in the beginning of this chapter. During and after the video recording of Marcelo Crivella, Pentecostal pastors joined forces to fight against the demons that evidently haunted the traficantes. However, as was already apparent in the previous chapter, the meaning of exorcism generally extends beyond the individual cases of the people involved. Just as traficantes are generally considered signs of the devil's presence in the favela, so is their exorcism considered a sign of the eradication of evil from the favela—a step toward its deliverance. The media of the churches generally supports such an idea. In the previous chapter I gave examples of the media of the Igreja Universal, but similar incorporations of mediated violence appeared in the print media of the Assembleia de Deus and other Pentecostal organizations.

Not long after the murder of Tim Lopes, the official magazine of the Assembleia de Deus, the *Mensageiro da Paz* (Peace messenger), opened its October 2002 issue with the front-page headline "Churches overcome violence in the morros." The large color photo on the front page showed a church of the Assembleia de Deus in Vila Cruzeiro, the favela where Lopes was murdered.[8] The article below the photo read,

> The preaching of the Gospel has diminished the occurrence of violence in several high-risk localities in Brazil, as social scientists throughout the country will verify. In places where public authority [*poder público*], the Roman Catholic Church, and NGOs do not penetrate, the evangelical churches, above all the Assembleia de Deus, make their mark with their presence as a Christian path to liberation [*libertação*]. . . . In the photo above, the Assembleia de Deus in Vila Cruzeiro in Rio de Janeiro, a high-risk neighborhood where the *Globo* journalist was murdered. The church [in the neighborhood] is one of the points to which the young people who run from the drugs and the criminality in the region turn.[9]

Further on in the *Mensageiro da Paz* the article continues, "There are countless testimonies of people whose lives have been transformed by the preaching of the Gospel in morros and favelas where organized crime reigns virtually supreme. In most of these places, the churches are the only alternative for those who do not want to opt for drugs or crime."

Markedly, the reputation of the power of the Assembleia de Deus to transform the lives of those involved in the tráfico reaches beyond Brazil. Take, for example, the July 3, 2000, issue of *Newsweek*, which features a photo of Pastor Demétrio Martins of the Assembleia de Deus on the cover, dressed in suit and tie, holding a Bible in his hands. The headline of the issue reads, "The holy war on drugs, Brazil. Street-smart preachers are taking the fight to crime-ridden neighborhoods." The article inside tells of the life of Demétrio Martins, whose abbreviated testimony I recounted in the introduction of this book. Demétrio Martins's appearance as one of the leading preachers during the cruzada evangelista in the favela Roda do Vento in 2011 tells us something about the lasting appeal of these kinds of exemplary conversions to favela residents.

Though it is certainly not the only evil that concerns Pentecostal adherents, in every church I visited at one time or another people emphasized Christianity's power to liberate people from a life of crime. Pastor Denilson generally stressed the power of the Lord to save those involved in the tráfico, and he occasionally invited guest preachers to do the same. During the cultos of his church, I witnessed several moving testimonies from such visitors. One testimony was given by a man who had come to tell of his experiences in the tráfico in São Paulo. He told us how he used to be a *gerente de boca de fumo* (manager of a drug trading point) in a neighborhood of São Paulo. He had been involved in armed confrontations with a rival gang in the neighborhood, and one night several men appeared and opened fire at him and his friends. He tried to duck down, but he was sure that his last moment on earth had come. Yet, when the shooting stopped, he saw that he was the only man alive at the scene. All the others had been killed by gunfire. The fact that they had missed him at such a short distance was truly miraculous, and at that moment he knew God had saved him. Hence he became a preacher, dedicated to telling his story to people all over Brazil. His emotional testimony was carefully crafted and delivered with passionate exclamations typical of Pentecostal preaching. The audience responded with cheers and hallelujahs.

In general, men and women of the Pentecostal churches in Visionário regularly approached the boys involved in the comando, telling them to come to church, hoping they would decide to step out of the life they were living and accept Jesus as their Savior. According to many, the boys acknowledged the righteousness of the crentes and respected the local Pentecostal churches. Take, for example, my landlady, who told me that the doors of her church—an Assembleia de Deus in Visionário—were always open for the boys involved in the tráfico: "Last Thursday a boy with a gun this large [holds out both hands far apart] entered the veranda of our church. He left his weapon on the veranda and entered to ask for a prayer." When I asked her why he asked for a prayer, she replied, "They believe in God. They just don't have the power to get out of the life they live. Many of them are the sons of crentes, they know the Word even though they are doing those things in the world, they know the Bible."

As also exemplified in the quote from the *Mensageiro da Paz* above, churches of the Assembleia de Deus were often imagined as sanctuaries against the evil that haunted the traficantes. An example of this kind of representation in which local Pentecostal churches are imagined as sacred places comes from *missionária* (missionary) Regina, who lived in a house at the foot of the morro, close to the boca de fumo where drugs were sold. The first time I talked to her while passing by on my way down to the asfalto, she explained that her house used to belong to the Comando Vermelho and that the boys used it to hide and store their drugs when the police would enter the morro. In a longer interview, she explained to me that she was sent by God to buy that house in order to preach the Gospel to those who had not heard it. She outlined her mission in an emotional tone not uncommon to preachers of the Assembleia de Deus: "I have a team of youngsters, ex-witches, ex-prostitutes, ex-criminals, ex-killers, who have done horrible things, but today they are cleansed [*limpo*] by the word of God and they are ministers of the Gospel of the Lord Jesus Christ here on Earth. . . . I have this team of youngsters that are sons in faith, produced by the word of God, recovered not with chemicals but with the power of Jesus Christ who is the liberator." When I asked her if there were no complications with the traficantes when she bought the house, she explained,

> When I bought it they came, and when I presented myself as the buyer they left the house. I did not encounter problems with them. I am praying for them that God will save them and He will save them in the name of the Lord Jesus. They only charge those that interfere with them, I am here praying . . . originally it was a hell here, and mind you, I am talking about different periods, it was a hell. Now there is peace in this place, a peace that Jesus Christ granted, before I came here, He had shown me He was going to send me to a place that was a hell and that would be transformed into heaven.

Though she explicitly stated that it was through her preaching and praying that people were saved by God, and through her that the house transformed from a hell into heaven, in fact there were no confrontations with the traficantes. She prayed for them. She did not interfere with their business, and they did not interfere with hers. Missionária Regina was quite a celebrity in the morro, and several people told me they converted after hearing her preach. She held cultos in her house and was trying hard to raise money to open more churches. Her success story was even featured in the Christian magazine *Defesa da Fé*, which she proudly showed me during our interview. In the small article, exactly the same testimony was summarized with these same words, demonstrating the standardization of her story into an instantly deliverable proof of her mediation of God's powers.

As becomes clear from the quotations above, the Pentecostal discourse of peace and redemption makes ample use of spatial metaphors (hell, heaven), which, among other things, allow for the imagination of individual conversions as a step toward the transformation of social space, as Jon Wolseth (2008) has also argued in relation to conversion in a popular neighborhood in Honduras. Drawing on Henri Lefebvre's (1991, 234–41) description of the creation of absolute space, Wolseth argues that Christian language and practice allows for the creation of (extralocal) sanctuary that protects Pentecostal youth from the gang violence that plagues their neighborhood.

As Lefebvre (236) notes, and Wolseth insightfully applies to his material in Honduras, churches and cemeteries are examples of absolute space; however, "considered in itself—'absolutely'—absolute space is located nowhere. It has no place because it embodies *all* places, and has a strictly symbolic existence. This is what makes it similar to the fictitious/real space of language, and that of mental space, magically (imaginarily) cut off from the spatial realm, where the conscious of the 'subject'—or 'self-consciousness'—takes form." According to Lefebvre, the space of the sanctuary *is* absolute space. Wolseth aptly describes how the persuasive use of spatial metaphors of the Pentecostal converts—being in the House of God, on the Path of God, and so forth—allows for the creation of social space, not necessarily fixed in a certain place, that protects them from being harmed by gang members. Wolseth's employment of Lefebvre's work gives us crucial insight to understand better the connection between Christian conversion and the experience of sanctuary in the favelas of Rio de Janeiro. The strict discursive separation between "being in the world" and "being of the world," which the evangelicals in the favelas employ, allows for the imagination and experience of a separate social space amid the people of the world yet protected from evil (see also Smilde 2007, 55–76). Not unlike in the neighborhood Wolseth describes, the belief in the protective powers of Pentecostalism in the favelas is heavily enforced by the fact that traficantes generally respect the unyielding manners of the crentes—if indeed they practice what they preach—and the general notion that traficantes frequently give up their hazardous life of crime to convert to the strict moral lifestyle of the crentes, which protects them in the here and now as well as in the hereafter.

However, here I wish to expand the insights of Wolseth in two other directions. First, in the morro, the imagination of sanctuary—firmly connected to the Christian discourse of peace and redemption—also rests on the homology between space in/of the favela and the bodies of its inhabitants, both of which are seen as the locus of the struggles between the devil and the Holy Spirit. Unlike the case Wolseth describes, Pentecostalism in the favelas of Rio de Janeiro is firmly entangled with Afro-Brazilian religious practices and, as we have seen, ideas about the origins of evil. Spiritual occupation should be understood in relation to the Afro-Brazilian deities, which Pentecostal adherents understand to be demons. This explains the public exorcism. Second, since absolute space is all space, the imagination of sanctuary can extend beyond specific places/churches in the favela to the favela as a whole (and beyond). In other words, the exorcism of a handful of traficantes can be imagined as a first step toward the deliverance of an entire favela.[10]

Deliverance

The attraction of the discourse of peace and redemption rests on the Pentecostal model of the subject and the practice of conversion, but also on the knowledge of spirit possession and the practice of deliverance. The Assembleia de Deus and Igreja Universal maintain similar distinctions between the worldly and the godly and similar ideas about the batalha espiritual between God and the devil. Nevertheless, the Igreja Universal gives much more attention to the possession and exorcism of *encostos* (demons) and the possible healing of mental and physical diseases or addictions. In many of my interviews with members of both churches, people would state that they used to drink alcohol and smoke cigarettes (or smoke marijuana or sniff cocaine) before they started to attend a Pentecostal church. Yet people of the Igreja Universal often explicitly stated that deliverance from demons was the first step to be taken. Therefore most of them initially started attending sessões de descarrego in the Igreja Universal before they completely "converted."

The weekly sessão de descarrego at the Igreja Universal—entirely dedicated to the deliverance of encostos—are generally spectacular and involve great emotional tension and catharsis. They are characterized by a gradual increase in the speed and volume of prayer that reaches a climax when several demons—recognizable as well-known Afro-Brazilian deities—manifest themselves in the crowd, after which the pastor or obreiros can exorcize them. The people who show no visible signs of possession are directed to place their hands on their head and say out loud, "Em nome de Jesus, *sai, sai, sai!*" (In the name of Jesus, *get out!*). Yet, when someone starts to scream or shake, one of the obreiros rushes forward to help before the demon fully manifests itself. The obreiro grasps the possessed person tightly by the head, after which he can exorcise the demon. Often, when obreiros cannot practice deliverance themselves, they escort the victim to the pulpit. Demonic possession is recognizable by the bodily postures of the victims, whose faces generally show signs of agony and loss of self-control. When "interrogated" by the pastor in front of the pulpit, the demons "confess" through the mouths of their victims that they were sent by the devil to destroy the lives of the people they possessed.

In an interview with Jorge, a man in his early forties, the trajectory of deliverance in the Igreja Universal was portrayed as follows: "If you are turning to *macumbaria* [Afro-Brazilian religions], *bruxaria* [witchery], and if you are searching for *feitiçaria* [sorcery], you are searching for something, you know, and what we are searching for in these places we did not find in alcohol, in drugs." "You mean marijuana?" I asked. "That is right," he replied. "Also cocaine?" I asked. He replied,

> Everything. What does that mean? We are searching for a solution to live, a real reason to live, and I did not find that anywhere until I started to go to the Igreja Universal. Then I went and I heard the pastor shout and it was something that I, thirty-two years of age, had never seen before. He was talking as if God was present there, and there you pass from something without emotion to feeling something supernatural. I am not telling you I was firm straightaway, but in the week thereafter I was longing for that experience once more . . . and I went there time and again and there I found myself, and there we were, starting on that straight and difficult path. If you want to stay on that path you have to be perceptive, very perceptive. I went there with a ruined life, I was addicted to drugs, and because of that my life was totally held up. The Bible says that the devil comes to destroy, steal, and kill. My life was infernal. There was only the aspect of destruction and death, I already had the job I have today but half of my salary was already spent before I received it because of debts and problems. I lived a miserable life, I wanted to win but I was conquered, so when I went to a culto it was a guerra espiritual. Because when I was there, brother [irmão], I participated in a culto and I received a prayer. In the first month I went I had no appetite for eating, I was very weak physically speaking, in terms of nutrition. Why? Because I lived for drugs and alcohol, addicted, and I had no time to eat anything, I drank instead of eating, you understand, brother, I was physically weakened. With those illnesses, both spiritual and physical, I went to the church. . . . When I went to church to receive the power of God, I ate a plate that had enough for three . . . I began to eat and eat . . . and not long after that the evil spirits manifested themselves. You see, spiritual evils began to manifest themselves, when I went to the church evil, evil, evil. First God began to repair me physically, but since I was suffering from physical and spiritual illnesses, spiritual evils began to manifest themselves, and then the struggle started, brother, a fight [luta], a fight of good against evil.

Here we see in more detail how the experience of physical transformation is connected to the imagination of a metaphysical fight between good and evil and the recurring practice of deliverance in the churches of the Igreja Universal. The public manifestation and exorcism of demons is a powerful confirmation of the doctrines of the Igreja Universal, not least because they are based on the knowledge and practice of Afro-Brazilian religions.

In Christianity at large there have been reinterpretations of religious traditions encountered throughout colonial history, and the constitution of an opposing deity as a manifestation of the devil has been widespread in South America (Taussig 1980), Southeast Asia (Keane 2007), and Africa (Meyer 1999). However, as Joel Robbins has suggested, Pentecostal and Charismatic churches distinguish themselves from other types of Christian movements because they generally preserve the existing spiritual ontologies and continually engage with the spirits that spring from them (Robbins 2004, 129).

This is the case for Brazil as well. Nevertheless, as with other Pentecostal and Charismatic churches around the globe, the Igreja Universal presents several innovations in the Brazilian context. The incorporation of spirits that are commonly worshipped and consulted in Afro-Brazilian religions such as Candomblé and Umbanda, in combination with its "health and wealth" theology, has introduced a dynamic that is different from the type of inclusion of existing spiritual ontologies in the other Pentecostal churches (Mariano 1999). In many other Pentecostal churches in Brazil, explicit possession of demons is much less common, and exorcism is not part of the standard ritual repertoire. Other churches do refer to Afro-Brazilian religious practices generally, but always in terms of macumba and never in such detailed ways as in the Igreja Universal.

Having said that, descriptions in this chapter provided thus far—the collective exorcism of traficantes, the testimony of Pastor Denilson—demonstrate that many adherents of the churches of the Assembleia de Deus also understand the practices of the traficantes in terms of possession by diabolical forces. Take, for example, the words of Marcus, leader of the *mocidade* (youngsters) of a local Assembleia de Deus:

> Angels surround us, but outside that circle is the enemy. We have to make sure the angels protect us against the enemy by praying, by going to the cultos so that the enemy does not breach the circle.... As we say, do not grant space to the devil. It is a constant struggle. If you look at the people here who are involved [in the tráfico], you see they don't shine [*não tem brilho*]. The devil is behind that, violence, famine. What he wants is that people will die without salvation. Talking about violence, many persons who have been brought up

with the evangelho are bandidos who know the word of God—well, they know the Bible, if you truly know the word of God, you would not do that.

Not unlike Marcus, many other people who attended the Assembleia de Deus envisaged relations in terms of the luta against demons, even though exorcism is much less common in the cultos and doctrines of the Assembleia de Deus. Leonildo, a man in his forties who had accepted Jesus only a few years before and was *presbítero* (elder) in the Assembleia de Deus, exemplifies this. According to Leonildo, after his conversion he no longer let certain kinds of people enter his house: "Before anybody could come in, but nowadays they have to stay on the threshold. They can bring demons in with them, like a dog that carries fleas. As a Christian you should not let all kinds of people inside. My neighbors, for example, do not live like Christians. You should not let people enter who don't have the same faith. The Bible says so." The widespread belief in demonic possession as the source of evil suggests that the pervasive message of the Igreja Universal resonates among adherents of other Pentecostal churches.

Spatial Purifications

Leonildo's remark points to a certain homology between the spiritual purification of bodies and spaces apparent in many of the religious practices in Brazil. In the sermons of the Igreja Universal a heavy emphasis is placed on things (pamphlets, envelopes, but also stones, salt, and other objects) and fluids (oil and water, mostly) as biblical mediators of the Holy Spirit and containers of curative and protective powers. By means of their words and prayers the bispos bless and consecrate these objects and fluids, after which the powers can be transmitted to individuals. The consecrated salt is supposed to be taken home to cleanse and protect the houses of the church attendants against the perceived evil that surrounds them. People are instructed to pour the salt on their doorsteps to safeguard the boundaries between the spiritually purified inside and the threatening outside. Similar practices of spatial demarcation of metaphysical domains of good and evil are also found in other evangelical practices, such as in the attachment of evangelical banners, stickers, and nameplates on walls, doors, and other entrances. These spatial markers serve to define a house or office as a "place of evangelicals" and simultaneously to purify and protect a space against invasion. An illustration of the imagination of demonic occupation comes form Dora, a young woman of eighteen. When I interviewed her at her home, she had recently joined the grupo jovem of the Igreja Universal and was determined to become an obreira:

> In this house we need an obreira, to expel the demons, my mother, she also manifested [a demon]. She was talking. I was doing very well in church and they explained that when you are close to a victory in a fight that has been going on for so long, the devil starts to raise himself. He does this so that people will topple into hell. So when I returned from church, my mother was already in full flight, attacking me, talking all kinds of things, swearing, saying things that had nothing to do with it. I did not even listen. Clearly I couldn't talk back. The word of God says I have to respect my parents. I can only read the Bible and tie down the devil [*amarrar o diabo*].

Many of the techniques of spatial purification encountered in the Igreja Universal and in several other Pentecostal churches demonstrate similarities with purification techniques of Afro-Brazilian religious movements and of the Catholic Church. *Sal grosso* (unrefined salt), for example, is commonly used in Umbanda and Candomblé to purify individuals and to protect them from harmful spirits. In these Afro-Brazilian movements salt is also often used for a *banho de descarrego* (ritual cleansing bath).[11] Likewise, the Brazilian Catholic tradition continues many practices meant to protect a place or a person against evil. Some Catholics in the favela, for example, had attached stickers with portraits of saints on their door to protect their house, but one could also think of the popular scapulars (*escapulários*), necklaces that feature portraits of Jesus, Mary, or saints on both the front and back side, thus fully closing off the body (fechar o corpo) against any potential threats.

All these practices that are used to purify and to protect bodies and/or spaces strike a chord with the important work of Mary Douglas. As Douglas taught us, practices of distinction and separation of the pure and the impure are universal ordering mechanisms, which often involve the body as a powerful metaphor for society. According to Douglas ([1966] 2002, 42), "The body is a model which can stand for any bounded system. Its boundaries can represent any boundaries which are threatened or precarious." As such, the powers and dangers credited to social structure are often reproduced in small on the human body.[12]

Especially in the favelas, the ideas about bodily impurity as a result of spirit possession are related to distinctions between groups of people and their mediated practices. Furthermore, Pentecostal ideas about bodily impurity on account of Catholic and Afro-Brazilian religious practices are enforced by the supposed connection between demonic possession and the presence of traficantes. The literal occupation of favelas by comandos supports the imagination of a diabolical occupation of space and enforces the homology between the spiritual purification of spaces and bodies. Whereas we should not rule out that other religious practices also offer persuasive rituals to counter evil, in my fieldwork I heard people explain this as a particularly powerful feature of Pentecostalism.

Testimony

Up until now I have described how adherents of Pentecostal churches generally perceive the spiritual battle as it takes place in the daily life-world of the favelas and how people try to separate themselves from other groups to carve out and produce a purified social space. In the remainder of this chapter I will focus on the process of conversion.[13] I will zoom in on the ways that adherents of the Pentecostal churches generally narrated their life experiences and their decisions to accept Jesus as their Savior.[14] I will argue that the Pentecostal message—particularly the religious testimonies that are reproduced in big and small media (Spitulnik 2001)—offers the people a persuasive religious message that compels them to regard the ability to change their life for the better in Pentecostal terms. This implies that they can intentionally change their lives and exercise their agency only by accepting that they have limited control because, ultimately, God and the devil are pulling the strings. In addition, many of the inhabitants described the transition to being a crente as sudden and definite, while in practice I witnessed that a good number of people started attending church services to see what they offered. Some of them were attracted and stayed, while others eventually went to other denominations. Plenty of people remained part of a church community for a while, after which they decided to stop attending for various reasons.

Many of the evangélicos I interviewed molded their life story according to the genre of the Christian testimony. Testimonies can be considered a Pentecostal genre in which life experiences are narrated according to an autobiography of salvation. During the first of a number of interviews with people who frequented Pentecostal churches in Rio de Janeiro, I did not know exactly what to make of the tone and structure of the narratives people presented. I would often arrive at their homes in the favela with my voice recorder and politely ask if I could record the conversation. To my initial surprise, the moment I would press the record button, quite a number of people took hold of the interview and left me no other option but to listen to their emotional life stories, without much chance to interrupt and ask questions. After some interviews I noticed that the structure and tone of the talks resembled the public testimonies I heard in the churches and at other evangelical occasions in the favela. In the interviews, people generally recounted their life stories before their acceptance of Jesus, the events that led to the moment in which they understood that God had clearly interfered in their life, and their acceptance of Jesus as their Savior.

Furthermore, some people began to talk in that specific rhythm common to speech in Pentecostal churches. They raised their voices, and their tone became somewhat solemn, yet heavy and melodic. Some of the recorded sessions involved personal stories about illnesses that were cured or loved ones who were saved, but many of the people also recounted their experiences with violence and the insecurities of life in the favela. An elderly woman recounted her loud prayers during the gunfights in the favela, while my evangelical landlady could only understand the severed head of a traficante, found in the alley of the favela, as diabolical. I began to understand that some people took the interview not only as an opportunity to convince me of the powers of the Lord, but also as a chance to weave together their experiences of the insecurities of life in the favela with biblical passages that were told and retold in the churches.

Furthermore, as time went by, I began to understand that the role of the voice recorder I used for my interviews and the recording of church services was not as neutral as I had thought. Some of the people I interviewed occasionally preached in the churches of the Assembleia de Deus inside and outside the favela, and a number of them asked me to copy the interview I had made so they could distribute the content and then perhaps even be invited to preach in other favelas or other cities. Also, I learned that audio recordings of testimonies of ex-traficantes who became evangelical preachers circulated among my male evangelical friends. Such recordings should be seen as part of a larger circuit of mediated stories about crime and conversion, such as those that are reproduced by the Assembleia de Deus dos Últimos Dias of the controversial pastor Marcos Pereira da Silva, whose traveling church spectacle includes live testimonies of ex-traficantes (see chapter 1).

Various people presented their decision to accept Jesus as their Savior as something that occurred at one particular moment in time, mostly after a moment of divine insight or contact with God. The testimony of Denilson, for example, shows that his decision was made after his understanding that God had saved his life. Other people retrospectively acknowledged that God had been present in their lives at crucial moments. In an interview, Tiago, an elder of an Assembleia de Deus in Visionário, explained that God first intervened in his life at the age of eleven. He was playing with wood at a large water tank when he fell in. He would have drowned had it not been for someone who appeared and rescued him. According to Tiago, "It was the hand of God. People who were working there came running up to the tank and pulled me out and called my grandmother. I remember that I almost died. Today I know that it was the hand of God in my life. At that time I did not know that. Today I can say it was the hand of God in my life, because when God has a plan with your life, things happen that must happen." When he was young he had attended the Baptist church for a while, but he stopped going and at the age of fourteen he got involved with the drug trade in the morro. He starting smoking marijuana, he sniffed cocaine, and he traded *barbitúricos* (barbiturates).[15] After using a while he noticed that he had been physically harmed, so he decided to stop using drugs:

> But today I also see that as the hand of God, again, even if you continue on that wrong path [*caminho errado*], you stop and do things differently. I should have known it was the hand of God because I was brought up in the church, but the enemy blinds our sight. Today I know it was the hand of God that made me understand I was doing something wrong and should change. I went on living without going to the house of God and without wanting to redeem myself. It was until 1997, when a missionária came to live here in the morro. I had gone to the Deus é Amor several times but I did not like it there. One day I passed the house of missionária Regina when there was a culto. She called me in and even while I declined she said, "A chair is reserved for you, none will sit in that chair except you." Not long after, I decided to go to a culto. I went with a thirst, with a desire to redeem myself because that whole week I had gone through such a friction in my soul. Within me there was the knowledge that I needed to be of Jesus. When I entered, she was glad and exclaimed "Gloria!" When she asked if there was someone who wanted to accept Jesus as his or her Savior, I was already on my knees in front of her before she could finish her sentence. Since then God has done very much in my life. I ended an illicit relationship with a woman who was not my wife, and from there on I started a new life.

Tiago's story presents an interesting structure. While he had been raised in a family of evangelicals, he did not accept Jesus as his Savior in his early adulthood. His story suggests that he was well aware he was leading a sinful life according to Pentecostal doctrines, and apparently this was bothering him more and more. Around the time he decided to accept Jesus as his Savior, he retrospectively understood that God's hand led him to his decision, and he realized that God had already intervened in his life at the age of eleven. Interestingly, even though Tiago was apparently aware of his sins and was contemplating his lifestyle consciously, according to him spiritual forces ultimately guided his perceptions and actions. The devil blinded him, but God led him to the right path.

One could interpret Tiago's choice to stop using and trading drugs and start attending church as a well-considered decision to change his life. The open arms of missionária Regina can be seen as a strong incentive to become a member of a congregation of the Assembleia de Deus, where he received a warm and caring welcome and plenty of emotional support. However, such an understanding of Tiago's story—and many others like his—favors an instrumental reading of the events that do not do justice to Tiago's worldview before his conversion and his perception that, in retrospect, God was already always present in his life. Even this small sample of Tiago's testimony shows that his acceptance of Jesus occurred after a period of contemplation and demonstrates that Pentecostalism offers him a rich symbolic reservoir for self-understanding. As David Smilde (2003, 327) has also argued about Latin American Pentecostalism,

> the notion of "instrumental" implies that a belief is a means to some external end—it is an "instrument" for attaining something else. But since the Pentecostal belief system is a bundle of narratives that includes a conceptualization of the way humans can live well, both means and ends are integral parts of the belief—being in communion with God is tantamount to overcoming one's problems. In addition, both while the conversion is occurring and in the consolidation process afterwards, the narrative conceptualizes key aspects of this process in such a way that the convert's agency is minimized, with the result that he or she no longer appears to be the primary source of that belief.

As we see in Tiago's testimony and several others I have described in this chapter, the adherents of the Pentecostal churches in the morro generally felt they gained control over their life and their harsh environment by accepting that they were never fully in control to begin with. As Smilde aptly describes, this conversion process generally occurs gradually rather than immediately, even though it is often narrated as such by adherents.

Giving and hearing testimony are key features of this gradual process of conversion. As Susan Harding (2000) has demonstrated vividly in the case of fundamentalist Baptists, testimonies often have a decisive emotional character, which invites the listeners to become part of a person's experience with God in situations of turmoil, grief, or distress. In the case of the inhabitants of the favelas, the intersubjective experiences of testimony giving and testimony receiving are supported by the shared experiences of life in similar circumstances. Having experienced the loss of family members due to the violence or the temptations of alcohol or drugs greatly enhances the intelligibility of the testimony and the willingness to listen to it. It is thus not the socio-material circumstance that necessarily leads one to convert, but it may very well lead a person to listen to the Gospel and believe the one who is telling it. As Harding aptly describes, "The membrane between disbelief and belief is much thinner than we think. All I had to do was to listen to my witness and to struggle to understand him. Just doing so did not make me a fundamental Baptist born-again believer, but it drew me across that membrane in tiny ways so that I began to acquire the knowledge and vision and sensibilities, to share the experience, of a believer" (58). Harding highlights the specificities of language, the sensibilities of the spoken word, the persuasion of the narrative structure, to argue for a more complex understanding of conversion: "If conversion is a process of acquiring a specific religious language and witnessing [giving testimony] is a conservative Protestant rite of conversion, then, if you are willing to be witnessed to, if you are seriously willing to listen to the gospel, you have begun to convert" (57).

Understanding conversion in terms of narratives people tell about themselves and through which they organize their lives opens up space to see conversion as a continuous process in which people are reworking themselves.[16] As Holstein and Gubrium (2000, 104) argue, "Considering the self in terms of narrative practice allows us to analyze the relation between the *hows* and *whats* of storytelling; analysis centers on storytellers engaged in the work of constructing identities and the circumstances of narration respectively. We can view the storytelling process as both actively constructive and locally constrained." This notion of the self highlights the processual and never-ending character of self-construction and acknowledges the constraining elements of language in use. Pertinently, it also leaves room for the multiplicity of available stories people might tell about themselves: "Their diverse and now seemingly ubiquitous narrative practices work to constitute subjectivities in accordance with local relevancies that link broadly with familiar experiential themes."[17]

The insights presented by the previous authors also give us a clue about how to understand the discrepancies between many of the Pentecostal tes- timonies in which acceptance of Jesus as Savior is presented as a decisive moment of transition, often marked by divine insight, and my observations of people who frequented the churches in favelas. Participation in church life in Visionário was often characterized by a gradual increase in attendance instead of a definite moment of transition from no participation to full participation. The people I knew who had converted recently before or during my research period often started to visit a church for a while to see if they were attracted. Those who liked a particular congregation and continued to attend the cultos gradually adopted the Pentecostal language and modes of conduct of that church until they accepted Jesus as their Savior and/or began behaving according to the Pentecostal norms of their church. This understanding of conversion strikes a chord with the seminal work of Lewis Rambo (1993, 5), who stated that "conversion is a process of religious change that takes place in a dynamic force field of people, events, ideologies, institutions, expectations, and orientations. . . . Conversion is a process over time, not a single event; . . . conversion is contextual and thereby influences and is influenced by a matrix of relationships, expectations, and situations; and . . . factors in the conversion process are multiple, interactive, and cumulative." The discrepancy between a Pentecostal representation of a definite and sudden break and the practical process of becoming (Engelke 2004) underscores the fact that conversion entails a gradual reinterpretation of events as divine moments that retrospectively mark the difference between old and new selves (see also Harding 2000).

Ambiguities

Besides the discussions about the (dis)continuity of (indigenous) cultural forms and practices within Pentecostal movements and about the discrepancy between the abruptness of divine calling and the gradual process of conversion, academics, Pentecostal adherents, and non-evangelicals also hold discussions about the authenticity of conversion. The popularity of Pentecostalism seems to have thoroughly shifted the relations between favela residents of different creeds. To some non-evangelical residents, Pentecostal missionary practices were experienced as intrusive, and some felt belittled by the principled tone of their Pentecostal neighbors.

During my research, adherents of Pentecostal churches often presented so-called demonic practices as something they had left behind for good. Many of their non-Pentecostal neighbors generally respected them for their disciplined lifestyle, yet some of the residents complained about the feigned righteousness of the crentes and doubted if all of them really had converted. Especially when Pentecostal adherents openly condemned their behavior and started pointing out their wrongdoings, these neighbors felt unjustly criticized. On occasion they exclaimed that these crentes had not exactly been saints in the past or that they occasionally saw them doing "ungodly" things themselves. Some residents stated that in the favela there were "real" crentes and those who could not really be qualified as such.

Instead of viewing the differences between what people say and what people do as hypocrisy (as a number of people in Visionário did), or reproducing distinctions between so-called sincere and insincere believers, I propose to see slips and controversies as insights into identification processes and into the mechanisms of power in the favelas of Rio de Janeiro. If we understand Pentecostal language and practice as one powerful performance among others, we could better ask what it means to present oneself as a crente or evangélico. Through which social mechanisms are identity claims enforced, contested, and disputed? What are the constraints and possibilities of the uttering of a specific discourse in a specific situation?

As I have argued in this chapter, in the context of the favela, identifying with a specific religion provides people with a philosophy of life, with conceptual tools to understand and deal with the phenomena that happen around them. Yet people also position themselves in a field of power relations. In the favelas of Rio de Janeiro there are different social pressures and sociopolitical implications tied to the performance of specific religious practices and identities.[18] Because of their denunciation of "worldly" pleasures and non-Christian lifestyles, adherents of the Pentecostal churches are generally assigned a special status in relation to the other inhabitants. They are often seen as honest people who practice what they preach (though certainly not always). This *status aparte* stand or falls by the demonstration of a certain amount of self-discipline in the eyes of other Pentecostal and non-Pentecostal inhabitants. Controversies over the authenticity of conversion tell us of the stakes that are on the table in relation to socioreligious identification in the favelas of Rio de Janeiro.

Whereas people know and feel what is at stake, this does not necessarily mean that the performative constitution of an evangelical identity is straightforward, clear, or unproblematic. Describing conversion as a process of becoming does not necessarily mean that the outcome is fixed. As Birgit Meyer (1998, 339) pointed out some time ago, churches "provide an intermediary space for members to move back and forth between the way of life they (wish to) leave behind and the one to which they aspire."[19] During my research I encountered plenty of people who felt the presence of God in their life but honestly expressed their difficulty in stopping certain behavior, or people who accepted Jesus and changed their lifestyle but gradually picked up certain worldly practices and stopped attending church shortly thereafter.

135

Some people went back and forth.[20] Roberto, a young man who lived in a wooden shack near Maria, told me he wanted to stop drinking: "I am trying cut down on my drinking and return to the church again." Instead of describing it as a clean break, he described going back to church as a gradual process in which he would slowly decrease his drinking while increasing his church visits. Some people had accepted Jesus as Savior in the past and had been part of a church community for a period of time, but did not feel at home any longer and temporarily stopped attending a specific church until they found a new one. I had a conversation with the brother of one of the inhabitants of the wooden shack near Maria's house. After he learned I was interested in Pentecostal churches, he started talking fervently: "I have already been in the Igreja Quadrangular, Presbiteriana, and Igreja Universal, but my church is the Assembleia de Deus. There the fire really comes down.[21] I think that the preaching in the Igreja Presbiteriana is lukewarm [morna] and so is the preaching in the Universal. If you go church you want to return in a blessed state. If you are still in doubt if you are blessed, that is bad. At this moment I am of the Assembleia de Deus, but I have deviated [afastado] a little bit."

Likewise, Maria's eldest daughter, Claudia, regularly frequented a local Assembleia de Deus in the morro. She had four children by three different fathers. She worked as a cleaner in a post office on the asfalto. During an interview at the beginning of my research she passionately told me about her recovered grounding in church life. She had been converted and baptized in the Holy Spirit at the age of sixteen but had lived a turbulent life in which she repeatedly joined and left the church. After a period of withdrawal from church life, the father of one of her children was killed while attending a baile funk, which gave her a strong incentive to return to church. Nevertheless, at a certain moment during my fieldwork she stopped attending church and began dating men who did not attend Pentecostal churches. When I asked her why she did this, she said, "Right now I am searching for a man to support me."

To some evangelical residents this type of behavior was unacceptable. One adherent of the local Baptist church in Visionário mockingly described her as *ioiô* (yo-yo) evangelical, one who went back and forth intermittently. Whereas some people I met over the years had been ardent church visitors in the past and completely stopped going at a certain point, social identification was less rigid than some of the categories might suppose. For instance, some of the movements and tensions between old and new lifestyles are incorporated into Pentecostal language and understanding. In the Pentecostal formulation people can, for example, be converted but still be *afastado* or *desviado* (distant or deviated) from God temporarily. The fight against deviation is conceptualized as a *batalha espiritual*. Furthermore, many people told me that the devil is primarily interested in seducing those who are in the church because they are close to salvation and are seen as bigger trophies than those who are not. For that reason, there is always the possibility of explaining sinful behavior or a temporary church departure in terms of demonic seduction.

Some inhabitants thought such claims should be considered false explanations that provided people with an easy but unacceptable possibility in order to maintain the *status aparte* of a crente while doing as they pleased. Though in some cases this might have been true, many of the evangelicals who were accused of displaying ungodly behavior by their neighbors and fellow church members generally experienced these accusations as troublesome. Often, the harsh conditions of favela life present people with dilemmas. Claudia's search for a supportive husband painfully exemplifies the conditions of the morro, for example. Many women have to raise their children alone, without the aid of fathers. Claudia's chances of finding a man in the local churches of the Assembleia de Deus were slim, since the majority of the members were women and most men were much younger. Undoubtedly, Claudia's departure from the church was beneficial to her love life, thereby increasing her possibilities to encounter someone who could support her. Nevertheless, despite such prospects, she still felt that returning to church life would solve many of her problems.

As I have attempted to show, Pentecostal churches present an environment in which people can experience a break between so-called worldly and godly lifestyles, but some structural conditions of the favelas of Rio de Janeiro make it hard to abide by the moral codes of the churches. While people say they have accepted Jesus and have been baptized, everything does not instantly change as soon as the words are uttered. Nonetheless, this does not mean it is necessary to go to the opposite extreme and describe Pentecostal language as mere rhetoric. This would hardly clarify how language, religion, power, and behavior interact in daily life. According to Michel Foucault (1978, 100), "We must not imagine a world of discourse divided between accepted discourse and excluded discourse, or between the dominant discourse and the dominated one; but as a multiplicity of discursive elements that can come into play in various strategies." The discrepancies between what people say and what people do, or what people say today and tomorrow, points to the fact that social identities are always in a state of flux and, perhaps more important, that they are closely related to mechanisms of inclusion and exclusion and to chances and obstacles. Moreover, as the small excerpt from my interview with Tiago shows, religious identification often involves a wide range of human affairs simultaneously, ranging from socio-ethical considerations to psychotherapeutic understandings of self and well-being.

Hypermediated Conversion

At this point it is good to recall some of the examples of chapters 2 and 3, in which I described how members of Pentecostal churches think about the sounds they hear and images they see in the favelas. Favelas are heterogeneous spaces where one encounters overlapping collectives whose self-ascribed members reproduce different ideas and practices governing how to dress, talk, behave, and so forth. Some of these collectives are generally described as religious (Catholic, Pentecostal, Afro-Brazilian), whereas others are described in terms of their musical preference (sambista, funkeiro). In practice, however, all of these collectives are seen to exhibit particular lifestyles and preferences for certain music and bodily comportment. Last but not least, identifications with one or the other collective is generally coupled to judgments concerning ethical behavior of oneself and others (Maffesoli 1996; Rommen 2007).

People I interviewed during the course of my research were very much aware of the lives of others and reproduced ideas about morally benevolent and malignant lifestyles in relation to their neighbors. As the reader might recall, Pentecostal adherents described certain music styles that were audible in the favela as spiritually damaging, and certain Pentecostal ideas about urban violence were supported by the personal experience of violence in their immediate surroundings *and* by the mass mediated images of the protagonists of urban dramas. This is perhaps best exemplified by Crivella's exorcism of local comando members I described in the opening of this chapter. Moreover, as I will describe in more detail in chapters 5 and 6, notions about the right kind of Christian life are firmly entangled with ideas and practices concerning media behavior and media effects.

These and other examples indicate that conversions in the context of favelas must been understood in light of a fragmentation, pluralization, and mediatization of social life. Contemporary religious conversions occur in heterogeneous religious arenas and—equally important—such conversions take place amid a plethora of lifestyles based on global religious and nonreligious cultural trends, sustained by media. I thus argue that it is best when we understand conversion in these contexts as hypermediated self-discipline and transformation. The term "hypermediated conversion" serves to indicate that current conversions take place in a context of cultural plurality and mediatization of everyday life (Hjarvard 2008) that complicates the stability of such self-transformations and asks for a continuous reworking of the self and for a continuous evaluation of the media and popular cultural products that people encounter on a regular basis.

The exigency to present this new concept to describe religious transformation stems from the fact that, generally, the anthropology of conversion (Buckser and Glazier 2003) has paid much attention to language but much less attention to (electronic) media as integral elements of the conversion process. Emphasis is often placed on the question of whether and how media have certain effects that lead to conversion; however, as I argue, this emphasis follows an evangelical preoccupation and occludes a more refined understanding of what role media play in religious transformation.

The concept of hypermediated conversion addresses the fact that different media (which may include rituals, traditional practice, etc.) sustain the "bundle of narratives" (Smilde 2003, 327) that supports Pentecostalism as a belief system. People refer to news programs and carioca funk to confirm the spiritual battle, for example. Media are more than transmitters of meaning, however, and the idea of hypermediated conversion also addresses the fact that media co-produce affect (Massumi 2002). Adopting Brian Massumi's work, Jon Bialecki (2015) has recently argued that affect is the appropriate term to understand better how the practices associated with Pentecostalism induce particular embodied states that produce the sensation of the presence of the Spirit and the devil. As Bialecki describes aptly, "Here, we will think of affect as the intensities and energies found in a particular moment or object that has consequences on others that it is in contact with in that moment" (97).

Lastly, the concept of hypermediated conversion addresses the fact that Pentecostal leaders and members offer favela residents a variety of techniques to deal with media and popular cultural forms. As people understand and feel that particular media are related to spiritual or demonic presence, questions arise about how to engage with these media. Whereas plain avoidance is one of the possibilities, Pentecostalism also offers residents a number of purifying techniques that can make certain popular cultural forms accessible for Christian consumption.

While I have already presented some examples of the entanglements among media, daily life, and Pentecostalism in chapters 2–4, chapters 5 and 6 will focus specifically on media practices and behavior. Looking at the perceived merits and dangers of music listening in chapter 5 and at the attraction and rejection of television viewing in chapter 6 will give us a more detailed understanding of hypermediated conversion.

Conclusion

In this chapter I have described some of the attractions of Pentecostal doctrines and practices in a life-world characterized by the threat of violence. Violence related to the presence of the comandos confirms that a spiritual battle is taking place in the favelas of Rio de Janeiro and supports the belief that deliverance—ideally followed by conversion—is the only viable method to bring peace. The belief that comando members are possessed by demons is enforced by their supposed involvement with Afro-Brazilian religious practices. As Crivella's recorded oração and his subsequent exorcism also indicate, this belief is heavily supported by the mediated messages of the Igreja Universal.

Pentecostal understandings of possession and deliverance facilitate the homology between the liberation of people and places and enforce the experience of personal and social sanctuary in the morro. Deliverance is predominantly seen as the condition and consequence of conversion, a process characterized by the gradual reworking of one's understanding of one's life and environment as part of the spiritual battle between God and the devil. Such gradual reworking is enhanced by the (mediated) testimonies that circulate among church members and inhabitants, which persuade people to think of their life in Pentecostal terms. Testimonies help to convince people that personal well-being and safety are dependent on forces that are apparently beyond control but nevertheless able to be influenced by living a pious life.

While stories of converted traficantes play an important role in the imagination of the end of the comando-related violence, Crivella's visit to the morro lucidly demonstrates the paradoxes at work. Ironically, the moment the young men of the comando approached the pastor to be exorcised, the cameras were lowered, demonstrating the widespread fear of shooting pictures of traficantes and verifying the enduring chokehold that informal sovereign actors exert on favela life. Moreover, one must doubt whether the ritual exercise itself leads the young men of the comando to pursue a different occupation. As Christina Vital da Cunha (2008), Cesar Pinheiro Teixeira (2011), and Edin Abumanssur (2015) have shown, comando members also regularly take up Pentecostal practices (and identities) in search of divine protection against the forces that threaten them (e.g., other comandos, the police, milícias). Instead of understanding this as a phenomenon that disproves the arguments made so far, I think the example demonstrates the capacity of Pentecostalism to incorporate that which is seemingly foreign to it or that which seems diametrically opposed to it. Furthermore, this phenomenon arguably points to the moral dilemmas of favela life. Many young people who live in Rio's favelas are confronted with widespread police corruption and police violence, and many of those who are involved in the comandos uphold religiously inspired notions of right and wrong behavior in the face of unjust state actors. As the example of Robson's liminal position—described in the introduction—shows, some comando members temporarily frequent Pentecostal churches in search for different life options or spiritual reflection, whereas others might give up their comando life entirely.

Also, we need to keep in mind that Pentecostalism is wrought with internal tensions and denominational rifts (see also Cunha 2008). The fact that crentes bandidos emerge in the favelas of Brazil does not necessarily mean that the imagined opposition between urban violence and Pentecostalism loses its appeal. During my research, a member of the Baptist church told me that a Pentecostal pastor of the morro started performing church services in the open air that attracted many comando members, but that other Pentecostal pastors in the favela opposed such an institutionalization of Pentecostal ritual for comando members. Such contestations remind us that lived religion and institutional religion are engaged in dialogue with one another, and that grassroots changes do not necessarily lead to institutional innovations.

With this chapter on conversion in the context of favela life, I have cleared the path to elaborate on the concept of "hypermediated conversion" in more detail. As I will discuss in the next two chapters, evangélicos consume radio and television with notions of spiritual contamination in mind, and their media consumption is influenced by social pressures to maintain a *status aparte* in the favela. As we will see, evangelical favela inhabitants not only watch and listen to radio and television to receive information or to be entertained, but they also use media to understand, feel, and demonstrate what the difference is between "being in the world" and "being of the world."

141

Spiritual Attunement

Pentecostalism and Listening

One Saturday morning I was helping Pastor Abrahão of an Assembleia de Deus in Visionário with construction work outside the church. The pastor was gradually improving the church building with the help of the congregants. Two young men, Bernardo and Tiago, were scraping the topsoil off the hillside, while I was loading it in a wheelbarrow. Bernardo and Tiago were making fun of me; according to them, they could see the gringo was not used to manual labor. The radio was on inside the church while we worked. The volume was quite low, but the background music provided an audible rhythm that eased the work. Nobody seemed to hear the lyrics.

At a certain moment, however, one of the men became conscious of the fact that the rhythm coming from the church was that of carioca funk. It was only at that moment that we became fully aware of the music that was playing. I had assumed it was a Christian broadcaster and, apparently, so had the others. When we started to listen carefully it was clear that the radio was tuned to the local radio station transmitting from directly below us. The pastor stopped working and ordered us to change the frequency and find a Christian radio channel. When I asked him why we could not listen to the community radio station, he replied, "That is the community radio. They play only baile funk music that has a lot of foul language [palavrão] and that talks about using drugs and prostitution." Abrahão stated that such music should not be heard, particularly not in a church. "What if people were to hear such music coming from our church?" he added. Bernardo quickly found the Christian radio station 93 FM, which was very popular among people who attended the Assembleia de Deus in Visionário.[1]

Initially I was a bit surprised that they were speaking negatively about the community radio coordinated by an inhabitant of the morro. Some people were proud of having a community radio station and liked listening to it. It broadcast a variety of programs featuring different music genres. That was exactly the problem for many evangélicos, however. There had been a gospel show on the station, and some people believed it had disappeared because people did not like the fact that the gospel show had to share the same air space with programs that featured funk or pagode music. Gilberto, Maria's youngest son, claimed the community radio stopped playing gospel music because listening to gospel on a station that broadcast funk afterward was not right: "The light does not combine with the darkness, that is why they play only gospel on El Shadai." Abrahão's and Gilberto's remarks made me aware of the perceived influences of music in the day-to-day life of the inhabitants and reminded me that, despite the enormous influence of television in Brazil—especially telenovelas—radio and amplified music were considered equally important to many of the adherents of the Pentecostal churches.

In this chapter I focus on the listening practices of these adherents and on their accounts of the importance of music, radio, and other electroacoustic devices. In several ways, this chapter follows up the arguments in chapter 2, where I argued that sound and music are essential to the constitution of identities in the favelas. In the density of the favelas, different groups try to exercise a politics of presence among others through the sounds they produce. Sound and music are important to evangélicos because they confirm distinctions between them and people "of the world." By and large, evangélicos oppose their "godly" sound and music to the "worldly" sounds of their neighbors and try to transmit the Holy Spirit to the other inhabitants in order to convert them to their faith. Whereas in chapter 2 I focused on the politics of presence, in this chapter I will focus on the role of radio, music, and sound in the lives of individual Pentecostal adherents.

At this juncture, I will argue that the relation between electroacoustic technology and Pentecostalism is characterized by an elective affinity. Building on the insights of Jacques Derrida (2001) and several other scholars, I suggest that electroacoustic technology used by Pentecostals produces an experience of non-mediation and touch that verifies the "real presence" of God. For the adherents of the churches, the emotional gospel music, the authoritative voices of the pastors, and the remediated testimonies share the quality that, when transmitted or played, they produce a feeling of intimate contact with God. Listening to gospel music envelops people in godly sound, protecting those who are "in the world" from the harmful sounds and influences "of the world," albeit only temporarily.

A second argument I present in this chapter is that tuning in to certain evangelical radio stations or playing specific gospel music should not be conceptualized as actions that sequentially follow the acceptance of Jesus as Savior or that such an acceptance is the effect of proselytic media. As I have described in the previous chapter, conversion is often characterized as a watershed moment marking the transition from the old self to the newborn self. Though often presented as a definitive break, people commonly change their behavior and worldview gradually and perceive their new situation as perilous because demonic seduction continues to haunt them. During the conversion process, they learn to recognize all kinds of cultural practices that are possibly dangerous. In the next chapter I will focus on television viewing, but in this chapter I focus on hearing and listening. The process of conversion generally involves a categorization of sounds that one hears and a discipline concerning what to listen to and what not. Electroacoustic media can be characterized as sensitive tools that people use self-reflexively. The concept of "hypermediated conversion" dictates that media technologies should not be separated from our analysis of conversion. Taken as devices of self-discipline, media do not merely provide channels for the distribution of proselytic messages, which may or may not convince people to convert; rather, they are integral parts of benign and malign religious experiences that either help people stay in touch with God or threaten their spiritual well-being.

Combining these two arguments, I argue that Pentecostal sound categorization and media behavior occur at the crossroads of cultural-religious conceptions of the power of music and of social identifications in the context of favela life. The acknowledgment that certain sounds are divine and should be regarded as transmitters of God's spiritual force, whereas other sounds are spiritually harmful, enforces Pentecostal notions about social distinctions in the favelas. Continuous efforts to separate worldly and godly practices in the name of salvation place the discussions of music (and radio) at the heart of identity politics. Part of the assertion of a Pentecostal identity in the favelas of Rio de Janeiro is the awareness of the significance and power of specific sounds in relation to self and others and learning to act accordingly. People use radio, MP3s, and CDs not only to receive positive spiritual energy but also to demonstrate the difference between "being in the world" and "being of the world." Consequently, listening to the "right" evangelical radio stations, CDs, and MP3s should not be regarded as evident outcomes of conversion but as continuous reassertions of an identity that is much less fixed than often presumed. A focus on conversion narratives highlights the importance of radio in Brazilian Pentecostalism and urges us to take seriously media practices that generally receive less attention.[2]

Evangelical Radio in Rio de Janeiro

Since the introduction of radio in Brazil, recorded music featuring Brazilian artists has been, and continues to be, very important to the medium's popularity (Cabral 1996). The first Brazilian record with national musicians was made in 1902 (8). Radio was introduced in Brazil in 1922, and the first transmitter was set up in Rio de Janeiro the following year (9). Initially, when there were not many radios and not much of a radio audience, broadcasts were mostly noncommercial. While popular music was heard on the radio during the 1920s, it was only after Getúlio Vargas became president in 1930 that commercial radio began to grow. In the 1930s, more radio transmitters were installed (Ortiz 1988), more music was recorded, and more money was reinvested in radio and in recordings. Sambas recorded in the time of carnival became very popular, as did the *radionovelas* (Cabral 1996; Ortiz 1988).

Radio flourished during the 1940s and 1950s, and since then it has established itself firmly as one of the most pervasive means of mass communication in Brazil, alongside television (Straubhaar 1995, 79). While the advent of television in 1950 changed the consumer market, as the new medium eventually surpassed radio in attracting advertising dollars, the number of radio stations kept growing during the latter part of the century. Most radio stations are privately owned and financed by advertising revenue. According to the Brazilian Association of Radio and Television Broadcasters (Associação Brasileira das Emissoras de Rádio e Televisão, or ABERT), between 2001 and 2009, about 88 percent of Brazilian houses owned a radio (which would mean approximately fifty million sets).[3] Since 2009, the prevalence of home radios has declined, but that does not mean fewer people listen to radio broadcasts. According to the Brazilian Secretariat for Social Communication (SECOM), more people listened to radio daily in 2015 than in 2014, and according to ABERT more people started to listen to radio on cell phones and via the Internet instead of a "traditional" radio.[4] Most of the music transmitted on the radio comes from Brazilian artists; furthermore, as Perrone and Dunn (2001, 30) confirm, the Brazilian music market is dominated by national acts: "All genres included, national product accounted for up to 70 percent of unit sales of sound recordings in 1998, and all the top-ten sellers were Brazilian acts."

The first evangelical radio program broadcast in Brazil was *A Voz Evangélica do Brasil* (The evangelical voice of Brazil) in May 1938 on Rádio Transmissora Brasileira (Bellotti 2009). The program was the result of a collaboration of Methodist, Presbyterian, Episcopal, and Baptist churches. The next program to reach a large audience in Brazil was transmitted in 1943, *A Voz da Profecia* (The voice of prophecy), hosted by Pastor Roberto Rabello and produced by the Associação Geral da Igreja Adventista, based in the United States (Fonseca 1997, 45). The first Pentecostal radio broadcast was transmitted in 1947 by a missionary of the Assembleia de Deus; not much later, the U.S.-based Igreja do Evangelho Quadrangular, also Pentecostal, started to work in Brazil (Freston 1995). In the period thereafter, several other Brazilian Pentecostal churches—including O Brasil Para Cristo (Brazil for Christ), founded by Manoel de Mello, and Deus é Amor (God Is Love), founded by David Miranda—began broadcasting in Brazil, and radio became one of the privileged evangelical media in the country (Campos 1997). Freston (1995, 128) states that the headquarters of Deus é Amor in São Paulo featured more than fifty plaques with names of radio stations on which Miranda's program could be heard.

Today, leaders of the Assembleia de Deus and the Igreja Universal both invest in radio. The Igreja Universal exerts much greater control over its own media channels, since it has a pyramid organizational structure, whereas the Assembleia de Deus consists of networks of semi-independent churches. The radio stations of the Igreja Universal are united in one overarching company called Rede Aleluia. In Rio de Janeiro, the Igreja Universal broadcasts its music and the messages of its pastors on 105 FM and Copacabana AM. While pastors and members of the Assembleia de Deus in Rio de Janeiro are involved in two popular radio stations—Rádio Melodia FM and 93 FM, formerly called El Shadai—the churches themselves do not control these stations in the same manner as the Igreja Universal controls its channels. Neither of them is directly linked to one evangelical or Pentecostal church in particular. Both stations broadcast Christian music as well as evangelical sermons and *debates* (opinion programs in which experts discuss how to comport oneself as an evangélico in an environment fraught with worldly attractions).

A closer look shows that the radio stations form part of larger media conglomerates (*redes*) associated with different politicians. Rádio Melodia is owned by Francisco Silva, a former federal deputy for the state of Rio de

Janeiro who is affiliated with the Assembleia de Deus de Madureira. The gospel station 93 FM is part of the company MK Publicitá, which also owns a record label and a publishing house that distributes the popular evangelical magazine *Enfoque*. It also produced the popular television show *Conexão Gospel* until 2007. MK Publicitá is headed by Arolde Oliveira, federal deputy for the state of Rio de Janeiro. Although Arolde de Oliveira congregates at the first Baptist church of Niterói, several of the stars contracted by MK Publicitá congregate at the Assembleia de Deus.

Strikingly, data derived from the Brazilian Institute of Public Opinion and Statistics (Instituto Brasileiro de Opinião Pública e Estatística, or IBOPE), the principal agency that researches audience ratings in Brazil, show that Rádio Melodia has been among the most popular radio stations in the metropolitan region of Rio de Janeiro for more than a decade, often reaching second place in overall radio audience ratings.[5] The gospel station 93 FM has slightly fewer listeners but has maintained its place among the most popular radio stations in the region during this period.[6] These numbers indicate the enormous popularity of evangelical radio in Rio de Janeiro in general.[7] Not only were these two outlets the most popular evangelical radio stations in the city, but they were also among the most popular of all radio stations in Rio de Janeiro.[8] The large audiences indicate the growing popularity of Pentecostalism in mainstream culture as well as the mergers between Pentecostalism, advertising, and political campaigning. According to Luther King de Andrade Santana (2005), this popularity is due to the strategies of religious media businessmen such as Arolde Oliveira (93 FM) and Francisco Silva (Melodia).

On the basis of a quantitative comparison of the three most popular evangelical radio stations in 1996—Rádio Melodia, 105 FM, and 93 FM—Alexandre Fonseca (1997) concluded that 105 FM had the most exclusive audience from one denomination. Those who tuned in were mostly people who attended the Igreja Universal (54 percent). That is not so surprising, as the radio station is explicitly linked to the Igreja Universal, while the other two are not linked to any denomination in particular. Yet Fonseca concluded that people of the Assembleia de Deus generally showed a slight preference for Melodia, and he linked this preference to the consumer-class positions of the audience and the genre of music transmitted. Fonseca postulated that the audience of 93 FM leans more toward the middle classes, and he connected this profile to the language and (pop) music of 93 FM, which resembles other popular FM radio stations more than Melodia does.[9] Conversely, "at Melodia the intersections with prayers are more constant and the music follows the patterns adopted in the Assembleia de Deus with popular rhythms (*baião, forró, lambada*) that always speak of 'fire' and 'power,' generally associated with 'the new heaven and the new earth'—common characteristics in the Assembleia de Deus" (91). My observations confirmed some of the preferences Fonseca describes. Broadly speaking, those people who attended the Igreja Universal listened to 105 FM, and those who attended the Assembleia de Deus listened to 93 FM or Melodia. The people I interviewed who attended churches of the Assembleia de Deus often mentioned both 93 FM and Melodia when I asked them about their listening habits.

Notwithstanding the advantages of statistical data gathering and analysis, ethnographic accounts of actual radio-listening practices are also important for various reasons. Questions that remain unasked in most quantitative research are why people tune in to a particular radio station, in what social circumstances radio functions, and how people engage with it. As I have argued thus far, most inhabitants of favelas experience differences between the sounds they find pleasing or like to listen to and the sounds they hear throughout the day and night. Such is the case, among other reasons, because many people hear the radios of their neighbors.

While radio listening is often described as an individual exercise, it is frequently not possible to control which broadcasts echo through the alleys of the favelas or are audible in a domestic context. As I will show later on in this chapter, such lack of control is often considered worrisome for members of Pentecostal churches. As I have explained in chapters 1 and 2, the dense life-worlds of the favelas are characterized by proximity, and households often consist of many relatives living together in small houses. People often share one television, computer, and sound system.[10] In practical terms this means everybody may have their own preferences, but they cannot always control what is on the radio or television in their own home.

For some that was not particularly problematic. Bernardo, the young man I introduced at the beginning of this chapter, lived in a small wooden shack with his friend Carlos; Carlos's fiancée, Elisa; and their baby. Elisa attended the Igreja Universal while Carlos attended the Assembleia de Deus together with Bernardo. Since Elisa was mostly at home and she liked listening to 105 FM, that station was on most of the time. The other inhabitants did not mind much, as long as it was a Christian broadcaster.

In other houses, people of different religious mindsets lived together. Under those circumstances evangélicos often had to cope with the (unpleasant) sounds of others and vice versa. Many of Maria's children went to different churches, yet not all of them considered themselves evangélicos.

Between the six of them who were living permanently in Maria's small house, they had to share one sound system; more than once I was present during heated arguments over the music that was on. One day Carla's youngest sister was listening to loud gospel music when, at a certain moment, Carla could no longer stand it. She ran to the radio and put it on another frequency while she shouted, "Enough of that church music!" Her sister ran back to the radio and turned it back to the gospel music. This continued while both got increasingly angry, until finally Maria turned the radio off and threatened that no one would listen any more if they did not resolve their differences. These examples point to the fact that radio listening can also be a social exercise that does not always run smoothly. Furthermore, as the example in the opening of this chapter indicates, radio sounds frequently extend beyond the personal or domestic realm into the public domains of the favelas.

Listening

I became aware of the specific place of radio in the lives of many evangélicos when I lived in the apartment of my evangelical landlord, José.[11] When climbing the small concrete stairs leading up to the apartments, we all had to pass the door of José and his wife. One could always tell when they were home because the radio would be on. He mostly listened to 93 FM or evangelical CDs. José and his wife liked to listen to the daily debate. Intriguingly, they had no television, which made them an exception in the morro. When I asked why, he said, "I don't like television, I don't have time for it. Besides, what I hear on the radio programs is that television does not fit well with a Christian life. I would rather read the Bible. The Bible is my television." Even though many Christians have a television and watch it regularly with pleasure, José felt that the television was problematic. He could not work while watching, and what it presented was not good in his estimation. Jose felt that watching television practically opposed Bible reading—it was either television or the Bible—whereas radio was not at all problematic. In fact, he trusted the evangelical experts on 93 FM when they said specific programs on television were bad for evangélicos.[12]

Like José, many people listened to the radio during work together with colleagues, but plenty of people also told me they listened to evangelical radio on their own. At home, people listened while they were cleaning, washing the dishes, or performing other household activities. Interestingly, I never heard anyone who said they substituted going to a church service with an evangelical radio program. When I asked people what they listened to on the radio, they generally told me they listened to the louvores and debates. People often pointed out that they learned a lot from the debates. These programs were considered useful to their *edificação* (edification) as well as their grounding in church doctrines and practices.

During my research I was fortunate to be able to visit the houses of many families on a regular basis. There, I could observe people watching television and listening to the radio, CDs, or MP3s. Maria's house proved to be a very fertile ground for observing the practical uses of radio, television, and other electro-technical devices. Like so many other households in the morro, Maria had one sound system with a radio, a CD player, and a double cassette player. Her sons, Gilberto and Paulo, who both attended the Assembleia de Deus, were very fond of the debates on 93 FM and listened to them frequently. Gilberto had dropped out of school and at the time was delivering errands for small businesses on the asfalto. Paulo had returned to school at night and was trying to get his business as an *estofador* (upholsterer) going. It was his wont to offer his services in the streets down the asfalto, hoping that pass-ersby would contract him. Both were at home in the morning, and I regularly found either one of them on the couch in the living room. Sometimes they would be watching video or television, but I also often found them listening to the debates with their eyes closed. When Paulo was not listening to the debates or evangelical music, he also loved to listen to Rádio Tupi (1280 AM) in the company of his mother, Maria. The program *Patrulha da Cidade* (City patrol), broadcast between 12:00 and 1:15, featured violent and spectacular stories of the city, such as robberies and assaults, but also amazing rescues and strange occurrences.

In general I found that the people who attended the Assembleia de Deus were pragmatic in their choices of sermon, compared to the people of the Igreja Universal. Most of the latter preferred the words of their leader, Edir Macedo, above all others. Young people of the Assembleia de Deus exchanged videos, DVDs, CDs, and cassette tapes, but they did not inten-sively debate preachers or specific sermons. Paulo, Gilberto, and many of their friends of the Assembleia de Deus owned several CDs of pastors of different Pentecostal churches, and they copied all kinds of audio mate-rial from friends and church members, including material from Pentecostal preachers affiliated with the Assembleia de Deus. Paulo and Gilberto, for example, particularly liked the CD *Táticas que o Diabo Usa parar Afastar-nos de Deus* (Tactics the devil uses to lead us astray from God) by R. R. Soares.[13] On one occasion they were listening to a tape of David Miranda, the charismatic leader of the Pentecostal church Deus é Amor, on the sound system in their home. On the tape Miranda preached fervently against watching television, when all of a sudden the family's television broke down. Despite the unfortunate loss of the television, everybody laughed out loud about the incident.

Besides the testimonies on radio and television, recorded testimonies were also quite popular. In some cases these testimonies were mentioned as decisive contributions to the acceptance of Jesus as Savior. Take the words of Paulo, for example:

P: I felt emptiness in my heart. Something was missing. I was going to the bailes, staying with the girls there, but I saw the crentes and I thought, "One day I will be part of those people." One day there was a pagode that went on the whole day, but I saw that the crentes were passing by. I was thinking of returning to Jesus. One day at home I was cleaning the house and I saw a tape on the floor and I decided to put it on, I thought it was a tape with funk music. But when I listened I discovered it wasn't funk, it was a testimony, and as I listened my eyes started to open. I was getting a different vision: If God is truly so powerful, I didn't know the power of God. We can only know it when we accept Him. Then we see who God really is. I only knew Him by name, but we only know Him really when we accept Him in our hearts and He is with me up to today, even if I have been through trials and tribulations. I am happy.

M: Do you remember which tape it was? Which testimony?

P: Alex Macedo, testimony of an ex-traficante. Every week he had to drink blood. He was macumbeiro. There were many other things. I remember he did an *arrastão*[14] on the beach while I was there surfing. I saw the arrastão that he committed, but then I didn't know it was him. When I listened to the tape I thought, if God changed his life . . . I had proof of what happened at the beach because I was there, it was an arrastão in which nothing was left. Everything was taken. I know it was a real testimony because I was there and I thought if God has done that in his life . . . and from there on it began. Jesus began to talk with me, a voice in my head said, "If you don't enter the church today you are going to regret it," and I was thinking, "Am I going crazy?" But I wasn't crazy, I was just ignorant. It was God talking to me, and today I am in the church.

Paulo's example demonstrates the entanglement between technology, religious knowledge, and the sociocultural environment of the favelas. Furthermore, in the words of Paulo we see confirmed the tight relationship between music, lifestyle, and morality. As Paulo recounts, he was already thinking of turning his back on the bailes, but the tape gave the final push. The conversion narrative of Alex Macedo reproduced on audiotape gives Paulo a different perspective on life. As he listens, he is caught. Clearly, he is even more impressed by the story because he has seen the very arrastão Alex Macedo described. Having been witness to the arrastão in which Macedo participated proved the sermon's worth. Paulo's new insights marked the beginning of his relationship with Jesus, who then started speaking to Paulo directly. At first he thought he was crazy, until he understood that this was part of his newly obtained relationship with God. This example indicates the complex relationship between the production of (religious) truth, mass media, and the senses (see also Schmidt 2000; Hirschkind 2004; Stolow 2005). Paulo's memory of the arrastão and the narrative on audiotape verified his knowledge of Pentecostalism. Subsequently, it allowed him to experience the presence of God, who spoke to him. Before we analyze this entanglement in more detail I briefly return to the importance of gospel music.

Gospel Music

For many adherents of Pentecostal churches, music is one of the most important features of their spiritual life. Inside and outside church, people listen to the songs of popular evangelical artists. Many youngsters who attend churches of the Assembleia de Deus sing or play an instrument and are eager to be part of the church band of musicians.

During church services I experienced firsthand the importance of music, since I often played the drums myself. Not unlike other Brazilian religions, it is the music that inspires people and sets in motion the emotional participation that leads to the reception of the Holy Spirit, demonstrated by people who start shaking, dancing, and speaking in tongues. Many times I witnessed how the interaction between musicians and other members would lead to an exalted state of being. The repetition of chords and lyrics and the increased tempo and loudness would set the tone and environment for the Word of God to be preached with the right fervor to move the people in the church. When the pastor began to preach in the emotional style that characterizes most Pentecostal sermons, people would respond with "Aleluia!" "Glória!" or "Jesus!"

Gospel music consists largely of songs of praise or worship, which Brazilians call louvores.[15] Somewhat different than the term "gospel" might suggest, the Brazilian use of the label generally refers to the entire spectrum

Figure 8 Live performance of the samba gospel group Labaredo de Fogo in a small church of the Assembleia de Deus in Zona Norte. Photo: author.

of contemporary Christian music. Though in theory Brazilian gospel music may include a wide variety of (global) music styles, in practice, discussions about the divine status of certain music recordings and performances revolve around differences among styles. For example, whereas now one may often hear gospel music with Afro-Brazilian samba rhythms, as I will discuss below, for a long time Pentecostal adherents agreed that gospel music styles could range from baladas românticos to up-tempo rock and pop songs but should not include Afro-Brazilian styles. Many Pentecostal adherents considered these typical Brazilian styles to be pagan or demonic. Nowadays, many Brazilian styles have been accepted in evangelical circles as legitimate forms of gospel music, just as rock gospel and hip-hip gospel have also become more accepted in Brazil. As Jacqueline Dolghie (2007) and Maxwell Fajardo (2015) confirm, in the 1960s and 1970s generational differences obstructed the use of certain instruments (guitars, drums) in evangelical church services in Brazil on account of their "worldly" character. Nevertheless, these instruments were gradually accepted and are at present seen as appropriate for louvores.

Many people who attend Pentecostal churches consider music an important means of communication with God. Take, for example, Gilberto, who told me, "God talks to you by means of louvor. It is louvor that is giving you the Word of God. You feel the power of God through louvor. God talks to you on these CDs, I brought this one by Cassiane. It is a blessing. It has the power of God as well. There is a louvor on this one in which God talks to you profoundly. The more you listen to these CDs the more you want to get closer to God." Gilberto adored the music of Cassiane.[16] The way he talked about her resembled the way other people would speak of a rock star or other celebrity: "I would do anything to watch a show of hers," he said. Franck, a young man of nineteen, who attended the Assembleia de Deus, also loved Cassiane's music. Franck told me,

> I watch *Conexão Gospel*, which is broadcast on channel 9. This program is very good, all the singers from MK, of Radio MK, feature there. *Conexão Gospel* is broadcast every Sunday and Thursday. It is very good. There are video clips and interviews with singers who have a new CD. Do you like louvor? Of louvor, lately I like very much Diante do Trono, but above all I like Cassiane. These are louvores in which you really feel an artist of God. These are singers who sing as though anointed, you know? It makes you say, yes, that is good.[17]

Contrary to those of the Assembleia de Deus, the services of the Igreja Universal do not often feature large bands of musicians, but some of the pastors were quite famous gospel singers and sold many records.[18] Pastor Marcelo Crivella of the Igreja Universal, who has appeared in several chapters of this book, was quite popular among the inhabitants of Visionário, and many experienced his music as genuinely dedicated to God. Take for example what Dona Dora, a woman of fifty-two who attended the Igreja Universal, said when I asked her if she liked to listen to any particular music: "I have more CDs of bispo Crivella. I like his music. He has a charisma. You feel that when he sings, they are very strong, his louvores, I like them very much. I feel the presence of God when he sings. I feel the presence of God in his music because he sings with his heart. You can feel he does it with love. He doesn't record for the sake of recording. He records with love." These quotes unequivocally show that music is an important aspect of Pentecostalism, but they also demonstrate that audio broadcasts and recordings are powerful mediators of the divine presence. To understand why broadcasts and recordings can be experienced as such, let us first take a closer look at the specific qualities of radio, after which we will turn to the elective affinities between electroacoustic technology and Pentecostalism.

The Qualities of Radio

The three popular radio stations—Melodia FM, 93 FM, and Radio 105 FM—all played gospel music throughout the day. However, they also featured pastors who delivered sermons or engaged in conversations with listeners. Melodia and 93 FM both broadcast debates between 11:00 and noon. In these debates contemporary social issues are discussed with (evangelical) experts in order to instruct listeners about how to practice their faith in a complex society. At night 93 FM broadcasts the program *Culto Doméstico* (Domestic church service) and Melodia broadcasts its *Projeto Cristo em Casa* (Christ at home project).[19] Radio 105 FM broadcasts the words of its charismatic leader, Edir Macedo, at noon and at night in a program called *Palavra Amiga* (A friendly word).[20] Markedly, two of the three titles refer to the intimate sphere of the domestic household, and one to the kindliness of the radio broadcast.

These titles remind us of the intricate connection between the development of radio and the establishment of the living room as the locus of family life (Lacey 2000; Moores 1993). Such a connection is important because it reveals the seemingly paradoxical experience of radio listening as a public *and* private affair, and it points to the often-experienced intimacy of radio. Consider the words of Kate Lacey (2000, 285):

> The radio offered access to a public world, compressing the distance in space between the listener and the event, and at the same time making the perception of that event accessible to a numberless audience of listeners, and celebrating the distance overcome in transmitting those events into the home. The microphone, like the camera, had traversed the aural landscape, giving the broadcast a sense of "second nature." The loudspeaker, often designed to blend with the fabric and furnishings of the home, offered the illusion of an equipment-free reproduction of reality. (Indeed, although the distance between spectator and object is always apparent in visual media, sounds, especially music, seem to enter the body and prompt a visceral response.)

Several authors have described similar qualities of radio listening. David Hendy, for example, has argued that the lack of images in radio listening provides a sense of greater emotional experience than is often the case with television watching (and listening). Building on the work of Susan Douglas (1999), Hendy (2000, 119) writes, "It is not just that radio 'stimulates the imagination,' but that the innate pleasurability of such cognitive activity helps forge a strong *emotional* attachment to the radio medium itself, even in a predominantly televisual age." Besides this cognitive faculty, Hendy argues that we generally relate quite differently to audiovisual technology than to electroacoustic technology. Sight "may allow us some power to gaze and dissect at a distance, to be apart from our surroundings" (120). According to Douglas (1999, 30), in contrast, "sound 'envelops' us, pouring into us whether we want it to or not, including us, involving us."

Nevertheless, as Shaun Moores (1993, 77) also urges, we should be cautious: "If broadcasting was to 'capture' a place in the times and spaces of everyday life—to win an accepted and taken-for-granted position in domestic cultures—then this victory was less than immediate." In the case of the introduction of the "wireless" in Britain, there were considerable disturbances in people's daily routines and among family members. Moreover, as the fights between Maria's daughters indicate, we should not assume that radio listening—or other media use—is unproblematic. Family relations are often renegotiated in the face of religious and cultural differences.

Strikingly, the producers of evangelical media are quite aware of the specific qualities of radio as an intimate medium. Take for example the words of Pastor Rodrigues of the Igreja Universal: "We discovered that radio is a means of communication that has no equal. There is nothing like radio. Television has the power of the image, but it does not have the force of radio. . . . Our dream is that the evangelical churches in Brazil will discover what it means to have a radio station."[21] The owner of the evangelical radio station 93 FM expressed similar thoughts on the qualities of radio in relation to television:

> Radio is a much warmer vehicle because it allows people to listen while doing other things. People may come together in groups. Moreover, radio is a warm communication instrument. Television is very cold because it is egotistical, television separates. Instead of uniting it separates. . . . Now, from the evangelical perspective it is not necessary for the medium to create communitarian bonds, because salvation is individual; it is personal; it is the framework of values of each and every individual, so television is a very strong instrument indeed. I have seen programs, sermons very well constructed, strong messages that touch . . . radio is warm . . . it has a much bigger appeal. With radio you feel much more involved with the communicator, there is intimacy.[22]

Whereas evangelical radio producers of Pentecostal inclination wholeheart-edly embrace radio as a privileged medium in the present, this was not always the case. As Karina Bellotti (2009) states, sectors of the Assembleia de Deus resisted the use of radio in the past on account of its worldly character. Moreover, acceptance of radio as an intimate vehicle of communication is the result of a complex process of both technological and sociocultural trans-formations. Bellotti has shown how Brazilian evangelical radio between 1940 and 1970 was marked by the inclusion of specific northeastern, rural cultural styles that addressed migrated listeners in urban environments and gave them a sense of familiarity. It was the new format of Protestant evangelical ideology and familiar cultural style that produced the warmth so cherished (Bellotti 2003, 87–89). Another important element has been the marriage of electroacoustic technology and Pentecostalism.

Elective Affinities

I was drawn more and more to evangelical radio when I discovered that many evangélicos who live in the favelas understand the medium as an instrument that puts them in touch with God, in order to achieve a divine state of being. For example, Rodrigo, one of my friends of the Assembleia de Deus, under-stood listening to the radio as part of his search for the Holy Spirit.[23] When I asked Rodrigo how this search proceeded, exactly, he told me the following:

> I began to fast. I began to separate myself. Sanctification, from saint [santo], means separated; to sanctify means to separate; sanctifica-tion means separation. I began to separate myself, fornication I already no longer indulged in, you know, Jesus had already liberated me. I said from now on only when I am married. That was already determined, that particular desire was taken from me. Then I began to search for the Holy Spirit, fasting, praying, reading the Bible. Early in the morning I woke up to pray. Sometimes I went to sleep very late because I was praying, listening to the word of God on the radio. I made a promise to God, I will only stop fasting after I am married. I kept searching. One week before I was married I received the Holy Spirit.

Rodrigo used radio to separate himself in the religious sense of the word.[24] According to Jacques Derrida (2001), there exists an elective affinity between Christianity and mass media. Derrida argued that, in contrast to Judaism or

Islam, the merger between Christianity and televisual technologies produces the "real presence" of something that is otherwise mostly spoken about. In the case of the televised Eucharist and televised miracles, "the thing itself, the event takes place in front of a camera . . . the thing actually takes place 'live' as a religious event, *as* a sacred event. In other religions religion is *spoken about*, but the sacred event itself does not take place in the very flesh of those who present themselves before the camera" (58). Derrida argues that the intersection of Christian movements and televisual media demonstrates a particular connection between faith and knowledge that hitherto was not as obvious:

> There is no need any more to believe, one can see. But seeing is always organized by a technical (mediatic and mediatizing) structure that supposes the appeal to faith. The simulation of "live" transmission which has you believe what you cannot manage to believe: that you are before "the thing itself"; you are there, at the Gulf War; there are reporters there, with their cameras, who transmit to you live, without intervention, without technical interposition! . . . Now one knows very well—and this is the most rudimentary knowledge concerning what television is in reality—that *there is never anything live*. All of that is *produced* [*monté*] in a fraction of a second, in studios where one can instantaneously frame, efface, reconstruct, manipulate [*truquer*]. The presumption remains, and with it, the common prejudice, the structural credulity that television, by contrast with printed newspapers and radio, allows you to *see* the thing itself, *to see what touches* with the Evangelical dimension: one can almost put one's finger on the wound, touching; you can touch; that's coming one day; we'll be able not only to see but to touch. Belief is both suspended in the name of intuition and of knowledge, and (at the same time, naturally) reinforced. . . . There is no need to believe; one believes; no effort is necessary because no doubt is possible. . . . This is the argumentative strategy that is actually used in all the milieus of proselytism, of conversion, of appeals to particular, determinate religions. . . . Believe me immediately because there is no need to believe blindly, since certitude is there, in the immediacy of the senses. (63–64)

If the promise of touch and of non-mediation ("real presence") lies at the root of this elective affinity between Christianity and the mass media, perhaps radio and other electroacoustic technologies deserve more attention than they are given in many studies about Pentecostalism in Brazil.[25] While it is clear that vision has a particular place in the historical discernments between faith and knowledge in modern society—and it is this discernment that Derrida is trying to unravel for us at here—I would argue that electroacoustic technology used by Pentecostals produces a similar experience of non-mediation and touch that verifies the "real presence" of the divine.[26]

Such a connection is plausible because many of the Pentecostals' spiritual encounters—negative and positive—are acoustic.[27] As the examples of Paulo, Gilberto, and Dona Dora show, people recount that God or the devil spoke to them. Often people said they literally heard voices, but even those people who did not recount hearing a voice said that God was trying to speak (*falar*) to them directly in such and such event.

I suggest here that the seemingly equipment-free reproduction and visceral experiences of sound connect well with the idea and experience that God is directly accessible through the Holy Spirit without any other mediation. Remember, for example, some of the people I presented in the second chapter who felt that through louvor they could transmit the Holy Spirit to other people in the morro. Moreover, I suggest that there is an elective affinity between the Pentecostal discourse, the emotional character of the Pentecostal speech and song, and electroacoustic technologies. The emotional experience of radio listening, the experience of nearness and intimacy that radio produces, is especially suitable to the emotional character of Pentecostal language, which is often addressed to an individual in distress or wracked by emotional problems.[28]

While she does not discuss the role of radio in particular, I believe it is no accident that Clara Mafra (2002) starts her book on the performative power of words in the Igreja Universal with a fragment of a radio conversation between a pastor and a "client." Besides Mafra, many authors who have written about the Igreja Universal in Brazil highlight the great importance of the performative language in rituals of the church. Kramer (2001b) and Campos (1997) also point to the power of language in relation to other practices of mediation in the Igreja Universal. The church places a heavy emphasis on objects and fluids (oil and water, mostly) as biblical mediators of the Holy Spirit and bearers of curative powers.[29] By means of their words and prayers the pastors bless and consecrate these objects and fluids, after which the powers can be transmitted to individuals (Kramer 2001b). Such powers of words to transform objects into mediators of the power of the Holy Spirit are also transmissible through radio and television. In television and radio broadcasts, the pastors of the Igreja Universal invite the audience to place a cup of water near the radio or on the television. Through the instrument of the *oração forte* (powerful prayer), the water obtains the curative powers of the Holy Spirit. At the end of the program, the audience is invited to drink the water together with the pastor and receive God's blessing. Campos (1997, 361) states, "In the IURD they believe that the temple [of the Igreja Universal] radiates [*irradia*] a 'vital fluid' channeled through Hertzian waves in the direction of radio or television receivers, materialized in the cup of water." Patricia Guimarães (1997, 24) tells the experience of a woman who was watching a program of the Igreja Universal on TV Record. A woman called to speak with the pastor who hosted the program. She began telling him that she suffered from an illness and that she was thinking of committing suicide. The pastor ordered her to put a cup of water on the television, after which they prayed together to bless the water. After she drank the water a demon manifested itself and took over the voice of the woman on the telephone. Unperturbed, the pastor began speaking firmly to the demon over the telephone: "Just by listening to the voice of the pastor on the telephone he [the demon] was burned [*queimado*]." Such transmissions of divine powers through radio waves and electroacoustic devices confirm a different kind of elective affinity between mass media and Pentecostalism.

Another example of such a link appears when reception of the Holy Spirit is imagined in relation to contemporary technological reception devices.[30] Here I would like to mention briefly the performance of Pastor Ouriel de Jesus, who preached at a *congresso de jovens* (youth congress) of the Assembleia de Deus, broadcast in the program *Cristo o Vencedor* on July 7, 2002. While the pastor preached to the crowd, he asked them to raise their hands as if they were an airwave reception dish (*antena parabólica*). He showed them how to raise their arms wide and shouted, "Are you seeing it? Are you seeing? Now receive!" While the program itself was broadcast on television, the reference to the antena parabólica suggests that the Holy Spirit is transmitted in the same way radio and television waves are, and that no other technological medium except the body is needed to receive the Spirit. In other words, the reception of sound, music, and voice reflect and duplicate the feeling of direct non-mediated reception of the Holy Spirit because electroacoustic technologies enhance a feeling of presence, nearness, directness, and intimacy. I suggest that it is this electroacoustic experience that enhances the imagination of the body as a receiver of the Holy Spirit in much the same way we receive sounds mediated by electroacoustic technology.

For many Pentecostal adherents, the search for an evangelical broadcaster was not motivated just by their quest for divine presence, however. As I mentioned in chapter 2, the meaning of Christian sounds cannot be detached from the significance of other popular sounds and music in the soundscapes of the favelas. Let me describe the consequences of our common understanding of the relation between conversion and media preference.

Moral Attunement

Up until this point I have discussed radio and music mostly in terms of a politics of presence. Here I will focus on listening practices, moral evaluations, and media behavior that are tightly related to daily life. Despite their genuine love for evangelical artists, the joy people generally experienced from gospel singers should be seen against the background of the normative separation between música do mundo and música evangélica that church leaders and adherents tried to maintain. By and large, a gospel song can be recognized by its Christian lyrics, although many people consider certain styles—principally carioca funk and pagode—incompatible with a sanctified Christian life, regardless of the lyrics. Take for example the words of Paula, who had joined a local Assembleia de Deus not long before our interview: "Your vision changes after you are in the church. You look at things differently; you see the world in a different light, totally different. From one minute to the other you change your personality. I adored funk, I loved funk, pagode, all these things, I did not miss one baile funk, I adored it. I lost the desire, I can't even sing the music, many things I did in the past, I don't do today." As Paula indicates, a sudden change in musical taste was one of the strong features of her newfound church life. Nevertheless, many people did not experience such a sudden dislike for these styles. Consider the following words of Marcus, a fellow member of the Assembleia de Deus:

> I like soccer, but because of an injury I had to stop. I think that if I were to continue I would be hurt. That is what the enemy wants, but God is so great that He changes things in such a way that you no longer feel the necessity. Look at the example of Luis. He is a *surfista* [surfer], but he has often said that the desire in his heart isn't the same as it was in the past, the wish to go the beach every day has disappeared. I also stopped drinking and lying. Music, I had to separate. I loved pagode. I sang, but God works in such a way that

you don't find that important anymore. Certainly, when you hear it you remember, but you won't pay it much attention.

When I asked whether he never missed pagode, Marcus replied:

> Let's put it like this. Our flesh, which is sinful, remembers certain things you did, very vividly sometimes. Today our fight is not against the flesh or the blood, but against the things we don't see. It can take us by surprise. I was at my work and there was a young girl and I heard a voice saying, "You can have her." But I was alone there. It was the enemy. He is like someone who conceals himself close by and says things such as, "Ah, you are beautiful," about this girl.

As we can see, Marcus explains his change in music taste in relation to sinful pleasures associated with them, and he graphically illustrates how the joys of the past continue to haunt him in the present. For him and many others, pagode is closely connected to the carnal pleasures the devil uses to seduce people to act immorally. Pertinently, adherents of Pentecostal churches related their disliking of pagode music to the lifestyles of the people who loved it, and they explained their promiscuous sexual behavior and love of *cachaça* (rum) as the result of demonic influence.

During my fieldwork, Pentecostal adherents often voiced their preoccupation with the transgression of boundaries between what they considered divine and worldly realms and the possible contamination of their spiritual purity as the result of listening to worldly music.[31] Moreover, people also often commented on the worldly aspects that could corrupt gospel music and the harmful effects such corruption might have on individuals and spaces. Therefore, even those people who had accepted Jesus and considered themselves crentes regarded radio and other electroacoustic devices as dangerous elements to be handled with care.[32] For the majority of the people, it is important to know what to listen to in order to get closer to God, but equally important to know what one should *not* consume.

Markedly, the concerns were not only about the inner experience of listening but also about the listener's identity as a devout Christian in relation to others. Let me recall the example with which I started this chapter. The pastor's concern about the music transmitted by the community radio was not only that he found it unpleasant. He was also worried that other people would hear such music coming from the church and, as a result, he would lose his moral authority to correct people who did not follow biblical prescriptions in the light of the Assembleia de Deus doctrines. In other words, he was worried about what it would do to his moral authority and that of his congregation.

Controversies concerning music styles in Brazilian evangelical circles tell us much about what Timothy Rommen (2007) has described as the "ethics of style." As Rommen demonstrates, evangelicals in Trinidad experience musical style as closely connected to habits and customs of particular groups. Consequently, the introduction of new gospel styles generates an array of ethical discussions about the lifestyles of others and the boundaries of religious communities. Rommen's analysis of the interplay among musical style, religious community, and ethics connects well with Birgit Meyer's (2009; 2010) conception of religious mediations in terms of "sensational forms." According to Meyer (2009, 13), sensational forms, which can be defined as "relatively fixed, authorized modes of invoking and organizing access to the transcendental," induce particular bodily sensations that bind practitioners with the divine and with one another. Meyer highlights the fact that sensational forms are not opposed to ethical norms. Aesthetic style structures religious experience and simultaneously clothes it as legitimate. The works of Rommen and Meyer underscore the importance of form in religious worship and begin to clarify why stylistic transgression can be experienced as extremely troublesome to Pentecostal adherents (see also Howard and Streck 1999). As we have seen, the experience of radio and music listening by Pentecostal adherents involves aesthetic and religious components on the one hand—people may or may not enjoy the music and feel connected to God—and what Hirschkind (2001, 624) calls a "moral attunement" on the other.

To be able to discuss this concept in detail, let me briefly repeat some of the things I explained in the previous chapters and point out the why the reception of mass media is important to Pentecostal identity in the favelas of Rio de Janeiro. Much has been written about the transition from "living in the world" to being a crente, in which the change in modes of conduct and dress and regular participation in church life are inward and outward signs of a new social identity.[33] All authors note that, apart from the specific norms outlined in the Bible, evangélicos stress the importance of particular modes of behavior: no drinking or smoking, no cursing and swearing, no illicit sexual affairs, no idolatry, and so on. In other words, in addition to the explicit sacred activities dictated by the Bible, one has to be aware not to perpetrate the mundane practices considered sinful or which could lead to a possible contamination of a Christian lifestyle. According to Burdick (1993, 83), for many evangélicos the consequences of the distinction between secular and Christian lifestyles can be observed in "leisure time" activities. The normative differences between godly and worldly lifestyles stimulate people to fill the few "free" hours they have with activities that bring them closer to the Lord: helping in church activities, listening to gospel music, or reading the Bible.

In the dense social spaces of the favelas, media are not merely the vehicles that deliver a Pentecostal message or enforce experiences of divine presence. They also function as tokens of a sanctified spiritual life. Media offer people the knowledge to formulate "new" identities, and these media can be used to demonstrate such an identity to others. Expressing that one listens to evangelical music and watches evangelical television is itself an important feature of favela identity politics.[34] Expressing love for gospel carries implicit religious and moral statements about life in the favelas and distinctions between spiritual and secular lifestyles.

As I have also explained in the previous chapters, the *status aparte* proclaimed by many of the evangélicos was precarious. As church leaders and co-congregants would often state, "Crente tem que ser diferente" (The believer has to be different). The only way they could claim a *status aparte* in the environment of the morro was to demonstrate that they truly practiced what they preached. This meant no partying at the baile funk, no smoking, no drinking, but also no deliberate listening to funk or pagode music. Regulation of media practices through normative statements and social control of co-congregants is thus not merely the result of an inward search for spiritual experience but also part of the collective effort to ensure that people who identify themselves as crentes are regarded as "sanctified" and truly different from the rest of the inhabitants. This is not merely the case in the favelas of my research. Talking about the crentes in the favela Dona Martha in Zona Sul of Rio de Janeiro, Clara Mafra (1998, 288) wrote that many people are driven by an ideal of "sanctification" and that "consumption is also regulated by this ideal of sanctification; it is common that friends and parents of crentes promote rigid control over the music that is heard, the TV programs that are permitted, the written messages that one reads."

If we take the regulation of media practices as a starting point, we might also understand that the relationship between media and evangelism should not predominantly be described in terms of causality. We would be misled if we follow a certain Christian conceptualization that describes evangelical media principally in terms of messages that reach people and affect them. Notwithstanding the fact that people often narrate their decision to accept

Jesus and join a congregation as something that took place at a definite time and place and is often described as permanent, the life trajectories of most people show that they go through a process of gradual transformation that involves a change in the evaluation of music that surrounds them. Remember the words of Paulo, who recounts that before joining the Assembleia de Deus he already thought differently about the baile funk and was considering following the example of the crentes who passed by the local pagode.

Joining a Pentecostal church can therefore better be understood as hypermediated conversion and as a self-disciplining performance that positions people in a field of power relations. Training oneself to be attentive to the kind of music one plays and listens to is part of identity politics. In the dense social spaces of the morro, social control over music and radio is exercised by friends and relatives but also by non-evangelical neighbors who question the sanctity of their fellow inhabitants. If conversion is an assertion of a Pentecostal identity through particular performances, rather than a clear break between past and present, tuning in to certain radio stations is not the outcome of, but rather an integral part of, conversion. The awareness of the significance and potential of specific sounds in relation to self and to others is crucial to the maintenance of a Pentecostal identity in the favelas of Rio de Janeiro. Public listening to radio, CDs, and MP3s is part of the continuous reassertion of an identity that is much less fixed than has been presumed. The following fragment comes from an interview with Franck, who appeared earlier in this chapter. This excerpt demonstrates the considerations and worries of many evangélicos concerning radio use and their self-disciplining media performances:

M: Do you listen to the radio?

F: Do I listen to the radio? If I could I would listen to the radio twenty-four hours a day, I love radio, it is my thing. Today a colleague will bring his radio to work. He will bring his *som* [sound system]. You know, you can put CDs on and [cassette] tapes. Tomorrow I have to work in the morning and I will take my CD box. I will take my tapes. I will work and listen the whole day, radio is my thing, 93, only 93 FM.

M: No other?

F: [clucks with his tongue] No other, only 93 FM. My CDs, my tapes, and nothing else, there is no other radio.

M: But 93 FM, that is only gospel.

F: Only gospel.

M: Do you never listen to other music?

F: Never to other music, only gospel, gospel, gospel. When I did not belong to the church, I liked pagode and samba very much, I danced the samba [*sambava*] a lot, but then I did not belong to the church.

M: Why don't you listen to pagode any more?

F: It doesn't edify me, no. Today, if you were to listen to the music of today, if you could hear rap or funk, if you would see the lyrics, these are things, I think a child should not hear the things they hear today. In the past the raps and the funk were like this for example: [starts rapping] "I went to the corner of the school where everything began, I was looking at her . . ." you know, that was how it went and nothing more. Today, I can't even tell you. You hear the pagode and the funk of today. They only talk about garbage. Let's see if I remember one of them, no, I don't want to sing it, no. You know when you hear it all the time you record [*grava*] it. The music is so indecent, I think it should not be sung. Rap is really absurd, it is a load of garbage that only leads people to prostitute themselves. When that music is heard people prostitute themselves faster, understand? I do not agree, I would rather not listen to it. As I told you, either you grant space to God or you grant space to the devil. That music doesn't take you to God. It doesn't make it to the throne of God. That's why I can't listen to that music. I prefer to listen to the louvores. It is difficult, you know why. If I were to arrive at work, for example, and I put pagode on, my colleagues who do not belong to the church would come in and hear that music, they would say, "Are you listening to this music, aren't you a crente?" I can't give them an opening to talk like that, they will judge you. Because a crente can't look at women, a crente can't listen to música do mundo, a crente can't dance, a crente can't go to a baile, he really can't, so when we give them the smallest opening people will take advantage of it: "Oh that crente there is listening to pagode." We would lose that authority, that thing of the Christians. We have to be cautious.

M: Who is judging you?

F: The *ímpios, ímpios* are the people who have not accepted Jesus. They can do it, but we can't. They judge. So afterward, when we want to talk about God, they say, "You are talking about God to me? You are no crente, you don't belong to the church, you were dancing there."

M: But that must be difficult here in the morro. There are always people from the church or *ímpios* in the vicinity?

F: That is why you have to be very careful.

M: How do you do that?

F: You have to make the separation. Grant space only to God. Try to do the good things, the things that please God. You understand, you should never again listen to worldly music. Don't put it on the radio. Surely we do hear worldly music, music that is not from the church, that isn't gospel. We hear it the moment we step out of the Assembleia de Deus. But not on my radio that is playing. I won't put it on. I am not singing it either. I won't arrive at home and put on a pagode, a samba, or a rap. I would never tune into a worldly radio channel on my radio. That is music that praises the devil. The music on my radio pleases God. It brings the Word to my brothers, the pastor gives a Word that educates, I want to improve every day and every moment in order to make sure that people won't see my failures and accuse me afterward when I pass by with my folders saying to the people that God loves them. They will attack me: "How can you say, 'God loves you,' when you are doing that?" They say that. It is better to be cautious. We are different.

The dynamic that becomes obvious in this quote resembles to a certain extent Hirschkind's (2001, 627) elaborate description of sermon listening in Egypt—as my emphasis on "moral attunement" indicates. Among my informants, the idea was widespread that listening to Pentecostal radio or music would instill certain Christian virtues, "enabling one to live more piously and avoid moral transgressions." Yet, unlike in the case of Hirschkind's informants, my informants did not recognize particular and elaborate bodily dispositions and emotional states in or during the actual act (performance) of listening. Certainly there were all kinds of emotional states people described; however, there were no widespread instructions about or techniques for how to listen to experience sermons correctly, as Hirschkind describes for his informants. In relation to my informants, moral attunement was literally related to the tuning of the radio to an evangelical broadcaster in order to demonstrate that one led a virtuous life. What becomes obvious is that listening is both a personal and social act for evangélicos in the morro. People search for a divine experience by listening to gospel music but are simultaneously aware that others are scrutinizing their listening preferences. Avoiding worldly sounds, specifically on one's own sound system, is important because demonic sounds are harmful and because neighbors and relatives may overhear and judge the music being played.

Flordelis

Franck's words give us insight into how amplified gospel music functions as a token and communicates to neighbors that someone is a crente and thus different from the rest. Occasionally, gospel music performers also reinforce connections between gospel music and Pentecostal identification in the context of favela life. The music and mass mediated life story of Flordelis—one of the Pentecostal performers presented in the introduction of this volume—give us insight into how gospel performers contribute to religious scripts that reinforce notions of the power of the Holy Spirit to save innocent lives in the favelas of Rio de Janeiro. Flordelis—born and raised in Jacarezinho, a favela in Rio de Janeiro—has become known throughout Brazil as the woman who "adopted" fifty underprivileged children. Many of the children had experienced traumatic encounters with violence, addiction, and poverty while growing up in the peripheries of Rio de Janeiro. In her attempts to rescue them, she acquired legal custody over all the children. Because of her struggles, her musical talent, and her religious message, TV Globo dedicated several programs to her in 2002, which boosted her fame and helped her career as a performer. Her growing celebrity culminated in multimedia exposure when a docudrama film about her life came out in 2009 and MK recorded and distributed her CD in 2010. On top of this success, a commercial publisher printed Flordelis's autobiography in 2011.

In her autobiography, Flordelis narrates her life as a pastor and singer, but a substantial part is dedicated to her childhood experiences surrounded by the violence of the tráfico and her dealings with young people involved in the movimento. As she explains, she often preached the Gospel in the early mornings in Jacarezinho: "Here was born the Evangelization of the Early Morning, as I called it. Each and every Friday, religiously, I was seen amid the youth at the bailes funk, forrós, and even at the bocas de fumo. My mission was to distribute folders of the church [Assembleia de Deus] and transmit [transmitir] the Word of God. I even went up to the boys of the tráfico when they were armed or drugged, to tell them that God had a different life for them in mind" (Flordelis 2011, 55). Besides re-narrating her evangelization practices in the favela, Flordelis also recounts how, by way of spiritual revelation (revelação) and courage, she saved multiple young men from the hands of comandos. According to her, in all cases, the young men had violated the rules and were informally sentenced to death when she intervened as a messenger of God to plea for the boys' release. During one of these confrontations, she intervened while gang members were torturing a young man named Marcos. According to Flordelis, she asked the chief of the gang to let Marcos go and said she would make sure he would never cross their path again. If he did, they could come and kill her, she offered. When they refused, Flordelis asked if she could say a prayer for Marcos and all of the men present. They let her and she began, "Lord, you are our aid in this moment of despair. You are the advocate of all advocates, the judge of judges. You are braver than the bravest and I am asking you, Lord, come and help me save this boy from death. . . . Come, great Father, to soften the hearts of all the young men here because you love them and you are not pleased to see them in the state they are" (82). When Flordelis ended her prayer, the chief told her he did not know if indeed it was God but that he would do as she requested and let Marcos go.

The excerpts of Flordelis's autobiography show us how celebrity gospel singers make use of religious testimonies to demonstrate their own status as exceptional people—as individuals capable of mediating the powers of the Lord while identifying themselves as people who come from identical life-worlds as their audience. In general, such identification can help create a strong sense of intimacy between performer and audience, and in the case of Flordelis's autobiography it also reinforces the idea that Pentecostalism is the most powerful answer to urban violence.

Gospel Funk

About a decade after my first fieldwork in Rio de Janeiro, a remarkable shift occurred in the field of Pentecostalism and popular music. Whereas during the initial years of research I did not hear anyone play gospel funk, by 2011 the popularity of this style was undeniable. Gospel funk MCs performed at gospel dance parties throughout the city, and many Pentecostal adolescents carried gospel funk on their MP3 players. Furthermore, Pentecostal artists also more frequently used other styles such as pagode and forró.

The popularity of gospel funk is noteworthy because its musical style is closely associated with what most evangelicals consider the gloomy and immoral sides of favela life. As I have demonstrated above, Pentecostal adherents in the favelas of Rio de Janeiro regularly describe carioca funk as a primary example of worldly music in opposition to gospel music. Carioca funk features explicit lyrics, and funk parties are generally accompanied by erotic dance moves. Furthermore, evangelical inhabitants understand the public consumption of drugs and alcohol during the funk parties as deeply immoral. The rise of gospel funk, therefore, begs for a deeper explanation that clarifies how the shift I described above could occur.

Several scholars analyze the recent expansion of gospel music in Brazil in terms of capitalist market dynamics and modern media culture, both of which slowly obfuscate stylistic borders between Christian and non-Christian music (Cunha 2007; Mendonça 2008). At the base of the dynamics of expansion stands the prevailing semiotic ideology (Keane 2007) that the form and content of a song can be separated, and that it is the latter which ultimately defines its spirituality. According to the scholars mentioned, the evangelical norm that a Christian song can be recognized by its lyrics allows for an unprecedented incorporation of musical styles (so long as the lyrics remain "Christian"). Whereas I largely agree that we should analyze change in religious practices in relation to economic life, I also think that religious transformations are ambiguous and involve more than the breaching of fortifications that hinder the free circulation of commodities.

Fierce debates take place among evangelicals in Rio de Janeiro about the changes in the gospel industry, and some of my Pentecostal informants (adamant gospel funk fans) criticized artists who seemed to have accepted Jesus only because the gospel market was booming. To picture Pentecostal adherents as people who naïvely follow the logic of the market deprives them of much of their agency and ethical judgment. Furthermore, not all popular gospel music in Brazil has the same status. While some considered gospel funk uncontroversial, not many people presented it as the music that should regularly be played in church, for example.

Though very popular, gospel funk was mostly presented as *estratégia* (strategy): music made to attract teenagers who would otherwise opt for the worldly equivalent of that style. It is risky to reason that so-called strategic gospel music will necessarily possess the same meaning or acquire the same status as other gospel music styles. In the social worlds of Brazilian Pentecostals, these styles are employed and evaluated differently. From a theoretical perspective we should be wary of teleological arguments about the power of the market to eventually include all genres as evenly fit for religious experience, because it obscures the ongoing power struggles and the open-endedness of their outcomes.

Nevertheless, young Pentecostal members expressed the desire to play funk and dance to it without being regarded as sinners, and several MCs were gaining more and more fans among the residents of Rio de Janeiro's favelas. As I argue, acceptance of gospel funk depends on a host of purifying techniques that extend beyond a mere transformation of lyrics, and this in fact shows in detail some of the intricate relations between music, life-worlds, and morality.

The evangelical adoption of carioca funk music started with Grupo Yehoshua in the early 1990s (Pinheiro 1998). During my research among adherents of Pentecostal churches in 2002, 2003, and 2009, I did not encounter a single adolescent who listened to gospel funk. Conversely, during my research in 2011, many teenagers expressed their enjoyment of gospel funk, and many of my informants, including several artists, agreed that it was MC Adriano Gospel Funk who paved the way for the broadened possibilities to perform and listen to gospel funk in Rio de Janeiro.

Adriano, born and raised in a small municipality on the border of the city of Rio de Janeiro and a member of the Igreja do Nazareno (Church of the Nazarene), started making gospel funk in 2003. Whereas Adriano congregates in an evangelical church that does not define itself as Pentecostal, he frequently performs at Pentecostal churches and venues. As he explained during an interview with me, it was incredibly hard early in his career to convince people that his music was appropriate for worship. People wrote him disapproving e-mails in which they accused him of making music "of the flesh" and urged him to convert. According to Adriano, people gradually began to accept him because they saw the fruits of his work. More and more teenagers claimed to have accepted Jesus or returned to the church after hearing Adriano's music; this, according to Adriano, is the irrefutable sign that the Lord has blessed his endeavor to use funk.

Interestingly, arguments against the use of carioca funk also provide Adriano and his gospel funk colleagues with a powerful counterargument. Carioca funk is the most popular music of the favela youth, and many Pentecostal favela residents understand funk parties as dangerous forms of entertainment that lead adolescents onto demonic paths. According to Adriano, his gospel funk gives teenagers a chance to participate in the popular culture of the favela without risk and with the prospect of eventually choosing the right path over the many seductions and dangers that favela life offers.

Adriano's drive to make gospel funk is propelled by a genuine desire to reach the people who have been brought up with carioca funk music in an attempt to "speak their language," to use the very same kind of music that potentially leads them astray to save them. However, as Adriano indicated himself, some evangélicos were particularly wary about his attempts to use carioca funk because it obfuscates the difference between genuine "music of God" and "music of the world." In response, Adriano explained that a number of crucial elements need to be safeguarded to distinguish gospel funk from ordinary carioca funk and to make sure the music can perform its spiritual function to heal and save people.

First, the lyrics should beyond a doubt communicate that a song is Christian. Weaving biblical phrases into the text or explicitly invoking the Lord is customary, but gospel lyrics also regularly remind listeners to be watchful of demonic seduction and to evaluate critically the people, practices, and things they encounter.

Strikingly, some of Adriano's gospel funk songs thus communicate the very same message that many evangelicals voiced in opposition to funk music. Many evangelicals regard funk as a suspicious style on account of its links to funk proibidão, the bailes funk, and the perceived immoral behavior of its audiences. As a consequence, critics of gospel funk doubt the carioca funk style can be used for worship. Adriano's songs cleverly respond to this critique by incorporating it. Adriano attempts to sever the existing relation between form and content by stressing that one should not be seduced by the "wrapping" but analyze whether God has blessed the content.[35]

Second, Adriano believes that the performer of the music should clearly be a person of God. Since the sacred condition of gospel music is partly dependent on the sanctified status of its performers, gospel artists do their best to demonstrate that they have accepted Jesus as their Savior. They generally preach against immoral behavior and take care not to display or encourage illicit sexual behavior or consume alcohol and drugs. It is also important that pastors and religious leaders authorize gospel funk artists as legitimate. For Adriano, it was very important that his pastor at the Church of the Nazarene gave his blessing to pursue his gospel funk career.

Lastly, the consecrated condition of gospel is also dependent on extramusical behavior during shows and performances. Specifically in relation to funk music, this concerns the erotic nature of dancing. Baile funk parties, funk lyrics, and representations of carioca funk are riddled with sexual connotations, sexual movements, and erotic encounters. Therefore, as Adriano and members of his crew told me, they all remain alert during gospel performances to prevent audience members from dancing erotically. Adriano is well aware of the tensions between the desire to earn income and his moral responsibilities as a gospel artist. Moreover, as we will see below, Adriano's considerations resonate with the ideas and practices of other gospel funk artists.

Another MC who had become popular in Pentecostal circles in Rio de Janeiro was LC Satrianny, who congregated at an Assembleia de Deus. In contrast to Adriano, Satrianny had made a modest career as a carioca funk artist before his turn to gospel funk in 2007. Satrianny then presented himself as "ex-MC Furacão 2000." (Furacão 2000 is one of the most popular organizations that produces baile funk parties in Rio de Janeiro. To perform at Furacão 2000 events generally means one has made it in the world of funk.) In Brazil, one regularly encounters gospel artists known as ex-pagodeiro (former pagode singer) or ex-funkeiro (former funk artist), presented in popular media as formerly belonging to "the world." While one might at first assume that such explicit display of one's worldly past hinders full acceptance as a consecrated artist, these labels generally serve the purpose of demonstrating the unlimited powers of the Lord to save the people who were once in the hands of the devil.

In compliance with the desire to maintain clear demarcations between funk artists *do mundo* (of the world) and gospel funk artists, Satrianny changed his artist name from MC Satrianny to LC Satrianny. As Satrianny explained, "I was *mestre de cerimônia* [master of ceremony] but now I am *Levita de Cristo* [Levite, gospel musician]." Besides modifying names, converted gospel artists commonly transform older songs into gospel songs by changing the lyrics. Satrianny, for example, took the song "Camarote e Pista" (Box and dance floor) he had performed during his Furacão 2000 period and transformed it into the song "Quem vai pra gloria" (Who aspires to glory). As Satrianny explained, with the alterations he transformed a "malediction [*maldição*] into a blessing [*benção*]."

According to Satrianny, it is very important to have gospel funk because favela teenagers adore funk music and want to dance. Evangelical teenagers should also have this opportunity. As Satrianny explained, this should not be regarded as the corrosion of Christian values; it is possible to "modernizar sem se mundanizar" (modernize without becoming worldly), to have "liberdade não libertinagem" (liberty but no licentiousness). Moreover, he told me, "Funk is an evangelical strategy. Funk is bait to fish for the youth who are lost in the world, to get them in here [the church]. The teenagers come to dance, but in the middle of the baile you stop to address them; urge them to drink some water and listen to the words of the pastor present."

Like Adriano, Satrianny highlights that the difference between worldly funk and gospel funk is visible in the way adolescents dance, and that he also considers it his responsibility to scrutinize the events where he performs. He regularly surveys the dance moves of his audiences but, in his opinion, people generally do not need much correction; girls do not rapidly lower their bottoms to the ground while dancing primarily because his lyrics do not call for such kinds of erotic behavior.

What we might learn from these two examples is that, in general, gospel singers and musicians who wish to incorporate new styles attempt to sever the rigid connections between the musical form (style) and the (lifestyles of the) groups associated with it, in order to make it spiritually appropriate for them and their audiences. In the case of carioca funk such incorporation is complicated because of its association with funk proibidão, the eroticism of baile funk parties, and the perils of favela life. However, according to gospel funk artists, the incorporation of carioca funk is desirable and justifiable because it lures teenagers away from the perceived dangers of the baile funk parties. Gospel funk performers attempt to rework the music by including critique of worldly phenomena in their gospel funk lyrics. In addition, gospel funk artists consider it their responsibility to safeguard the boundaries between ordinary carioca funk and gospel funk by inspecting dance moves during gospel parties.

Conclusion

Accounts of adherents of Pentecostal churches in the morro regarding their listening practices reveal an elective affinity between electroacoustic technology and Pentecostalism. It is often through mediated gospel sounds and music that people discern the voice of God or feel the Holy Spirit. By itself this confirms an important insight of Tanya Luhrmann regarding evangelical Christian perceptions of the world. While the majority of Brazilian Pentecostal churches promote a modern type of individualism on account of its emphasis on personal (individual) salvation, Pentecostal ideas and practices also reproduce what Luhrmann (2012, 62) has called a "participatory theory of mind": "This new Christian theory of mind . . . asks congregants to experience the mind-world barrier as porous, in a specific, limited way." While Luhrmann focuses on God's "voice," she occasionally mentions music as powerful channel through which God talks to the people she interviewed, and I believe much of her analysis corresponds with my analysis of the "spiritual attunement" of Pentecostal adherents in the favela.[36]

In this chapter I have focused on radio and music listening practices, and I have argued that the experience of divine presence through electroacoustic technology is enforced by the separation between música do mundo and música evangélica. The efforts to separate worldly and godly

174

domains place the discussions of music (and radio speech) at the heart of identity politics. Mass media are not only important bearers of Pentecostal messages (the Gospel) but are also the instruments through which religiosity is expressed and experienced. Sound systems are sensitive tools that people use self-reflexively to feel and demonstrate the difference between the worldly and the godly. The examples presented in this chapter show how identity politics and enchantment intersect and what hypermediated conversion entails.

The fact that certain genres are marked as godly and others as demonic—thus allowing for experiential boundaries between the two—does not mean that we are dealing with static phenomena. The Pentecostal semiotic ideology (Keane 2007), which presents a song's lyrics as the defining feature of its spirituality, tentatively allows for the incorporation of formerly demonized music. This process upsets and challenges prevailing notions about the perceived differences between worldly and godly music and underscores the fact that adherents need to remain alert. In the next chapter we will see that this also holds for television, though in a slightly different manner.

"Written by the Devil"
Suspicious Television

During my conversations with evangélicos in Rio de Janeiro, I frequently asked their opinion about television. Usually, I hinted at some of the evangelical television programs broadcast on one of the open channels, hoping they would tell me about their importance. To my initial surprise, instead of enlightening me about evangelical television programs, many of my interlocutors started to describe the devastating effect certain television programs have on Brazilian people and the society at large. In particular, telenovelas, a Brazilian type of soap opera, were often brought to the forefront as deplorable programs that demonstrated the miserable state of the world and contributed absolutely nothing to the well-being of their viewers. What was even more surprising was that some of the self-proclaimed evangélicos started to explain in detail what was wrong with telenovelas by detailing the plot twists and social drama of a particular program running at the time. I could only deduce from such detailed critique that the complainant clearly had watched much of the telenovela, maybe even every episode.

While for a period I continued trying to get more information about evangelical television programs, it was only after a while that I understood that my initial perspective on religion media was shortsighted. Having understood that Pentecostal media are part of a "communicative ecology" (Slater and Tacchi 2004), I began to see that if I wanted to understand the relationship between religion and media, my inquiries into this relationship should not be focused on evangelical media alone. All kinds of programs were important to the people of the evangelical churches, albeit in different ways from what I had imagined beforehand.

The negative stance adopted toward some mass media among the evangélicos in Rio de Janeiro resembles Quentin Schultze's description of evangelicals in the United States. In his study on televangelism in the United States, Schultze (1991, 61–73) argues that among evangelicals there are two views on mass media. One is the optimistic view that mass media can be used for the purpose of spreading the Gospel effectively and changing American culture for the better; the other is the pessimistic view that the mass media threaten the values and beliefs of the evangelical community. What struck me when looking over the opinions of evangélicos in Rio de Janeiro was not only that Brazilian evangélicos generally expressed the same two opinions, but also that evangélicos, academics, and journalists seem to be concerned with the same question, namely: What are the effects of certain programs on the audience? While such a question is legitimate, the various parties generally suspect that there are particular effects that occur immediately.

In Brazil, for example, journalists are especially concerned with the effect of evangelical media on the behavior of potential voters. The idea that evangelical churches and politicians are trying to use media for political gain is widespread, as is the idea that evangelical media persuade "believers" to vote for them. While media and political power are of course intricately connected, models that suppose straightforward effects of mass media on audiences tend to overlook the fact that specific media are part of a broader communicative ecology that reproduces broad notions of what the world looks like and how it functions. Moreover, I also hold that investigating the nature of the relation between Pentecostalism and media in Brazil means that we should try to understand what media mean to people who live in urban contexts in Brazil and describe what "structures of feeling" (Williams 1961, 48) we might recognize.

In the previous chapters I have sketched the life-world of the people who live in the favelas of Rio de Janeiro, in order to give the reader insight into the meaning of media to the evangelical inhabitants. In chapter 3 I described several news programs that people watch regularly in relation to evangelical newspapers, to demonstrate that the anxieties of everyday life are reproduced by broadcast media at large. Churches magnify some of these anxieties without being able to resolve permanently the tensions they themselves reproduce. In the previous chapter, in order to understand how media are related to religious doctrines and practices, I followed Derrida's insights into the elective affinities between Christianity and mass media. I have showed that electroacoustic technology specifically enforces an intimate, emotional connection with God while also being considered an important vehicle to express identity and evangelical presence in relation to other groups.

In this last chapter I turn my focus to television in relation to religion. In this chapter several important threads of the book come together. As I have shown in the preceding chapters, for many adherents of Pentecostal churches, conversion implies acquiring a different perspective on the world because they start to perceive the spiritual battle between God and the devil that is taking place all around them. During my observations and interviews it became apparent that an a priori analytic separation between media and daily favela life obscures the ways media are experienced as transmitters and as mirrors. To people in the favelas, television and radio broadcasts, websites, and music were often experienced as remediations and confirmations of what they had seen or heard elsewhere. Moreover, as I have also shown in the previous chapter, these individuals experience electronic media, objects, and other people as possible transmitters of spiritual forces.

At this point I will describe television as part of the daily life of the people in the favelas of Rio de Janeiro, and I will demonstrate how evangélicos position themselves in relation to its content. By showing some of the different spectator positions evangélicos may take when watching telenovelas and reality shows such as *Big Brother Brasil*, I will argue that television viewing involves a dynamic of attraction and rejection, which for evangélicos is related to Pentecostal bodily disciplines and practices. Moreover, attraction and rejection cannot be categorized simply into spiritual programs that attract and worldly programs that repel. People can also be attracted to watching so-called demonic programs in order to identify the work of the devil, for example. Moreover, boundaries between "healthy" or educational programs and harmful ones are often hard to establish once and for all. Interpretations and evaluations of television in relation to Pentecostal discipline are part of what I call "hypermediated conversion," which involves new understandings of the self in relation to cultural practices—including mass media.

Among other things, this means that an ethnographic exploration of the relation between Pentecostalism and mass media cannot be defined only by that which adherents of Pentecostal churches say they watch, but also by that which they say they do not watch. As my example above demonstrated, telenovelas are important examples because they are part of the popular cultural representations that can be considered common knowledge in Brazil. They represent features of society that are considered typical of Brazilian culture but which many crentes perceive as sinful and diabolical. As I will show, the attraction and rejection of certain images and narratives in telenovelas are not only related to the "reading" of those programs' messages, but also to the physical and spiritual experiences of viewing such shows. For many evangélicos, experiences of watching are directly related to the presence of the devil and the Holy Spirit. Lastly, I will argue that these experiences are related to the prevailing popular mythology that TV Globo, the main producer of telenovelas in Brazil, is linked to the devil.

Selective Iconoclasm

If one examines evangelical discourse on television and radio in Brazil, one will find recurring accusations of the putative idolatry of other religious institutions. The Igreja Universal, for example, is known for its fierce opposition to the veneration of Catholic saints. The best example of such opposition is the infamous *chute na santa*—the televised vilipending of a statue of the Brazilian patron saint, Nossa Senhora Aparecida. During a national television broadcast from the studios of TV Record, bispo Sérgio Von Helder of the Igreja Universal desecrated a plaster statue of the Catholic saint. In his attempt to demonstrate that it was merely a plaster image and not a saint he assaulted the statue, resulting in a lawsuit in which he was accused and found guilty of vilipending religious symbols and of inciting religious prejudice and discrimination (Kramer 2001a). The broadcast on TV Record was not the immediate cause of the scandal. Only after edited clips of the incident were broadcast on the nightly news of TV Globo did the potentially disturbing images cause an outrage (45).[1] Nevertheless, one should be careful not to misread the accusations of idolatry on the part of the adherents of the Igreja Universal as a total ban on the use of images in religious doctrine or practice.

Given its history of aversion to idolatry, Protestantism and religious currents springing from it are often represented as iconoclastic. Yet, as David Morgan (1998; 2005) convincingly argues, this is not an accurate picture. While Protestants indeed "expressed disdain for religious imagery in religious practice," as Morgan (1998, 117) puts it, they generally replaced it with "alternative forms of material culture that provide a different form of iconicity."[2] Protestant groups in the United States use all kinds of images, including representations of Jesus, to create what Morgan (58) describes as "the embodiment of belief in response to the image as a real presence." In his work on popular religious artworks in the United States, Morgan (3) argues that looking at images "constitutes a powerful practice of belief."[3]

It is not only in the United States that one encounters such an intricate relationship between vision and Protestantism. Based on her research on Pentecostalism in Ghana, Birgit Meyer (2006) also argues that we should pay attention to the ways Pentecostal imagery constitutes belief. She argues that while Protestantism is centered on the word, it would be a mistake to disregard the importance that images have in the creation of Pentecostal meaning. In Pentecostalism in Ghana, the relation between the Bible and the image is one of mutual dependence. Images and objects are interpreted with reference to the Bible, but at the same time these images visualize the written word and "affirm the Bible's power to explain" (301). In other words, Pentecostal doctrines and practices involve a Pentecostal visual culture, in which looking is informed by Pentecostal notions of reality and, mutatis mutandis, Pentecostalism is confirmed by what is seen. In addition, both Meyer and Morgan argue that religious visual culture is influenced by a belief in the power of images to act on the spectator (see also Freedberg 1989). Subsequently, both of them contend that analysis of religious visual culture should go beyond the common notion that images *represent* the metaphysical; instead, for the religious spectator the metaphysical is present *in* the image (Meyer 2006; Morgan 2005).

While the bispo of the Igreja Universal might be thought of as an iconoclast, the Igreja Universal is certainly not against the use of imagery in religious practice. As I have shown extensively in chapter 3, the Igreja Universal and many other evangelical churches make ample use of photo and film to produce iconic images of heroes and villains, and I have even witnessed the use of feature films in church services of the Igreja Universal. Besides the use of visual imagery, the Igreja Universal produces all kinds of images and objects that function as religious artifacts linking adherents to biblical narratives and symbols (see also Kramer 2001b).

The church produces small objects and paraphernalia such as (empty) crosses, a replica of the cave tomb of Jesus, and innumerable types of folders and colorful envelopes, which serve as "contact points" to "awaken the faith" of the adherents (Campos 1997, 81). Many of the objects and symbols are common to other religious traditions in Brazil. Oil and unrefined salt are used in cleansing rituals both in the Igreja Universal and in Afro-Brazilian religious practices, for instance. According to Leonildo Silveira Campos, the use of objects and the rituals in which they are involved characterize the church's distinction from iconoclastic Protestant denominations in Brazil.[4] Nevertheless, notwithstanding the use of images and objects as vehicles for divine communication, the church remains conscious of the limits of representation. As Eric Kramer (2001b, 118) has noted, "Macedo does take care to point out that the symbols used in the Universal Church are taken from the Bible and that the practice of manipulating these material representations is not 'anti-biblical' but 'extra-biblical'—not explicitly condemned by the Bible and thus licit."

Whereas the Assembleia de Deus makes less use of religious paraphernalia in their church services, among members and in evangelical boutiques a range of objects and representations circulate that form part of what might be called a Pentecostal material culture. For example, many adherents of the Assembleia de Deus I encountered owned paintings of a white dove—symbol of the Holy Spirit—and a quick look at the website of the major publishing house of the church, the Casa Publicadora das Assembleias de Deus, will show the kinds of visual imagery featured in books, CDs, and DVDs.[5]

Yet how can we relate such observations to television, the most popular medium in Brazil? This chapter builds on the work of the authors mentioned but also suggests that we analyze the relation between evangelical ideologies and imagery in a somewhat broader perspective—including in our explorations the wide array of objects and representations not necessarily produced or remediated in evangelical and Pentecostal circles but also in media that form part of the daily surroundings of people in Rio de Janeiro.

Television in the Favelas of Rio de Janeiro

In the highly mediatic society that is Brazil, people are bombarded with sounds and images that scream for attention. Every bar in Rio de Janeiro has a television turned on from opening time to closing time, and every shop has a radio that transmits programs to customers or passersby. When looking out over the favelas of Rio de Janeiro one is struck by the vast number of dish-shaped antennas on top of the brick buildings, marking the importance of television in the lives of the people. Although inhabitants of favelas are poor in relation to the well-to-do neighborhoods of Zona Sul, many favela households have at least one television, often placed in the center of the living room. Walking through the alleys of favelas I would always hear the sounds of television sets, marking TV's continuous presence as part of the daily environment.

The most popular channel among inhabitants of the favelas of Rio de Janeiro is undoubtedly TV Globo. Known for its telenovelas, TV Globo is watched by millions of people every day. The first telenovela of the day generally starts between five and six in the evening and the last ends between ten and eleven at night.[6] Besides the three to four novelas that run every day of the week, TV Globo offers news programs, soccer matches, talk shows, and reality programs. During the time of my research in Visionário, the reality program *Big Brother Brasil* in particular was very popular. Besides TV Globo, other popular channels in Rio de Janeiro are TV Record, SBT, Band, and Rede TV. All stations broadcast largely the same type of programs during the day, with some small differences among them.[7] They all offer Brazilian-made programs along with movies from the United States, and all of them broadcast telenovelas in the evening.[8]

In particular, telenovelas form an important part of the social setting of Brazilians from childhood to maturity. Telenovelas are soap series about love and conflict, and they "treat a series of characteristic conflicts and problems, most often about status reversals—especially upward mobility—and usually with urban settings" (Kottak 1990, 39). In contrast to the American soaps, which run for years on end during the day, the telenovelas last six to seven months and are shown between 5:00 and 11:00 p.m. (Vink 1988; Kottak 1990).

Regardless of whether one likes telenovelas, they form part of the daily reality of images and narratives that influence people. As Esther Hamburger (1998) has shown, people constantly discuss telenovelas. In the house, on the street, in other television programs, in journals, and on the radio, telenovelas are the topic of conversation between people of all social classes. Hamburger goes beyond a telenovela approach to highlight the distinctiveness in interpretation according to each region, class, or gender and argues that the telenovela must be considered a "shared repertoire." Hamburger (483) suggests that "given the proto-interactive character of the novelas, the ways in which the public appropriates these programs and interprets them in their everyday life can be better understood if the reception was approached as part of a dynamic which during the years has consolidated the formal conventions of the narratives which are mastered by the public." People know *how* to watch telenovelas, and even when in their discussions about the shows they differ in interpretation or judgment, they share the common repertoire, which makes these discussions possible. Indubitably telenovelas are part of the everyday life of people—individuals copy the language, the clothes, and the styles. In the programs they see a mirror image (although often distorted) of Brazilian society and of themselves. As such, telenovelas mobilize "a network of communication and polemics of exceptional reach" (482), which transgresses the borders between telenovelas and everyday life and has remarkable potential to connect spaces otherwise treated as separate.

In the favelas of Rio de Janeiro this potential is certainly strengthened by socio-geographical characteristics. Houses are small, built close to or on top of one another, with very little space between them. Moreover, many people have to share these small spaces with many relatives who do not always adhere to the same faith. Many people watch or take notice of the programs that are on the television at a particular moment. Furthermore, the power to decide which programs are watched often resides with particular people—for example, the head of the household—which implies that people cannot always control what is offered to them on the screen.

Popular Evangelical Television

Remarkably, people of the Assembleia de Deus I interviewed did not give consistent answers to the question of which evangelical television programs they watched.[9] Overall, the programs evangélicos liked appeared on open channels such as Rede TV and Band. The only program that was mentioned by almost all adherents of Pentecostal churches was that of Pastor Romildo Ribeiro Soares, who originally established the Igreja Universal with Edir Macedo but founded his own neo-Pentecostal church—the Igreja Internacional da Graça de Deus—in 1980. The Igreja Internacional da Graça de Deus resembles the Igreja Universal in its theological component. Both focus on deliverance and divine healing, and both preach a prosperity gospel and revolve around a charismatic leader. Despite this, the Igreja Internacional da Graça de Deus has much fewer churches and is much more focused on televangelism (Fonseca 2003; Mariano 1999). The church has been broadcasting since the 1980s and remains able to do so by means of audience donations. R. R. Soares was probably the best-known media pastor among the people who attended all kinds of Pentecostal churches in Visionário. His show was aired multiple times a day.[10]

From my observations and conversations in Visionário and other favelas I conclude that people of the Assembleia de Deus like to watch the R. R. Soares show primarily because it is one of the few Pentecostal television programs that offers a straightforward church service. During the broadcast, Soares delivers a sermon and reads and explains passages from the Bible. The reason for its success among adherents of the Assembleia de Deus seems to be the informative nature of the program. Since the show is not exclusively aimed at drawing people to the churches—as is often the case with the programs of the Igreja Universal—viewers can simply enjoy this evangelical program, learn something from it, and continue to congregate at an Assembleia de Deus in the vicinity.

Most adherents of the Igreja Universal I interviewed said they watched the evangelical programs of their own church, broadcast on TV Record. TV Record has been quite successful in attracting popular TV hosts and professionals, which has elevated the network's standards rapidly. It has continually improved its infrastructure since the 1990s and become one of the leading networks in Brazil. TV Record broadcasts a mix of programs. In the afternoon it generally shows movies; in the evening it starts with news programs, followed by telenovelas.

One of the often-mentioned programs of the Igreja Universal on TV Record during the early phase of my research was *O Ponto de Luz* (The moment of clarity), of which the "S.O.S. Espiritual" was a prominent feature.[11] *Ponto de Luz* often presented an ex-feiticeira or ex-macumbeira (mostly women) who talked about how her life had been ruined by her past involvement in Candomblé or Umbanda. Sometimes *Ponto de Luz* would show dark and hazy images of people with candles skulking in cemeteries, representing the Candomblé rituals deemed extremely harmful.

The "S.O.S. Espiritual" part of the program offered the audience a chance to call the studio and ask a pastor for spiritual advice, and a great deal of the program was dedicated to conversations between callers and the pastor. When I asked a young obreiro from Visionário which persons he thought watched "S.O.S. Espiritual," he said, "These programs are more for those who don't sleep, who are depressed. They put on the television and there they see it. They look at 'S.O.S. Espiritual,' then they call, looking for help."[12] Another obreiro of the Igreja Universal saw this program as an excellent tutorial to learn how to talk to other people, and he watched it primarily in order to acquire the techniques himself:

> *Ponto de Luz.* I try to watch that. I try to learn something from it. I try to sum up the program to study how to converse with the youngsters. Because I am not the only one who watches it, the youngsters also watch it. I have to understand that preaching so I can pass it to the youngsters. . . . *Ponto de Luz* is a program that shows you the truth. They try to attend [*atendender*] people "live." They try to demonstrate the truth, the difference between good and bad. There is a God who can do everything, but there is also the bad that unfortunately can also do everything, or almost at least. It is a program that helps you spiritually, it informs you, and it also functions as a lesson. You learn how to deal with certain situations. If you watch

Figure 9 Watching evangelical television in the morro. Photo: author.

that program it often shows you what to do. I think that is the most important program of the day.

What becomes apparent here is that the young obreiros occupied a different spectator position than generally presumed. Though watching the program regularly, the young men perceived that its message was not directed at them but at the people who had not yet accepted Jesus. The second obreiro, especially, liked to watch the practices of the pastors in the program because they provided him with examples—and techniques—that would help him convert youngsters in the favela. Meanwhile, he also experienced it as confirmation of a truth he already held dear.

This example demonstrates that it is important to analyze the interplay between television programs and spectators from a variety of angles, leaving room not only for different readings of the meaning of a particular narrative but also for the spectator's (dis)identification with the presumed public, which subsequently allows for a different appraisal of the content. As we will see in other examples below, such a perspective produces a more complex interplay between religious ideology, spectators, and self-discipline than is often reproduced in talk about media and religious life. These examples, and others that will follow, show that differences in spectator position in relation to the presumed public are structured according to the Pentecostal separation between the people of the world at whom the Gospel is addressed and the people who have accepted Jesus and have the responsibility of preaching the Gospel to as many as possible. Whereas this structure is at a play during the viewing of Pentecostal programs such as *Ponto de Luz*, it also operates when Pentecostal adherents watch non-evangelical programs. Before returning to this separation, let me first sketch the non-evangelical television programs that often became the subject of my talks with favela residents.

Big Brother Brasil

To analyze the relations between Pentecostalism and popular media (including telenovelas), it is worthwhile to say something about the popular reality show *Big Brother Brasil* (or simply *BBB*) and repeat here some of the appraisals voiced during the first years after its debut.[13] My second period of fieldwork in Rio de Janeiro coincided with the airing of the first Brazilian episode.[14] *BBB* is a reality-soap that consists of the constant camera surveillance of a group of selected people who voluntarily live together in a secluded house. All participants must try to survive sixty-four days of confinement. The program is not just a reality-soap, however—it has an added contest element. Every week, inhabitants must nominate another inhabitant to leave the house. After this initial nomination, the judgment of the television audience is sought. Spectators may phone in and vote for which one of the nominated inhabitants must leave. When there are only three members left, spectators may phone and choose the winner of the program, who receives a substantial amount of prize money.

While *Big Brother* can be seen as part of the "reality" television trend that started in the 1990s, the twenty-four-hour-a-day surveillance in the form of an interactive game show presented quite an innovation. Wherever the show was broadcast, fierce debates followed. As in other countries, the introduction of *Big Brother Brasil*,[15] and the rising popularity of the program in the weeks thereafter,[16] elicited a variety of reactions. Newspapers and magazines started writing about the program, and people started talking about it in the streets. In the Brazilian print media *BBB* became the focal point of discussions about television and society. After the first couple of episodes, various journalists and representatives of Brazilian organizations, both religious and nonreligious, used its popularity to criticize Brazilian television and Brazilian society as a whole.

The core of the criticism was aimed at the display of intimacy, nudity, and sex on public television, which, according to many journalists, was to be understood as an effect of the search for sheer profit shorn of any moral considerations. In the journal *O Pasquim 21*, for example, several journalists argued that the search for an ever-larger audience had caused a commoditization of sex and led to the downfall of quality television. One reporter even ended his arguments against programs such as *BBB* by stating, "Marshall McLuhan was right: the medium is the message. Global village, universal degradation."[17] In *Carta Capital*, a well-read weekly magazine, an article in a special edition about television featured the header "Programs from Bad to Worse: The Commercial Success of *Big Brother* and *Casa dos Artistas* Indicates that Quality Programs Are Losing Space."[18] Many of the critics portrayed television as a mass medium that is "misused" for entertainment instead of supporting "high culture," and they presumed a direct relationship between the content of television programs and the knowledge and behavior of viewers.[19] Take for example the following words from a journalist at the daily newspaper *Jornal do Brasil*: "We cannot allow TV to become yet another domestic device in the home of a semiliterate Brazilian, who keeps watching *Ratinho*, *Big Brother*, Luciana Gimenez, *Show do Milhão*, João Kleber, Sergio Malandro, the bathtub of Guga, and a lot of other nonsense. This means degradation, selling the soul to the devil. And in this case the devil is the easy audience."[20] Although unintentionally correct in bringing in the devil as an important force (as I will show below), the journalist in my view misunderstands the dynamic of watching television. *BBB* is popular precisely because it offers spectators the possibility of morally evaluating the behavior of the protagonists involved. The possibility for the spectator to act on his or her moral feelings, to call the network and vote off those people he or she dislikes, is what makes *BBB* so interesting. When I talked about the program with a Brazilian friend, she said that the people in the *Big Brother* house could be seen as "television neighbors." From this point of view, the contestants are seen as the "family next door," about which one gossips and complains, yet this family is known by viewers nationwide. In other words, part of the success of the program seems to be that it provokes people to discuss and evaluate the behavior of the program's contestants.

Pentecostal Ideology and Popular Television in Rio de Janeiro

Like those in the Brazilian press who scorned *BBB*, Pentecostal leaders in Rio de Janeiro were very disapproving of it. Nevertheless, as we will see, the format of the program in fact allows for fusion with a Pentecostal worldview. To understand the different positions Pentecostal adherents may take in relation to such programs, it is worthwhile to take a closer look at some of the evangelical reactions to *BBB* in the print media and describe some of the Pentecostal evaluations of Brazilian mass media and culture. As we will see, the introduction of *BBB* provoked Pentecostal authorities to attempt to discipline the viewing behavior of their followers, yet simultaneously allowed them to appropriate the popular program as a mirror of Brazilian society.

In the weeks after the show's introduction, several reactions to *BBB* appeared in the evangelical print media. The magazine *Enfoque* reacted to the "reality" programs *Big Brother* and *Casa dos Artistas* with a long article about the tendency to show "private" behavior on television and the question of how evangélicos should react to these kinds of programs: "This new tendency [exposing intimacy] is causing an enormous headache for pastors and Protestant leaders. Could it be that this exposure, motivated by exhibitionism, need, narcissism, marketing, or all of them together, is an obstacle to the Christian faith? To what extent does this gossip mania hurt biblical principles? The polemic is in the air."[21] The fact that the polemic about *Big Brother* was literally *in the air* was brought home to me when I visited José, my Pentecostal landlord in Visionário, who congregated at the Assembleia de Deus. When I asked him whether he watched *BBB*, he said, "No, I don't watch that kind of program, I always listen to radio El Shadai [93 FM] and it had a discussion about *Big Brother* and *Casa dos Artistas*. It recounted the things they show on these programs. *Big Brother* has scenes that don't accord well with a Christian life. I'd rather read the Bible." Not surprisingly, *BBB* was received by many evangélicos as the kind of program that could not bring much good.

Though considered suspect from the start, especially because it was introduced as a "juicy" program with a "voyeuristic" side, the Pentecostal media condemned it outright after the first signs of nudity, some "kisses," and a bit of swearing. An example of Pentecostal reactions to the program can be found in the following text from Pastor Carlos Rodrigues of the Igreja Universal, printed in the *Folha Universal*:

> *Big Brother* and *Casa dos Artistas*, everyone is naked. Dear brothers, the lack of shame is apparent on national television. The infamy has become common and public. It is enough to turn on our television and be given a lesson in coarse behavior, swearing and cursing, obscene gestures, intrigues, and weaponry, all in the name

of money. . . . In both cases, in *Big Brother* and *Casa dos Artistas*, we observe scant clothing in the house and no clothing outside it. We are watching the stimulation of pornography, the fight at any cost to make money and obtain fleeting fame. . . . No one worries about education. Programs that present culture, information, and healthy leisure are rare on our television. Sex has become banal and very vulgar. We have to fight against this. We cannot permit our families to be inundated by so much banality. The result of all that is shown on our television is reflected immediately in our society. It is sad to witness such a decline of morality and ethics.[22]

These quotes indicate that Pentecostal churches generally take *BBB* as an example of the media programs threatening the values of the Pentecostal community and demonstrating the deplorable state of the country at large. In 2012, ten years after the introduction of *BBB*, Silas Malafaia—an influential Assembleia de Deus pastor—took a scandal surrounding alleged sexual abuse in the program as an opportunity to restate this Pentecostal interpretation: "*Big Brother* is garbage. How is it possible that there are crentes still wasting their time with it? They should convert all over again. . . . This program is promoting *baixaria*, immorality, and all of the most destructive things for society. It openly stimulates drinking, sensuality, promiscuity, and infidelity. Where will we end up when such a ridiculous and immoral program is among the most watched in our country?"[23] These examples of the moral outrage of pastors of the Igreja Universal and Assembleia de Deus prompt the question of how evangelical viewers in Visionário dealt with *BBB* and the telenovelas.

Handling Television

For many evangélicos in Rio de Janeiro, television is a medium that must be approached carefully. As with radio and the perceived threat of certain sounds, Pentecostal churches acknowledge the potential threat of illicit images that circulate outside the established religious domains; moreover, as we have seen, they devote quite a lot of time and space in their own media to discussing the potential menace of harmful programs. Not unlike the warnings concerning worldly music (see chapters 2 and 5), discussions about the banality and dangers of popular television can be read as attempts to discipline the viewing practices of evangelical adherents.

This interpretation is strengthened by the fact that many television channels broadcast evangelical programs but none of them is exclusively evangelical.[24] Therefore, watching television often presents the Pentecostal-minded spectator with the question of whether a program causes a possible "contamination" of a Christian lifestyle (again, see also chapters 2 and 5). While Globo and SBT—the networks of *BBB* and *Casa dos Artistas*, respectively—have been among the most popular television stations of Rio de Janeiro for decades, in evangelical circles they do not often receive a positive mention. During my interviews with members of Pentecostal churches in Visionário, these two television networks mostly came up as producers of harmful programs; besides their reality programs, telenovelas of the two networks were also often mentioned as potentially dangerous.

Strikingly, as I showed in the beginning of this chapter, the fact that certain programs are condemned in evangelical print media and in church sermons does not mean that evangélicos are unaware of their content. The fact that people say they condemn certain shows does not mean they never watch. Whereas quite a few Pentecostal adherents in Rio de Janeiro think ill of *BBB* and similar programs, this does not mean they do not play an important part in the constitution of their Pentecostal ideology and experience.

Although some evangelical leaders maintain that the decision not to watch garbage is simple, the evaluation of television programs is not as straightforward as might be expected. Appraisal of television programs generally depends on the media ideologies at play (Gershon 2010), the status of the programs as truthful representations of society, the Pentecostal framework of interpretation, and the (dis)identification with the presumed public. Building on the work of Webb Keane (2007), among others, Ilana Gershon (2010, 283) describes media ideology as the way people on the ground think about the relations between medium and message: "*Media ideologies* as a term can sharpen a focus on how people understand both the communicative possibilities and the material limitations of a specific channel, and how they conceive of channels in general."

As a number of scholars have shown, religious evaluations of communication bring to light the media ideologies at play, because in many religious traditions the material aspects of such communication are important elements of the presumed qualities and effects of a medium (think of the amplified gospel I described in chapters 2 and 5, for instance). Almost all the evangélicos I interviewed in Visionário criticized telenovelas, yet their readings of the effects differed considerably, which consequently affected their appraisal of the programs.

Some viewers judged programs on the basis of the particular images shown, concluding that since these were sensual images one should not watch the program at all. Others evaluated the narrative of the telenovela and the supposed example it set for the viewers. Again, others judged the behavior of the individual characters in the program. Many of those who judged the behavior of the characters commented on and discussed the behavior of the people in the telenovela as if they were living in a parallel, real world. Images, behavior, and narrative were evaluated according to the Pentecostal interpretation of the Holy Bible, but in all cases contradictions emerged.

For example, one telenovela that showed the life of a family in which the elder daughter had a drug habit was interpreted by some of my Pentecostal interlocutors as "good" because it showed the dangers of drug abuse, while others interpreted it as "bad" because it showed drug abuse at all. Here, the difference in appraisal is the result of different media ideologies, specifically the differing beliefs about the effects of the displayed behavior on audiences. According to the first category, contextual embeddedness of the displayed drug abuse transforms the appraisal of the telenovela episode from negative to positive, since the telenovela shows the devastating effects of drug abuse. According to the second category, however, no contextual framing can undo the harmful effects of showing drug abuse on television. People, in other words, have different ideas about the power of a medium to affect people and hence different notions about which media are potentially harmful.

In one interview I asked a man who frequented the Assembleia de Deus whether he watched *BBB*. He replied, "I watched it, it was a mistake, but I watched it. It was a mistake because it is a kind of program that teaches you nothing, sitting in front of the television, prying on people . . . when I watched it I forgot God and so I had to stop watching." When I asked why he watched it and whether he could describe the attraction, he said, "The attraction, it embraces you like a lion. It swallows you up. You even ignore the people who talk to you. How can you remember God that way? So I stopped watching *Big Brother* and I asked God to forgive me. Only God can forgive our sins, *Glória Deus*." Here, the appraisal of the television show is primarily related to the qualities of the medium to hold viewers captive and thus divert their attention from godly matters. Other people recounted similar experiences concerning the power of television to attract, yet they were less alarmed by this power and more concerned with the content and the programs' perceived power to persuade viewers to accept immoral behavior. Daniela, a woman in her early twenties, felt particularly that the telenovelas of Globo supported prostitution, but for her it was hard to stop watching. She explained in detail how Globo tried to persuade the spectators to excuse the characters' sinful behavior: "In the Globo novelas the next thing happens: as

I told you, it stereotypes people a lot and, for example, in the Globo novelas the men have their mistresses and their wives at home are always the ugly ones, the fat and the bad tempered, and the mistresses are always beautiful, independent, nice. The Globo novelas excuse so much. We end up hoping that the guy stays with his mistress and not with his . . . that he leaves his family." When I asked her why she watched, even though she criticized the telenovelas, she replied, "I also think there is no problem in watching television because I don't want to be alienated. I don't want to stay closed only in my world, but really there are things I could avoid watching and which I don't keep away from, I can't do it." Daniela's remarks indicate that she grants substantial power to telenovelas to form the moral opinions of viewers. Nevertheless, her remarks also show that that attraction and rejection are part of the dynamic of watching television. Unquestionably, the young woman felt there were things she could better avoid, but the feeling that television programs offered her a "window to the world" often prevailed.

Many of the men and women who had recently accepted Jesus mentioned television watching as a practice they started to regard differently during their learning process. In Pentecostal doctrine and practice, the reception of the Holy Ghost and the fight against the devil both occupy an important place. The personal fight against the temptation of illicit pleasures is often portrayed as a fight against the devil, in which victory can only be achieved with the help of God. The devil works cunningly in various ways, however, and he is always and everywhere busy trying to "steal, kill, and destroy," as many people told me. Just as God may work through television—in evangelical programs, mostly—the devil also works through television, especially by seducing men and women with images of sinful carnal pleasures.

Demonized television programs, which feature infidelity, nudity, or sex, are often believed to teach women to prostitute themselves and men to commit adultery. The television spectator should therefore be very careful not to get caught in the trap, for the flesh is weak. Many evangélicos told me that televised images and narratives are the work of demons trying to lure people away from the straight and narrow way by offering them pleasures that might be attractive but eventually lead to death and destruction. While television news was generally considered objective and harmless, other programs were seen as potentially threatening.

Among the Pentecostal adherents I interviewed, telenovelas were most often mentioned as programs they learned to perceive with suspicion. Common topics of the telenovelas (relationships, sex, intimacy, marriage), once considered attractive yet harmless, were now seen as potentially dangerous. Take for example the opinion of Regina, Maria's older sister, who regularly attended the Igreja Universal:

> I am going to tell you that today the government is doing something very wrong because before there was much more censure, you can see so much today, even on the television. The television is garbage. You don't see anything that pleases you. Sometimes this may be more or less, and because you like that actor, you end up watching a bit, but in itself the novela has nothing more to offer you. This is because the novela presents only the destruction of the family, the only thing it passes on is the destruction of the family. For example, when the husband has a problem with the family, with the wife, he is already looking at his sister-in-law, or the other way around, the mother leaves the husband and finds a new boyfriend. You know, it is prostitution in the novela itself, it really is.

Regina rejected telenovelas because she was convinced they show only prostitution, which leads to the destruction of the nuclear family. However, despite these deep-rooted objections, Regina admitted to being tempted to watch because she liked a particular actor/actress. This shows that telenovelas can attract and repel spectators simultaneously.

Watching something that at first sight might be seen harmless, in light of Pentecostal morality and spirituality, occasionally confronts believers with images they experience as troublesome. When I asked Renato—a young man who attended an Assembleia de Deus—what he does when watching television and suddenly sees scenes that display nudity or sex, he replied, "The correct thing to do is, as with a horror movie, close your eyes. That is the most correct thing to do, understand, a strong crente closes his eyes or turns off the television." Renato's response tells us what an evangelical could and should do when illicit images appear on television: turn off the television program or close or cover one's eyes momentarily. During the interview he showed how he put his hands in front of his eyes to protect himself from a "shocking" image.

Watch and Judge

As mentioned above, people do not always have control over what is turned on or off, but more important here, Brazilian television, like television in many other places, presents contradictory images and narratives, dreams and desires. Many of the programs despised in the evangelical press are designed as relational dramas inviting spectators to morally evaluate the behavior of the protagonists. In particular, telenovelas are designed to involve the spectator to watch and judge. As the Brazilian television critic Eugênio Bucci wrote (1997, 136), "The telespectator is the voyeur of evilness. If everything ends well, everything is all right. And there are the novelas with their almost happy endings. Nobody makes a novela to show philanthropy. Novelas are written with the worst intentions and that is why they are fun. It is that way, filled with rottenness, that they can reinforce the idea that good will triumph over evil. Novelas are written by the Devil and finished by God." Such a reading of telenovelas concurs with the illuminating work of Tim Dant (2012), who argues that soaps and reality programs are among the television programs that invite viewers to imagine themselves in situations of moral ambiguity where they have to decide what is right and wrong. As such, soaps form part of a larger body of television programs that reproduce society's common moral framework but also leave room for a diversity of moral opinions.

I became specifically interested in the reactions of Pentecostal spectators to *Big Brother Brasil* when I understood that Bucci's interpretation of telenovelas also applies to certain reality programs. Consider how the host of the reality-soap *BBB* invited the audience to cast their vote for one or the other participant, who then had to leave the palm-fringed gardens of the *Big Brother* house: "We do not know who told the truth and who lied. What the people need is a vision of God, but in this case God is you, the spectator."[25] Courtesy of the omnipresent and omniscient directors of *BBB*, the nationwide audience was allowed to experience some of their divine powers. They were presented with some recorded "scenes" from the *Big Brother* house, so that they, the spectators, could see and judge who was right and who was wrong.

Bucci's reading of the spectator's involvement with television attains a particular evangelical twist when we look at the reactions of the evangelical audience. When I was watching *BBB* with a young girl attending the Igreja Universal, she grabbed the phone to call the network to vote off one of the inhabitants of the *Big Brother* house. When I asked her why she wanted that particular person to leave the house, she replied that the girl in question had a tendency to swear and curse too much and should therefore leave. What struck me was the fact that the girl did not reject the program as a whole on moral or religious grounds—a reaction I had also witnessed. Unlike some other members of the same church, who told me not to watch the program because they deemed its content non-Christian, she admitted to liking the program. From my observation, I concluded that she was attracted above all because *BBB* offers its spectators the possibility to interact with the program. This allowed her to condemn the immoral behavior of the players, to act on her own judgments, and to vote off the person who showed explicit, public, immoral behavior.

During my research among evangélicos in Rio de Janeiro, I noticed that while *BBB* was one of the few programs that actually provided this interactive possibility, people actively engaged with telenovelas in a similar fashion. Surely, *BBB* ineluctably belongs to a different genre of television programs. Contrary to the novelas, "real" people are involved and the opposition between "right" and "wrong" is not always clear. The lure is that putting six men and women together in one house and promising them prize money will eventually lead to some kind "immoral" behavior. The fun lies exactly in the fact that spectators can disagree about who was "right" and who was "wrong." This means that many people commented on the gossip, treason, and sexual behavior of the contestants. Who was siding with whom at the hour of the votes? Who was trying to flirt with whom and how far did they go? Herein lay the spice of this program.

Yet, for *BBB* and the telenovelas, it holds that people do not watch because they have no moral values. They are not an audience possessed by the devil, as the journalist quoted earlier suggested. The position of the omniscient spectator somewhat resembles the imagined viewing position of God. Through the constant camera registration, people finally have the chance to see whether the person practices what he preaches, whether he or she lies or cheats. Spectators of *BBB* do nothing but judge the behavior of people in the program. In other words, the possibility of rejecting certain images, behaviors, and narratives while watching the program is incorporated in its format and in the position the spectator occupies. It offers the spectator the possibility to "watch and judge" from the perspective of a variety of moral frameworks, religious or not. Clearly, immoral behavior can become attractive because it shows "evil" at work and provides the religious spectator with the possibility of judging this illicit behavior according to an evangelical/ Pentecostal moral framework.[26] Birgit Meyer (2003) has described a similar process. According to her, many popular Ghanaian films portray the demonic in order to reinforce Pentecostal morals: "What appears to be at work here is a combination of morality and prurience: for the sake of morality, the films offer audiences the possibility to engage with the Powers of Darkness as voyeurs. In this sense, the assertion of morality requires transgression, very much in the same way that, in Pentecostal churches, belief in God allows for an obsessive, voyeuristic interest in the machinations of the Devil" (26). Seen from this perspective, *BBB* and telenovelas can be watched by evangélicos precisely because they provide microcosms of lamentable behavior. By watching these programs people learn to identify the work of the devil and how to protect oneself against his demons.

Programs such as *BBB* can be watched and enjoyed by faithful Pentecostal adherents as long as they do not fear the sight of evil and know they will not be tempted by it. This means that one has to be sure that one has the power to discern and decide when to switch off the television (or close the eyes). For example, a young man, a leader of the grupo jovem of the Igreja Universal, who had just explained to me that his behavior should be impeccable because he served as an example to others, was quite disappointed with *BBB*: "I was hoping for a turbulent show, you know, but it was a bit boring. In the other program they showed fighting and all that, and there was a married woman who got involved with someone else in the house. I was expecting more scandals like that." When I asked him whether he thought watching *BBB* might be dangerous since the unwary could be exposed to certain seductive images, he said, "You have to know when it is time to stop watching."

This last message points to the problems some evangélicos experience with the kind of television programs discussed here. Although the dynamic of attraction and rejection seems to be the most important reason people, including Pentecostal spectators, tune in to *BBB* and the like, watching television has a dangerous side to it. Not everything can be watched for the sake of confirming that it is not congruent with a Christian life. Such a spectator position is only attainable for those who are *firme* (firm believers) and in control of their own emotional-physical response.[27]

Strikingly, some people used certain television programs as a testing ground to see whether they could maintain a "holy" spectator position and remain in control. One Pentecostal friend in Visionário told me that one night he was watching the sensual program *Noite afora* presented by Monique Evans on Rede TV. The show was about the lives of two lesbians:

You see scenes. It also has reports. It is even interesting. About lesbians. God forbids this kind of practice. God wants a man and a woman. It's one thing only, a man and a woman. There is no other, even that with multiple persons cannot be. What they call *bacchanalia*. It is all evil. They were talking about how she got to like women. I said, "Lord . . ." but then there was the sensual part of the program and the flesh already. . . . I put it in my head that I would do a test to see if I could resist these images, but it didn't help, I had to turn the television off and ask the Lord for forgiveness and He forgave me because I am human. If you see a beautiful woman what happens . . . ha ha, that is why you should not tempt the flesh, because you are flesh.

This example demonstrates that the man uses a Christian distinction between the flesh and the spirit to explain that he only wanted to watch in order to judge. Resolute though he was, he became aroused by the images and disciplined himself by turning off the television and asking for forgiveness.

Television, the Body, and the Holy Spirit

The example clearly illustrates that images can create both desire and repulsion. This type of physical engagement with television is often associated with male sexuality. However, other examples and other works suggest that emotional engagement with the image is certainly not confined to the male gaze. In his investigation of "haptic screens" and our "corporeal eye," Jojada Verrips criticizes the cultural bias on the eyes and on vision when thinking about the interaction between screens and humans. By restating the importance of McLuhan's observations on the sensuous effects of watching television, Verrips (2002, 22) sets out "to show there is a lot more involved than sheer vision when watching screens or that it is not only our eyes which are touched by what we see on film, TV and PC screens, but our whole body." Scholars of film studies have put forward similar arguments about the physical sensuality of the film experience. Most interesting in this respect are Laura Marks's (2000) theories of "haptic visuality" and "tactile memory" and Vivian Sobchack's (2004) work on "carnal thoughts." Both authors analyze the multisensory experience of the image, and both argue that looking at an image triggers embodied memories of touch, taste, and smell. Sobchack's emphasis on embodied memories in sensual perception especially demonstrates that sensual perception is prestructured by acquired, cultural dispositions. According to Sobchack, "We do not experience any movie only through our eyes. We see and comprehend and feel films with our entire bodily being, informed by the full history and carnal knowledge of our acculturated sensorium" (63).

The engagement of Pentecostal spectators with television also points to the affective relationship that people maintain with the images. If we return once again to the quote of Renato, who believed crentes should close their eyes when sensual images appear, just as one occasionally closes one's eyes during the watching of a horror movie, it becomes clear that televised images have the ability to "shock" the evangelical viewer. This small example indicates that we come to a better understanding of the relation between religion and television when we pay attention to the nexus between bodily experience, television viewing, and Pentecostal moral frameworks.

As I explained in previous chapters, in many Pentecostal churches in Rio de Janeiro the body is the locus of attention. There is a wide range of bodily techniques, postures, and disciplines that should be learned if one wants to achieve the right inward disposition to be blessed by God. Of central importance in the relationship between the individual and God is the Holy Spirit. Since the body is regarded as a vessel for the Holy Spirit, it becomes the carrier of the inward and outward signs of the individual relationship with God, both in the church community and in the community of favela inhabitants in general. According to the common conception among most crentes, not everyone can be baptized in the Holy Spirit at will, because one's body should be "clean" for the Holy Spirit to reside in it. In studies of telenovelas there seems to be plenty of "reading" of their meaning.[28] Yet the accounts of evangélicos watching telenovelas support the idea that it is also a very physical experience. Incontrovertibly, our analysis of the evangelical meaning of television must also take the body into account.

Although reactions to television programs were related in part to the differences in doctrines and practices of the Pentecostal churches, images that were undoubtedly considered sinful provoked similar reactions, often directly related to the body. Men were generally concerned with television programs that showed nudity because that could arouse them and lead to impure thoughts and feelings, which might cause the Holy Spirit to abandon them. A good example comes from Renato, who was a great fan of the Globo telenovelas *Malhação* (Workout) and *Esperança* (Hope).[29] When I asked him which programs he would not watch, he mentioned the Globo miniseries *A presença de Anita* (Anita's presence), in which an adolescent girl is involved in a sexual relationship with an older man:

M: What is the difference between *A presença de Anita* and *Malhação*?

R: In *Malhação* you don't see a woman exposed for the people to see naked. *Malhação* does not show that, so it is very different to what you see in *Presença de Anita*. In *Malhação* you may hear certain things that may harm, but you hear them only, you don't see it happening, so it is very different.

M: Did you watch *A presença de Anita*?

R: I have seen it once. I have seen it once and I know that this will not bring me any further. It does not bring me anything edifying, you know? It edifies me in nothing. It will only drive the Holy Spirit out of my life because the Holy Spirit cannot reside in a filthy temple. From the moment I put grief and resentment in my heart, the Holy Spirit cannot stay in my life; me, hurt in this way, the Holy Spirit cannot stay in my life because I am in sin. It will leave me, understand, if I watch *Presença de Anita*. The Holy Spirit will certainly remove itself from my life. It will go, if it has become a place of our enemy, the devil. I can't stay, because the Bible says we cannot worship two gods. I cannot worship God and the devil; it is God or the devil.

199

This example is an unequivocal demonstration that the reception of the Holy Spirit and the fight against the devil both occupy an important place in evangelical/Pentecostal doctrine and practice. The personal fight against the temptations of illicit pleasures or sinful behavior is often portrayed as the fight against the devil, in which victory can only be achieved with the help of God. Many of the evangélicos I interviewed believe that television programs that seduce the spectator with illicit images and narratives are the work of demons trying to lure people away from the "straight path" by offering them gifts and pleasures that might seem attractive, but eventually lead to death and destruction. The devil mostly works through television, seducing men and women with images of carnal pleasures.

In the examples above, the corporeal effects of television watching are primarily related to male sexuality and the fear that the spectator will become "impure" and therefore will lose his contact with the Holy Spirit. In the next cases we will see that the relationship between television, the devil, the Holy Spirit, and the body is not confined to male sexuality alone.

In my interview with Paula—a twenty-six-year-old woman who had recently started to attend the Assembleia de Deus—she told of the time she was watching a debate with the contestants of *BBB*. One contestant was telling about her adoration of Saint George, two others were cursing and swearing, and the directors of the debate were showing what the contestants did behind one another's backs in the *Big Brother* house. According to Paula, she suddenly felt something poking in her side and in her stomach. At first she did not understand what it was until she realized it was the Holy Spirit letting her know that she should not be watching those television programs. Paula explained, "I cannot watch everything. The Holy Spirit, it disturbs me. If you want to have this intimacy with Him and to know really it is Him, you need to have communion with God." When I asked her if there were other programs she could not watch, she mentioned one telenovela in particular: *O Beijo de Vampiro* (The kiss of the vampire). This Globo telenovela about a vampire lord and his family featured many scenes that showed the "dark powers" of vampires. Generally, Pentecostal spectators I interviewed did not dismiss these kinds of powers to the realm of the fantastic. Instead, many took them for the very real presence of feitiçaria and macumba and therefore interpreted them as the work of the devil. Paula told me the following:

> Now let me put on this vampire thing, my God in heaven, I certainly cannot watch that. If I have to watch something like that, my eyes don't cope. . . . No. I say no. I have to change channels because I know it will disturb me. It will mess with me. I watch the news, but novelas no, I don't watch novelas . . . I cannot watch this vampire novela. It is worse than *Big Brother* because it has things I have to avoid because if I begin to watch, I already feel that it will mess with me. It deals a lot with witchcraft. What they talk about, these supernatural powers, that disturbs me. When I keep watching, I know I will be so disturbed. I cannot watch it.

What becomes clear is that the internalization of Pentecostal doctrines in relation to popular cultural products in many cases leads to a transformation of media practices and experiences. What becomes tangible is that this internalization prescribes new ways of engaging with the world, which also profoundly changes the relationship with television.

Because television watching is a multisensual experience that provides physical engagement with the screen, Pentecostal visual culture is strongly related to the body. For many Pentecostal adherents, watching television provides physical experiences that are understood by means of Pentecostal frameworks and are perceived to have spiritual/material consequences. This reminds us that we should not focus primarily on the "seeing" and "reading" of television programs as texts or symbolic images. Especially in the case of Pentecostalism—whose doctrines and practices are so centered on corporeal experiences—we should avoid describing the relationship between religion and television primarily in terms of "reading" proselytic messages or telenovela narratives. As the examples suggest, watching television involves what Christopher Pinney (2001, 158) has coined a "corpothetics": "the bodily engagement that most people . . . have with artworks." Whereas my interviews generally showed that positive spiritual experiences were related to music, negative spiritual experiences were often connected to pictures, images, film, and television.

Many Pentecostal spectators regarded popular television suspiciously because its programs held the power to act on the viewer.[30] Television can arouse the Pentecostal viewer and remind him that he is not (yet) stronger than the flesh or the devil. It can make the Holy Spirit disappear or demonic presence felt. In any case, the examples make clear that the attraction and rejection of television programs are intricately related to bodily experiences that are intelligible in relation to Pentecostal understandings of popular television in Rio de Janeiro.

Globo, Telenovelas, and the Devil

As I found out during my research, speaking about telenovelas with evangélicos meant speaking about Rede Globo. Most interviewees watched and commented on telenovelas produced by TV Globo, and many saw this network as part of the "evil empire" Rede Globo.

Globo has had a hegemonic position in the Brazilian public sphere for almost forty years. According to Birman and Lehmann (1999, 151), Globo has been criticized for presenting a false image of Brazilian society through its telenovelas. It neutralizes the differences between rich and poor people by presenting a "fantasy world of rich but unhappy people." Pentecostal spectators in the morro generally disliked Globo for a different reason, however: broadly speaking, they thought that Globo's power was directly related to its connection with the devil. This demonization of Globo has a particular history.

When Edir Macedo, leader of the Igreja Universal, bought the TV network of Rede Record in 1990, the church not only entered the arena of competitive television networks but also commenced what Birman and Lehmann have described as the "battle for ideological hegemony." In their analysis Birman and Lehmann show that the purchase of TV Record was also an attempt to oppose the Catholic imagery of Brazilian society, as represented by TV Globo. The political struggle over ideological hegemony that followed was visible in a series of disputes in which Globo and the Igreja

Universal played leading roles. First, the purchase itself was questioned. In 1991, articles appeared in the press in which Edir Macedo was accused of having funded the purchase with drug money. The Brazilian Federal Police pursued an investigation and arrested Macedo (though on other charges). They released him shortly after heavy protests by followers of the church. The accusations against Macedo in the press marked the beginning of a series of counteraccusations and conflicts played out in the media: "It was noted—not least by the followers of the church themselves—that Leopoldo Collor, brother of then President Fernando Collor, was a Director of TV Globo, and they linked this to the mysterious leaks and smears, believing that Globo was trying to undermine the competition represented by TV Record in the mass media market" (Birman and Lehmann 1999, 148).

In 1995 Globo launched a miniseries called *Decadência* (Decadence), in which it mimicked Macedo and his Igreja Universal and presented a charlatan bispo enriching himself: "TV Record had responded to the *Decadência* miniseries with attacks on the violence and adultery featured in the telenovelas screened by Globo and watched daily by millions of Brazilians" (150). The fights culminated in the infamous *chute na santa* (kicking of the saint). This was followed by an incident involving bispo Gonçalves of the Igreja Universal. Gonçalves appeared in two video clips broadcast by Globo to expose leaders of the Igreja Universal as charlatans. In one he appeared with several other people in a hotel in Jerusalem, laughingly threatening to unbutton his pants, and in the other he and other church leaders were counting dollars in New York (allegedly these dollars were donations made by poor church attendees). In response to these clips, Gonçalves (1996, 40) himself claims Globo tried to show "that I might have homosexual tendencies; that the leaders of the Igreja meet in Israel to have orgies. Presenting me as if I were a bad person who exploits people, linking my name to financial problems. . . . Globo and its followers went against IURD and Record, with all the strength it could muster. It was a very powerful marketing strategy, a genius diabolical play, that we admit." The mediatized fight against the "diabolical" Globo continued when TV Record attempted to use Globo's own weapons against it. TV Record launched its own telenovela, *A Filha do Demônio* (The daughter of the demon), in 1996 in an attempt to use the popular genre not only to proselytize but also to unmask Globo (Fonseca 1997). Bispo Carlos Rodrigues said, "Seeing those actors who are not evangelicals collaborating to reveal the work of the devil made me think how marvelous the hand of God is. Globo has been using these actors for decades to teach perversion and the degradation of the Brazilian family. TV Record is now using the same vehicle to glorify the name of the Lord Jesus, to unmask the demons that demonstrate how to destroy the family, and to show how evangelicals are present in the hour of despair" (Fonseca 1997, 202). Strikingly, during my research, I did not encounter anyone who referred to these evangelical telenovelas. During the writing of this book, TV Record produced the first conventional telenovela based on a biblical story. *Os Dez Mandamentos* (The Ten Commandments), which is slated to run for 150 episodes, has already proven to be among the most popular telenovelas of TV Record of all time, at times even beating the audience ratings of the telenovela of Globo, aired at the same time.[31] To what extent this success may rearrange popular sentiments and break the hegemony of Globo remains to be seen.

What became clear during my research is that this popular mythology around Globo had drawn a response from Pentecostal members of different denominations. Various adherents of the Assembleia de Deus and the Igreja Universal used it as an argument against watching telenovelas. They not only blamed Globo for making non-Christian programs, but they also mistrusted TV Globo's sincere intentions to make these programs, the conditions under which they were made, and how they became popular. When I asked Geraldo, a young man of twenty-three who attended the Assembleia de Deus, if there were any programs on television he did not watch, he also referred to *Beijo de Vampiro*:

> What I don't watch no way? The seven o'clock novela, for example. *Beijo de Vampiro*, no way. Programs of Globo I hardly watch. Why not Globo? Because Globo is always giving an opportunity to . . . Roberto Marinho, president of Globo, [who] is *pai-de-santo* [a male Candomblé priest], and in Globo he has a temple, a chair, he sits there on the day of worship of the devil. I know because working in publicity I have access to TV Globo. I am there sometimes and I have learned this, but today after a long fight there is also a room for meetings of evangélicos as well, for the evangelical actors. It [Globo] has, that is what they say, that it has a pact with the devil to make a program every year especially to worship him, the media itself, and this year it is *Beijo de Vampiro*.

Geraldo perceived this telenovela not only as an adoration of the devil but as the direct intent of Globo's president, Roberto Marinho, to make these telenovelas in exchange for the devil's help in ensuring the success of Globo's television programs. Geraldo's suspicions concerning Globo point to a common perception that wealth and social position are acquired with the help of divine powers (see also Comaroff and Comaroff 2000). In a very simplified version of the applied logic, to become rich, famous, or powerful, hard work is not enough; one needs to be "blessed," or in any case some metaphysical power is needed. Since certain television stars do not identify themselves as evangélicos, they are thought to have made a pact with the devil to ensure their success and wealth. When I asked a young man who attended the Assembleia de Deus why he thought of Globo as macumbaria, he said:

> Because of him, of Roberto Marinho, you understand, he has to have made some sort of pact with the devil or something, because he does all sorts of things with macumba. He was macumbeira, you understand? In the same way Xuxa made a pact with the devil. Today the people who want to be famous make a pact with the devil, to become famous. Xuxa has made a pact, when she had her program. She has had to do it because of him, being the boss of Globo. People who get in there also end up involved. The owner is their boss, they have to be involved. Unquestionably he has made a law in there, you know, for his employees.

Remarkably, it is Xuxa—Maria da Graça Meneghel, the host of very popular children's programs and one of Globo's biggest television stars in the past— who stands at the center of spiritual controversy here. In many circles, Xuxa is considered a highly favored Brazilian TV personality. Nevertheless, to this young man, her star status makes her suspect of being aligned with the devil. To certain people in Visionário, their suspicion of Xuxa's involvement with the devil was verified when they were affected negatively as a result of watching her programs. A young man of nineteen who attended the Assembleia de Deus said the following when I asked him about the suspicions that Xuxa had made a pact with the devil:

> She has. It was on television once because, look, my little nephew was watching the tape of Xuxa. He watched the tape so much that he became disturbed. The boy could not sleep. He stayed up all day, all night. My aunt, she went to sister Regina, missionária Regina, preacher Regina, servant of God. She went there, prayed for him, and said that it was a demon that did not let him sleep, a demon. My aunt said that he had been watching the Xuxa tape, and Regina

said that he should not watch that tape anymore. It was disturbing. She did not let him watch it anymore and up to today he hasn't seen it again and he sleeps quietly at home.

In this description of the physical effects of a Xuxa tape, several aspects I have described come to the fore. According to a Pentecostal understanding of television, one can be negatively affected by demonic forces transmitted by means of sound and image. In particular, the television programs of TV Globo were to be approached with suspicion because its owner and famous personalities had supposedly made pacts with the devil.[32]

Conclusion

In this chapter, several of this book's threads have come together. As I have shown, people who convert and reflexively reconceptualize their relation to the world in Pentecostal terms become aware that the spiritual battle between God and the devil takes place all around them, including in the domain of electronic media. In previous chapters I have explained that this generally means they become attentive to the sounds they hear, the music they play, and the radio they enjoy. In this chapter I have focused on television in an attempt to unravel to what extent media confirm the genuine state of the world in the eyes and ears of Pentecostal adherents and to understand the perceived power of media to transmit godly and demonic presence. When we regard television from the Pentecostal perspective I have described, general evangelical opinions about the mass media described by Quentin Schultze (1991) acquire a different meaning. It not just that mass media can be used for the purpose of effectively spreading the Gospel and changing the culture for the better, or that the mass media threaten the values and beliefs of the evangelical community. Programs that supposedly threaten the evangelical community are integral parts of the materialization and confirmation of the spiritual battle, and as such they form an essential part of what Pentecostalism means to people. Threatening programs confirm the presence of the devil.

The fact that spokespeople of Pentecostal institutions continually warn their audiences not to watch worldly telenovelas and reality shows does not mean these people never watch them. So-called diabolical programs such as telenovelas, *Big Brother Brasil*, or erotic shows should be seen as important programs that allow Pentecostal viewers to imagine and feel how the devil operates. They are, as Birgit Meyer (2010) has coined it, the "sensational forms" through which the spiritual battle becomes intelligible. Those who are tempted to watch the dangerous programs experience firsthand the power of the devil to attract people and lead them astray. For our common understanding of the relation between media and religion, that means we should not only focus on the relation between audiences and mass media produced by religious agents. Images that are not produced in the context of a specific religious institution, or are not religious per se, might very well attain a religious meaning or experience in the process of their perception (see also Schofield Clark 2003). As we have seen, telenovelas can attain a religious meaning by way of a visual culture informed by Pentecostalism. Moreover, it is not merely that evangélicos observe the spiritual battle from a distance; television regularly touches them and reminds them that they are involved in this battle personally.

By this point it should be clear what the term "hypermediated conversion" entails in the context of favela life. Those who are attracted to Pentecostal understandings of the world gradually adopt different relations with the media that surround them. Depending on the perceived relations between godly and demonic sources and techniques of transmission, Pentecostal believers discern different spiritual circuits that can either nourish them or harm them. Conversion—explained here as a process of self-transformation—involves the acquisition of new perceptual schemes and sensibilities in relation to different media.

Conclusion

One of the main questions I have attempted to answer in this volume is why Pentecostalism is so appealing to the inhabitants of the favelas of Rio de Janeiro. Before summarizing the answers I have proposed, let me recall several of the public Pentecostal manifestations I described in this volume: the cruzada evangelista in Roda do Vento in the introduction, the church service of Pastor Marcos Pereira da Silva (ADUD) in chapter 1, and the deliverance ritual performed by Marcelo Crivella (IURD) in Visionário in chapter 4. While performed by Pentecostal leaders of varying denominations, all three events presented strikingly similar fusions of representations of violence and Pentecostal schemes of deliverance, enmeshed with electronic media with affective capacity. During two events, artists and preachers delivered detailed testemunhos of personal suffering related to the presence of comandos in the favelas of Rio de Janeiro, alternating with cathartic spiritual moments enhanced by music and deliverance rituals. In the third case, young men of the local comando joined the ranks to be spiritually healed by Crivella and local Assembleia de Deus pastors.

The last case exemplifies why practices of the members of the Assembleia de Deus and the Igreja Universal stand at the center of this work and why I have not sharply differentiated between the two groups of congregants for this research. While I am conscious of the structural differences between the two churches, my work has been influenced by the "lived religion" approach (Orsi 1999), which highlights the workings of religious ideas and practices in daily life. Though the organizational structures of the two churches that feature in this volume display great differences and their doctrinal positions are not entirely the same, my inquiries on media and social life showed that adherents of the churches share several basic ideas about the spiritual battle between God and the devil and the way this battle manifests itself in their daily urban surroundings and media.

The appealing message of both Pentecostal churches is deeply related to the social schism between the world of affluent people who live in secured areas and that of the favela inhabitants. As described in this book, members of Pentecostal churches in the favelas present conversion and deliverance as viable means to end the comando-related violence in Rio de Janeiro. People of the Pentecostal churches are represented as agents of God who make up for the failure of other institutions to counter the violence in the favelas. Though comando-related violence is certainly not the only or principal social circumstance that gives meaning to Pentecostal events in the favelas of Rio de Janeiro, it is one of the more invasive life experiences that structure collective stories of suffering (Silva 2008; Perlman 2010; Zaluar 1998).

Pentecostal churches present alternative utopias and life projects for individuals who aspire to a better condition. These life projects involve new ways of looking and listening to the world and a new understanding of self and community. Pentecostal churches generally propose rigid distinctions between good and evil. The pastors preach that only the acceptance of Jesus as one's personal Savior offers redemption from social and personal problems. As I have shown, deliverance and conversion offer the inhabitants of the favelas a sense of divine protection—sanctuary—from the violence associated with the comandos and milícias.

This relationship between Pentecostalism and urban violence is not particular to Rio de Janeiro or Brazil. The work of Jon Wolseth (2008) about evangelicals in a popular neighborhood in Honduras and the work of David Smilde (2007) about evangelicals in Venezuela demonstrate that similar mechanisms are at work in different Latin American cities suffering from the rise of the "new violence" since the 1990s (see also Sánchez 2008). As my work and the works of others show, many Pentecostal and evangelical converts understand their crossing from a "worldly" lifestyle to a "godly" lifestyle as a way to protect themselves from the harsh circumstances of life in urban areas of Latin America.

While the narratives presented in this volume resemble the findings of authors who have worked in other Latin American cities, one of the distinguishable local features of Pentecostalism in Brazil is the widespread belief in demonic possession caused by Afro-Brazilian religious practices. Enforcing historical prejudice against such cultural traditions, Pentecostal churches and Pentecostal mass media demonize popular Afro-Brazilian customs. Aided by literal readings of the Bible, these religious practices are depicted as idolatrous devil worship. In the favelas of my research, the devil was often associated with Afro-Brazilian religious practices, and subsequently evangélicos were inclined to align the violence of the traficantes with such practices.

This alignment has several social effects. Contrary to those cariocas who think all bandidos should be locked up without trial, Pentecostal adherents often regard comando members as fallible humans who can repent and change their ways. Nevertheless, such an understanding of the relation between religion and violence reproduces a one-dimensional image of Afro-Brazilian practices and sets up underprivileged people against one another instead of uniting them in the face of the unequal distribution of income and security (Oro and Semán 1999).

As I have described in chapter 4, knowledge of and experience with Afro-Brazilian religious practices allow for the perceived homology between demonic possession of people and spaces. In turn, this homology supports a Pentecostal idea that individual deliverance is a means to heal the favela at large. I am not claiming that similar homologies do not appear in other places in the world; rather, I am arguing that the particular entanglements with Afro-Brazilian traditions and its demonization produce local variants of Pentecostalism and have reconfigured relations between crime, violence, and religion.

Since Pentecostalism offers inhabitants a sense of sanctuary, one is tempted to see the churches as forces that protect people, helping them order their lives and come to terms with their harsh reality. As I have tried to demonstrate, we should not take this celebratory self-description of the churches at face value. Pentecostalism is fraught with paradoxes and tensions. It is said that accepting Jesus puts one on the safe side of the spiritual battle, yet the devil lurks close by and is ready to take advantage of anyone who slips. Paradoxically, Pentecostal churches continuously invoke the evildoings of the devil and hence reproduce anxiety themselves (Meyer 1999). As I have demonstrated in chapter 3, such a contrast also becomes apparent when one examines the images and narratives presented in the churches' mass media and the congregants' reactions. The Igreja Universal proposes to resolve the violence in the city and restore in the individual the belief that the world can be manipulated and is not arbitrary, but it produces an image of a society that is inherently evil.

Pentecostal churches do not just mend the gaps; in fact, they have developed an antagonistic attitude toward many popular Brazilian practices. In an attempt to break down the cultural hegemony of such popular practices, Pentecostal movements have launched aggressive media campaigns against other religious and cultural practices in Brazil (Birman and Lehmann 1999;

Silva 2007). Such fierce opposition against cultural practices that are deemed immoral and un-Christian is in some aspects similar to the cultural opposition of the religious right in the United States (Harding 2000; Gormly 2003).

The Pentecostal churches preach against the evil of the comandos, but they do not actually oppose the actions of the latter or hinder their business. In general, the binary ethical codes of Pentecostalism oppose the *jogo de cintura* (wheeling and dealing) of daily life, and some people do indeed radically change their life after an encounter with God. Nevertheless, we should not uncritically adopt the self-description of Pentecostal adherents. Conversion to Pentecostalism is attractive because it offers experiences of empowerment through collective rituals in combination with a newborn identity in the complex power relations of the favelas. The trope of the spiritual battle is crucial to understanding the nature of the conversions but also their inherent paradoxes. While the newborn identity is described as God-given, it is also an identity they must perform every day. The *status aparte* is generally granted by other favela residents, but only when crentes indeed show the signs of God's grace and do not engage in the behavior they condemn in others. This demands extra awareness and a multitude of self-disciplinary performances. Self-ascribed Pentecostals should no longer practice those diabolical things they did before: no more baile funk, samba, or pagode, and no more adultery, drinking, or smoking. Conversion restores the feeling of power over their destiny but also heightens the responsibility to behave according to biblical norms.

Whereas the self-disciplinary practices can be thorough, they are not totalizing and may have different outcomes over time. Some people are attracted to the strict codes certain Pentecostal churches prescribe; others see such stipulations as too much limitation on their freedom. What may be seen as empowering from the perspective of the convert at a certain moment may be experienced as a limitation at another. Regardless of the extent to which schemes of self-styling produce and limit agency (see Mahmood 2009), Jeff Garmany (2010) rightly describes Pentecostal institutions in favelas in terms of the Foucauldian notion of governmentality (Foucault [1978] 1991). Understanding Pentecostalism as governmentality, among other things, highlights that it reproduces particular modes of self-styling and spatiotemporal orderings that have lasting effects on the organization of favela life (see also Lanz 2007).

The styles and traditions of the churches are presented as contrasts to the cultural practices associated with immoral behavior and the devil. Música evangélica is opposed to música do mundo—samba, pagode, and carioca funk—because that is the popular music of parties at which people court, drink, and dance without obeying the strict moral prescriptions of the Bible. Instead of interpreting the excitement as a well-deserved escape from the complex day-to-day life of the favelas, many evangélicos understand these cultural practices to be the root of all social and individual problems. Only by breaking with those practices can one be blessed in this life and saved in the hereafter. As such, Joel Robbins is right to argue that discontinuity is at the heart of the Pentecostal message. Likewise, my description of the attitudes of Pentecostal favela residents confirms Robbins's (2004, 127–28) suggestion that the "open-ended range of referents" of the dualism between the divine and the satanic allows for the global spread of Pentecostalism that, nevertheless, maintains clearly distinguishable local characteristics. However, I have argued that we should push Robbins's insights further to include in our scope the popular culture that forms part of daily life in places such as the favelas I have described. That means including in our notions of locality the body of cultural productions (music, radio, television, print media) that co-produce local ways of living.

Understanding Pentecostalism as governmentality also offers better possibilities to comprehend current overlaps between evangelical and non-evangelical audiences and to understand contemporary intersections between evangelical music production and security measures in the favelas of Rio de Janeiro. As Carly Machado (2013) has shown, in 2011 municipal governmental organizations, the police, and non-evangelical broadcasters cooperated to stage one of the nation's most popular evangelical bands— Diante do Trono—in one of Rio's most infamous favelas, the Complexo do Alemão, in an effort to enforce the transition of the favela from "hotbed of crime" to "pacified" place. The concert, which drew a considerable crowd of evangelical and non-evangelical residents to one of the few open areas in the favela, demonstrated that governmental organizations are susceptible to the evangelical understanding of gospel music as inherently soothing and are willing to add gospel music to their repertoire of security techniques.

As this volume has tried to demonstrate, self-understanding and world-view are not dependent on the local spatio-material surrounding alone or the specific governmental structures related to the economic situation of slum dwellers. Favelas, like many other Latin American urban areas, are characterized by a plethora of media that reproduce and reconfigure residents' understandings of life and their place in it.

Starting from the assumptions that media technologies are constitutive of local worlds (Mazzarella 2004) and that media are part of the constitution of contemporary everyday life (Dant 2012; Hjarvard 2008), this volume has attempted to contribute to the anthropology of religion and to discussions concerning the global spread of Pentecostalism. As I have tried to show in the preceding chapters, the acknowledgment that electronic media reproduce pervasive notions of self and society means that we cannot study conversion as a response to material circumstances alone. Rather, we should extend our notions of conversion beyond the transformations that are generally mentioned in relation to Pentecostalism—such as, for example, change of dress, language, and substance consumption. The individuals I interviewed for this volume based their notions of the world on an eclectic sampling of television and radio programs; in the conversion process, these individuals acquired new understandings of how to deal with the media that surround them.

Thus, if anything, this volume has tried to broaden the discussions concerning religious conversion in the context of life-worlds such as the favelas of Rio de Janeiro. As I have argued, Pentecostal ideology and practice become meaningful and powerful because they are framed against the background of popular cultural practices that are thoroughly mediatized. Instead of analyzing media, society, and religion separately, I have examined their intersections from the perspective of the daily lives of favela residents. Media and daily life enforce the Pentecostal vision of the world that a spiritual battle is taking place, and it is within the media-saturated environments of the favelas that Pentecostal images and narratives become significant. Both in the public space of the morro and inside their houses, inhabitants watch, read, and listen to a variety of media, which concurrently produce a "reality effect" (Schwartz 1995, 316).

Notwithstanding the importance of the power of media to confirm and reproduce world*views*, the material presented here has also tried to push our understanding of the power of media beyond their capacity to *picture* the world. Pentecostal churches have appropriated the technological means to distribute their cosmology and theology, but they have also copied and invented new styles and formats to communicate the divine. These styles are essential to the establishment of a sense of belonging and the formation of communities in the age of mass media (Keil and Feld 1994; Maffesoli 1996). Styles of behavior, clothing, and music intersect with the power relations in the favelas and in Brazilian society at large. In a Pentecostal division of the world, the sonic battle between music styles articulates with the spiritual battle between God and the devil.

The development of electronic mass media has influenced the intersections between popular culture and Pentecostalism, but also the very nature of the religious experiences. Instead of understanding technology and religion as discrete domains, religion can be comprehended as a practice of mediation (Vries 2001). Such a conceptualization of religion helps us understand through which religious didactics (Meyer 2006) people become responsive to specific sensory perceptions that signal and authenticate divine presence. The investigation of religious disciplines and experiences can thus clarify through which media practices "enchantment manifests itself" (Pinney 2001, 157).

As I have argued in chapters 2 and 5, electroacoustic media are essential to the Pentecostal experiences of people in the favelas. People use their sound systems to understand, feel, and demonstrate the difference between "being in the world" and "being of the world." Inhabitants feel profoundly touched by the sounds in the favela. When properly tuned in, amplified louvor and broadcast gospel can call forth and make present the Holy Spirit. Such electroacoustic experiences of divine presence demonstrate that communication technology is part of the reproduction of religious experience (Abreu 2005), but it also demonstrates that technological mediation itself tends to disappear out of sight (or hearing) in the process, thus facilitating the experience of immediate connection with the divine (Eisenlohr 2009).

Television offers people an instrument through which they perceive the work of God and the devil, but they also feel those presences physically (see chapter 6). The physical experiences that occur during television watching support the critique that several scholars have voiced against the assumption that religious devotees tend to regard images as inanimate representations of the objects depicted, while religious spectators feel that pictures and objects contain elements of the transcendent or are experienced as the materialization of the deity in question (Morgan 2005). Whereas music was often mentioned as the medium that best transmitted the healing powers of the Holy Spirit, television programs were often singled out as media that transmitted the destructive power of the devil. Several Pentecostal adherents I interviewed thought the devil helped produce the telenovelas so that spectators were persuaded to commit sins. Some even felt that the Holy Spirit gave physical signals to warn for possible dangers. Strikingly, the fear of the diabolical consequences of watching closely resembles the widely held opinion among journalists, scientists, and the like that television programs—gospel, entertainment, advertisements—have clearly discernible effects that can be singled out and measured.

Television attracts and frightens Pentecostal spectators. While some programs are perceived as harmless, a variety of programs—such as telenovelas—are watched with great suspicion. This is partly related to the medium itself. As in film, editing techniques (e.g., montage) used in television programs like the telenovelas connect separate images to one another and allow for the construction of complex narrative sequences that can place similar objects, images, or occurrences in different perspectives (Manovich 2001). Some worldly images are incorporated within evangelical media, as we saw in chapter 3, but in other instances it is not entirely clear to the spectator whether a particular program is dangerous, because the worldly content can also be perceived from an evangelical standpoint. As we saw in chapter 6, evangelicals can also adopt a Pentecostal spectator position and critically judge the worldly program from a moral standpoint congruent with evangelical doctrines. The variety of spectator positions and possible affective experiences call for detailed approaches to the relationship between technology, religion, and (visual) culture in studies of Brazilian Pentecostalism.

The religious experiences and interpretations of telenovelas, news programs, and reality shows indicate that the relation between religion and media should not start or stop with the investigation of media produced by religious actors and institutions. Instead, we should examine how religious institutions attempt to demarcate and authenticate the separation between so-called religious and nonreligious media, while referring to and building on the audience's knowledge of the mass media at large. Pentecostal institutions in Brazil, paradoxically, make ample use of intertextual techniques that connect worldly and godly media to each other in their attempt to separate the two permanently.

The dialectical relationship between the fictional or dramatized mass media and the everyday life of the inhabitants urges us to take seriously the role of fantasy and the power of imagination, as Appadurai (1996) and Meyer (2003) have also argued. The public presence of Pentecostalism and its contemporary political growth do not just question recurring assumptions that religion will disappear from the public realm; the examples I have shown also argue for a political analysis that takes seriously the appeal of the Pentecostal worldview in the age of mass media. The global availability of mass communication technologies has spurred mass mediated religious imaginations that incite political actions in many parts of the world.

Especially in liberal-capitalist societies with high income inequality and a disproportionate protection of civil rights, particular religious movements gain popularity. Comaroff and Comaroff (2000) have argued, for instance, that global capitalism in its present form engenders notions of occult forces such as magic, sorcery, and witchcraft in a wide range of politico-economic activities around the globe. Similarly, according to David Martin (2002, 15), "There is a discernible consonance between Pentecostalism and the simultaneous (indeed, related) advance of global liberal capitalism." André Corten and Ruth Marshall-Fratani have argued that the contemporary success of local varieties of Pentecostalism can be understood as the result of the diffusion of mass media, accompanied by new forms of wealth and accumulation. According to Corten and Marshall-Fratani (2001, 3) this process opens up "wide vistas of possible lives, inciting desire and fantasy, but also anxiety, frustration, downward mobility and insecurity."

The material presented here demonstrates that Pentecostal churches in Brazil intersect with other mass media in the representation of a violent, apocalyptic society by means of spectacular images and narratives of urban warfare. These images and narratives fuel the Pentecostal experience of a society assailed by demonic forces. The examples of the deliverance of traficantes by Pastor Marcos and Marcelo Crivella demonstrate that the relationship between Pentecostalism, politics, and mass media generates spaces for a type of populism that envisions worldly progress for "the people" through spiritual interventions mediated by pastor-politicians. Such an imagination of society is highly credible to inhabitants of the favelas who are confronted with violence and insecurity daily and who experience limited control over the circumstances of their lives, while television programs fuel both their dreams of limitless consumption and their nightmares of misery and suffering.

Notes

The epigraph to this book quotes DJ Alpiste, "Vencer o Mal" (Overcome Evil), from the album *Efésios Cap. 6 vs. 12*. *Traficante* can be translated as drug dealer and *crente* as evangelical believer.

All translations of Portuguese-Brazilian texts are by the author.

Introduction

1. The names of the two favelas of my research—Roda do Vento and Visionário—are invented. I have substituted them to protect the identity of the favela inhabitants. *Cruzada evangelista* is the popular name for public evangelical events in Rio de Janeiro.

2. *Gospel* is the Brazilian term for worship music and includes different styles of contemporary popular music.

3. *Testemunhar* is Portuguese for witnessing. For an elaborate description of the relation between conversion and witnessing in evangelical culture, see the work of Susan Harding (2000) and chapter 4 of this book.

4. People who belong to Protestant or Pentecostal Christian churches often define themselves as *evangélicos*.

5. Unless stated differently, I conducted all interviews in this book. Throughout I use aliases to protect the identity of the people involved.

6. See also Anderson et al. 2010; Beyer 2006; Coleman and Hackett 2015; Csordas 2009; Robeck and Yong 2014.

7. The Brazilian government, social scientists, and journalists commonly use the term *evangélico* to describe a heterogeneous group of Protestant/Pentecostal members, consumers, and "voters."

8. See the 2010 census data of the Instituto Brasileiro de Geografia e Estatística (Brazilian Institute of Geography and Statistics), http://biblioteca.ibge.gov.br /visualizacao/periodicos/94/cd_2010_reli giao_deficiencia.pdf. See also "Assembleia de Deus atrai 3,9 milhões de novos evangélicos," *Folha de São Paulo*, June 30, 2012, http:// www1.folha.uol.com.br/fsp/poder/51844- assembleia-de-deus-atrai-39-milhoes- de-novos-evangelicos.shtml.

9. Marc Krell (2003, 6) employs the term "dialectic symbiosis" to analyze the constitution of Christian and Jewish identity in response and opposition to each other.

10. See the 2010 census data of the Instituto Brasileiro de Geografia e Estatística, http://biblioteca.ibge.gov.br/ visualizacao/periodicos/94/cd_2010_reli giao_deficiencia.pdf, and the 2000 census data of the Instituto Brasileiro de Geografia e Estatística, http://biblioteca.ibge.gov.br /visualizacao/periodicos/83/cd_2000_carac teristicas_populacao_amostra.pdf.

11. CEB is the acronym for Comunidade Eclesial de Base (Ecclesial Base Community).

12. See also Gay 2010; Lanz 2007; Silva 2008; Zaluar and Conceição 2007.

13. See the website of the research group Media, Religion, and Culture of the Methodist University of São Paulo, http://www.metodista.br/midiareligiaopolitica/index.php/composicao-bancada-evangelica.

14. In the period leading up to the elections of 2002, the Partido dos Trabalhadores (PT) of the elected president, Luiz Inacio Lula da Silva, opted for an alliance with the Partido Liberal (PL). At the time, the Partido Liberal was generally known for the number of Igreja Universal pastors among its supporters.

15. See "Templo de Salomão é inaugurado em São Paulo," *O Globo*, July 31, 2014, http://g1.globo.com/sao-paulo/noticia/2014/07/templo-de-salomao-e-inaugurado-em-sao-paulo.html.

16. The mergers between religion and media in Brazil are paralleled by similar developments in other countries. In Latin America, Pentecostal groups have actively sought involvement in sociopolitical processes (Boudewijnse, Droogers, and Kamsteeg 1998; Garrard-Burnett and Stoll 1993; Martin 1990; Stoll 1990), often by acquiring mass media outlets. Religious groups around the world have adopted techniques of mass communication to present themselves to the wider public (Meyer and Moors 2006; Hirschkind and Larkin 2008).

17. See http://www.universal.org/institucional/historia-da-universal.html.

18. Ibid.

19. The collection of churches of the Assembleia de Deus consists of subgroups known as Ministérios. In this work, congregations are all subsumed under the common name Assembleia de Deus.

20. See the 2010 census data of the Instituto Brasileiro de Geografia e Estatística, http://biblioteca.ibge.gov.br/visualizacao/periodicos/94/cd_2010_religiao_deficiencia.pdf.

21. See, for example, Campos 1997; Conrado 2001; Freston 1994, 2008; Fonseca 2008; Novaes 2002; Sá Martino 2002; Oro 2003.

22. See Machado and Mariz 2004; Oro 2003.

23. See also Birman 2006; Kramer 2005.

24. *Sessão de descarrego*—literally, "unloading session"—is a deliverance service.

25. *Encostar* literally means "to lean on"; therefore, *encostos* could be translated as spiritual entities that "lean" on people.

26. Some even criticize soccer because the "passion" (*paixão*) some people have for it may hinder their church presence or replace their zeal for the Lord. See, for example, the evangelical magazine *Enfoque*, no. 11 (2002).

27. The presumed effects of proselytizing media in Brazil often resemble ideas on the effects of mass media in general. Such effects have often been framed in terms of dominance and resistance (Fiske 1989).

28. See also Hirschkind and Larkin 2008; Meyer and Moors 2006.

29. See, for example, Conrado 2001; Dantas 2008; Machado and Mariz 2004; Novaes 2002; Oro 2003.

30. See Campbell 2010; Hoover 2006; Meyer and Moors 2006; Port 2011.

31. See Eisenlohr 2009; Engelke 2007; Meyer 2009; Stolow 2005.

32. Similarly, scholars who have their roots in research on religion and media have argued for an interdisciplinary approach to analyze the intersection of culture, religion, and media (Hoover and Lundby 1997; Hoover and Schofield Clark 2002).

33. See Burdick 2013; Cox 1995; Hackett 1998; Ingalls and Yong 2015.

Chapter 1

1. The term "community" (*comunidade*) is generally used by inhabitants of favelas and occasionally by outsiders. See the work of Patricia Birman (2008) for an elaborate analysis of the term *comunidade*.

2. In 2013 the pastor was accused of having connections with leaders of the criminal organization Comando Vermelho and of sexually molesting a member of his church. He was convicted for the second accusation and imprisoned in Rio de Janeiro from 2013 to 2014.

3. One may wonder about the effect of the installment of the UPPs and whether such "pacification" programs address the many structural conditions related to the persistence of criminal gangs and the

predicaments that inhabitants face. See the dissertation of Palloma Menezes (2015) on the effects of UPP installments in Rio de Janeiro between 2008 and 2014.

4. See Rafael Galdo, "Rio é a cidade com maior população em favelas do Brasil," *O Globo*, December 21, 2011, http://oglobo.globo.com/brasil/rio-a-cidade-com-maior-populacao-em-favelas-do-brasil-3489272.

5. See Alvito 2001; Arias 2006; Gay 1994, 2005; Lanz 2007; Perlman 2010.

6. See Burdick 1993; Hunt 2010; Mariz 1994.

7. Research done in 1994 (Fernandes et al. 1998) showed that of all the people who frequent Protestant churches in Rio de Janeiro, those who attend the Pentecostal churches Assembleia de Deus and the Igreja Universal generally earn the lowest incomes in the city. The majority of those who attended the two churches earned twice the minimum income.

8. See Campos 1997; Mariano 1999; Mariz 1994; Kramer 2001b.

9. See Arias 2006; Gay 2005; Goldstein 2003; Velho 2009.

10. See Burdick 1998; Mariano 2007.

11. See also Gordon 1991; Lemke 2001.

12. *Cariocas* is the Brazilian term to describe the people of Rio de Janeiro. It is also used locally to describe Rio de Janeiro as a place of birth or of identity vis-à-vis other regions or cities in Brazil.

13. Scholars disagree about the origin of this name. Nunes (1976, 19) says that the soldiers who came to live on the Morro da Providênçia probably used the name *favela* as an allusion to a plant that grew in the dry hinterlands of Bahia. Enders (2002, 203) also states that the name refers to a "thorny" plant that grows in the dry hinterland. However, she says the name was given by the soldiers to a strategic hill used to conquer the Citadel of Canudos. Souto de Oliveira and Marcier (1998, 65) state that wives of the soldiers, natives of a mountain range called Favela, introduced the name in Rio de Janeiro.

14. According to Valladares (1978), in 1948 there were 105 favelas in Rio de Janeiro with a population of roughly 139,000. Nunes (1976) writes that in 1960 there were 147 favelas with a total population of 335,000,

and in 1970 there were 300 favelas with a total population of one million people.

15. According to research done in 1981, presented in the *ficha cadastral* (cadastral file) of the favela, obtained at the Cadastro das Favelas do Município do Rio de Janeiro. This municipal favela cadastre was organized and maintained by the Instituto de Planejamento Municipal do Rio de Janeiro, now called the Instituto Municipal de Urbanismo Pereira Passos.

16. For a detailed description of the birth of the Falange Vermelho, which later became Comando Vermelho, see Lima 1991; Amorim 1993.

17. See also Perlman 2010.

18. When cocaine became available for the domestic market, it was at first sold primarily to the rich and later became popular among all classes.

19. See Alvito 2001; Arias 2006; Leeds 1996; Misse et al. 2013; Soares 2000; Zaluar 1998.

20. See Gay 2005; Leeds 1996; Oliveira and Carvalho 1993.

21. This is also suggested in the book *Favelas e as organizações comunitarias* (Oliveira and Carvalho 1993).

22. I have never heard the term used to describe women.

23. See Alessandro Lo-Bianco, "Justiça decreta prisão de seis PMs acusados de matar dois moradores em Santa Teresa," *O Globo*, July 28 2014, http://oglobo.globo.com/rio/justica-decreta-prisao-de-seis-pms-acusados-de-matar-dois-moradores-em-santa-teresa-13409458.

24. One of the members of the Catholic parish claimed that the diminished fear of removal could be attributed to the organization Pastoral de Favelas of the Catholic Church, created in 1977. This organization helped inhabitants of favelas fight for the legalization of their dwellings.

25. *Obreiros* are uniformed volunteers of the Igreja Universal who carry out many tasks during the *cultos* (services). Many young men and women in the morro were or aspired to become obreiros.

26. During my residence up the morro, the Igreja Universal had no church in the favela, though occasionally there had been a *núcleo* (a semiformal meeting place).

27. Enforcing the existing pejorative use of the term, Edir Macedo (2000, 63) of the

Igreja Universal refers to *macumba* as the generic name for all spiritualist traditions and spirit-possession practices.

28. *Mãe de santo* (mother of the saint) is the woman who heads the terreiro and is thus highest in rank.

Chapter 2

1. *Pagode* is a type of popular music I will describe in detail in this chapter.

2. *Forró* is a type of popular music associated with people from the northeastern region of Brazil.

3. *Funk*, also known as *funk carioca* or *baile funk*, differs from the style commonly referred to as funk in the West. Funk carioca is related to a genre known as Miami bass and is perhaps best described as a combination of electronic dance music and hip-hop music. I will describe the music in more detail later in this chapter.

4. This is confirmed by the quantitative research of Alexandre Fonseca (1997, 90), who showed that the people from the Igreja Universal mostly tuned in to the radio stations owned by their church instead of those owned by other churches.

5. For insights on Pentecostalism and music, see Burdick 2013; Cox 1995; Hackett 1998; Ingalls and Yong 2015; and Miller and Yamamori 2007.

6. In line with Feld's arguments we might follow Steven Connor (2004), Patrick Eisenlohr (2006), Veit Erlmann (2004), and Charles Hirschkind (2001), who all strive to pay more attention to the faculty of hearing/listening in the constitution of modern (religious) subjectivity.

7. I will not be able to do justice to the literature on ethnomusicology or to give detailed descriptions of the different musical genres and performances I encountered in the favelas.

8. Salome Voegelin (2014, 2) makes a similar point when she states that "listening is never separate from the social relationships that build the fleeting circumstance of hearing."

9. See Frith 1996; Rommen 2007; Stokes 1994; Turino 2008.

10. Following Martin Stokes (1994, 6), I understand people's presentations of "authentic music styles" as performances

that allow for the creation and enforcement of boundaries between groups.

11. See Brubaker 2004; Latour 2005; Stokes 1994; Turino 2008. Obviously, some of these group identities overlap and/or portray both dominant and demotic discourses *of* and *within* groups (communities) (Baumann 1996).

12. Such an approach is clearly indebted to the work of Judith Butler ([1990] 1999). According to Butler, gender identity should not be regarded as the expression of an inner truth, but rather as the *appearance of substance*, which is the result of the performance of certain stylized acts (173–80).

13. Paraíba is a state in northeastern Brazil.

14. Associação das Escolas da Cidade do RJ (Association of Schools of the City of Rio de Janeiro).

15. The lyrics continue with this summary of favelas in Rio de Janeiro where Comando Vermelho gangs rule.

16. In chapter 5 I will describe the importance that people ascribe to Pentecostal music and sound for their individual sacred experiences.

17. Mary Hancock and Smriti Srinivas (2008, 620) describe the present socio-spatial mediation of religion in cities in Asia and Africa. They argue against the persistent notion within urban studies to read the practice of religion as "a parochial contamination of cosmopolitan life worlds." Instead, they argue, we should acknowledge that religion is part of urban modernity.

18. According to Ash Amin and Nigel Thrift (2002, 41–48), the constitution of contemporary urban communities relies heavily on technological mediation.

19. In the case of gospel, a clear-cut distinction between live music and reproduced music—schizophonia, as Shäfer (1994) has coined it—is disputable. Instead of treating schizophonia merely as a one-way process—from original sound to its reproduction—it would be better to look at it as a circular process (Feld 1994, 260).

20. Shaun Moores (2004, 22) argues that he prefers to use the concept "trans-localized" when speaking of the effects of broadcast media on our experiences of simultaneity and "immediacy."

21. *Louvor* could be translated as worship or musical laudation of the Lord.

22. In 2012 Sony Music signed the popular gospel singer Irmão Lázaro, originally part of the well-known Afro-Brazilian percussion group Olodum. After a period without a contract, Irmão Lázaro returned to Sony Music in 2016. See the Sony website, https://www.gospelsonymusic.com.br /irmao-lazaro-retorna-para-cast-sony-music. In January 2014 Som Livre for the first time signed a well-known Brazilian Pentecostal singer, Andrea Fontes, formerly contracted by the record company MK Music. See "Andrea Fontes assina contrato com a Som Livre," *Desktop Gospel*, January 2014, http:// www.desktopgospel.com.br/2014/01 /andrea-fontes-assina-contrato-com-som .html.

23. See chapter 5 for a discussion of the individual experiences of music in relation to Pentecostalism.

24. Remember my encounter with Robson, described in the introduction.

25. A small string instrument used for samba and pagode.

26. See the evangelical magazine *Enfoque*, no. 9 (2002): 58.

Chapter 3

1. Teresa Caldeira (2000) describes a similar paradox in relation to the daily talk of crime in urban São Paulo.

2. Clearly the intricate confirmation of the "reality" of mass media in everyday life, and vice versa, is not reserved for Brazilian evangelicals. See Carroll 1998; Dant 2012; Garnham 1992; Hjarvard 2008; Silverstone 2002.

3. See the *Folha Universal* website, http:// www.universal.org/folha-universal.

4. One of the three languages Schmalzbauer distinguishes as multivocal is that of "justice and peace." The language of peace and justice is an articulation of ethically engaged journalism and religious activism. This categorization fits in well with the social-religious language in the *Folha Universal*.

5. Sá Martino's (2002) sharp distinction between religious and nonreligious constructions of reality obscures the fact that while religious discourses can be very dominant, they are never completely self-contained or totalizing (Asad 1993).

6. Bispo Alceu Nieckarz in the *Folha Universal*, June 16–22, 2002.

7. See Coimbra 2001; Jovchelovitch 2000; Leite 1997; Rondelli 1994.

8. During the year 2002 I collected and compared the *Jornal do Brasil* and *O Globo* on a daily basis. I base my generalizations on the representation of violence that year, taking into account that Jovchelovitch (2000) and Coimbra (2001) have come up with similar conclusions as I have.

9. See "A década sofrida: Imagens mostram como a violência se tornou rotina na cidade ao longo dos anos," *O Globo*, June 16, 2002.

10. See "Identificado corpo de Tim," *O Globo*, July 6, 2002.

11. See Antônio de Almeida, "Retrospectiva 2002," *Folha Universal*, January 5–11, 2003.

12. According to Andrew Tolson (1996, 38), "As a type of syntagmatic structure, montage works through juxtaposition. These juxtapositions may be emphasizing conceptual similarities or contrasts . . . but the crucial point is that the connections between the signs in a montage structure are implicit, not explicit. A montage therefore involves the reader/viewer in an active process of working out the logic (if any) implicit in the interconnections."

13. This evangelical framing and interpretation of the news resembles Paul S. Boyer's (2005) description of the Christian dispensationalist understanding of world news events as confirmations of biblical prophecies in the United States.

14. See Almeida, "Retrospectiva 2002."

15. Tim Lopes, the murdered journalist, appeared on the inside of the *IstoÉ* issue, not on the cover.

16. Rede Record is the broadcast network owned by Edir Macedo, the charismatic leader of the Igreja Universal. According to Silvia Ramos and Anabela Paiva (2007, 17), Rede Record stopped airing the program *Cidade Alerta* in 2006; together with the disappearance of several of the popular daily journals with spectacular "bloody" photos and reports, they take this as a sign that the spectacularization of crime news has diminished. However, the program *Cidade Alerta* returned to the air in 2007 and is still very popular in 2017. See http://noti cias.r7.com/cidade-alerta.

17. Pastors often address the people present during a service as *igreja* (church).

18. The Igreja Universal tries to influence the political affinities of its members in cultos and by means of its mass media (Conrado 2001; Fonseca 1998).

19. I do not share Schultze's (1991, 92–95) concerns about the possible dangers of such personality cults for either the churches or society.

20. Kramer takes up this notion from Coleman (2000, 150; cited in Kramer 2005).

21. The fame of some bispos is not unlike that of other religious celebrities of Brazil, such as Marcello Rossi (Abreu 2002; 2005).

22. See http://marcelocrivella.com.br.

Chapter 4

1. Orações are often held collectively.

2. This type of exorcism is very common in the services of the Igreja Universal, especially during the *sessão de descarrego* (deliverance service). I will elaborate on the practices of this church service below.

3. The *Bíblia de Estudo Pentecostal* (Pentecostal study Bible) is a Portuguese translation of the 1995 edition of the *Full Life Study Bible New Testament* (King James Version) that offers commentaries and interpretations by Donald C. Stamps and J. Wesley Adams. The Brazilian publisher is Casa Publicadora das Assembleias de Deus.

4. See also Burdick 1993; Novaes 1985; Mafra 2001.

5. Clara Mafra (1998) argued that the explanation for why traficantes and evangélicos both flourish in favelas must be sought in the similarities of their symbolic systems, especially the similarity of their conceptions: the bandidos use weapons as an affirmation of power, and the crentes use the Word.

6. See also the work of David Smilde (2007, 70), who describes the evangelical belief in God's protection against crime and violence in Caracas, one of the most violent cities in Latin America.

7. Literally, you "close" (*fechar*) your body to safeguard it against evil spirits.

8. For a discussion of the case of the murdered reporter Tim Lopes, see chapter 3.

9. *Mensageiro da Paz*, October 2002.

10. The imagined limitless possession of space is arguably strengthened by the particular spatiotemporal actions of the Holy Spirit (see Sánchez 2008).

11. The purification rituals of the Igreja Universal exemplify their seemingly paradoxical projects in which they heavily oppose Catholic and Afro-Brazilian religious practices yet incorporate many of their popular beliefs, practices, tokens, and symbols.

12. As Zygmunt Bauman (2000, 184) has argued, body and community are often perceived as "the last defensive outposts" amid the uncertainty and insecurity so characteristic of "liquid modernity." According to Bauman, "The body's new primacy is reflected in the tendency to shape the image of community . . . after the pattern of the ideally protected body."

13. I approach conversion here according to Talal Asad's (1996, 266) insightful claim that the study of conversion is best described as the examination of "the narratives by which people apprehended and described a radical change in the significance of their lives."

14. I cannot go into the longstanding debates in the conversion literature here. The encounters between colonizers and native inhabitants regularly involved conversion practices and the reworking of local religious practices (Comaroff and Comaroff 1991; Hefner 1993; Veer 1996; Meyer 1999; Engelke 2004). Yet many Brazilians who convert to Pentecostal movements nowadays are already familiar with Catholicism and the Bible, even though they approach it differently after their conversion.

15. Pharmaceutical drugs often prescribed for people with sleeping disorders.

16. Such an understanding of conversion concurs with the work of Diane Austin-Broos (2003, 2), who argues, "To be converted is to reidentify, to learn, reorder, and reorient. It involves interrelated modes of transformation that generally continue over time and define a consistent course. Not mere syncretism, neither can conversion involve a simple and absolute break with a previous social life. Learning anew proceeds over time and requires a process of integrating knowledge and experience."

17. Such a view does not lead to open-ended storytelling. Rightfully, in my opinion, the authors stress that people do not construct stories on their own terms. Race, class, and gender, for example, are

"deep reservoirs of self-construction resources comprising influential conditions for self-narration" (Holstein and Gubrium 2000, 105).

18. My approach is indebted to the work of Judith Butler ([1990] 1999, 173–80), who argued that (gender) identity should be regarded as the appearance of substance, which is the result of the performance of certain stylized acts.

19. See also the work of Engelke (2004, 106).

20. The movement in which people enter and leave a church community has also been described as a "revolving door" process (Martin 2002, 112).

21. In Matthew 3:11–12, John the Baptist mentions both the baptism of the Holy Spirit and the baptism of fire. The popular expression *o fogo desce* (the fire comes down), often used in the morro, indicates the emotional and vivid character of the cultos.

Chapter 5

1. 93 FM is a popular evangelical radio station in Rio de Janeiro that forms part of the record company MK Publicitá. See http://www.mkpublicita.com.br.

2. Media studies scholars observe that radio and the practice of listening have been neglected fields of academic inquiry (Bessire and Fischer 2013; Lacey 2000; Tacchi 2000).

3. See the ABERT website, http://www.abert.org.br/web/index.php/bibliote cas/2013–05–22–13–32–13/category /pesquisas-sobre-o-setor-de-radiodifusao.

4. See the SECOM website, http:/www.secom.gov.br/atuacao/pesquisa/lista-de -pesquisas-quantitativas-e-qualitativas -de-contratos-atuais/pesquisa-brasileira -de-midia-pbm-2015.pdf.

5. According to its own representation of the IBOPE figures, Rádio Melodia was the second most popular FM radio station of Rio de Janeiro's metropolitan area during the month of March 2005, with an average of 194,016 listeners per minute, an audience share of 1.41: http://www.melodia.com.br /pages/audiencia.php, accessed April 25, 2005. Ten years later, it was still in that position, according to the IBOPE rankings: http://www.ouvintes.com.br/#!RJ-Ranking -Ibope-%E2%80%93-O-Dia-e-Melodia-se

-destacam-na-briga-pela-lideran%C3%A7a /c24ue/5580fa300cf299727821db3d, accessed August 5, 2015.

6. In March 2005, 93 FM was the fourth most popular FM radio station in Rio de Janeiro's metropolitan area with 86,506 listeners per minute. In 2016 it ranked sixth, with 145,488 listeners per minute. See http://www .radiodeverdade.com/destaques/2016/11/10 /ranking-radios-do-rio-de-janeiro/.

7. Alexandre Fonseca (1997, 88) notes that in the months of July and August 1996, two of the three most popular radio stations in Rio de Janeiro were evangelical.

8. On its own website, Rádio Melodia claims that the station has been the most popular broadcaster in the whole region between 2011 and 2016 among people above twenty-five years of age. See http://www .melodia.com.br/a-radio.

9. Brazilian research categorizes five consumer groups from A to E, of which A is the "wealthiest." According to Fonseca (1997), the audience of Melodia consisted of 9 percent AB, 29 percent C, and 62 percent DE, while 93 FM had 8 percent AB, 56 per- cent C, and 36 percent DE. This pattern has changed. Listeners generally have more to spend twenty years later. Between October and December 2016 Melodia had 14.1 percent AB, 54.6 percent C, and 31.3 percent DE, while in October 2016, 93 FM had 20 percent AB, 63 percent C, and 17 percent DE. See http://www.melodia.com.br/a-radio and http://radio93.com.br/comercial.

10. According to the data Janice Perlman (2003) collected in five favelas in Rio de Janeiro, the percentage of people who had a sound system in their house went up from 25 percent in 1969 to 79 percent in 2001. This means that during her research in 2001, roughly four out of every five households had such a setup. Sound systems generally consist of a radio, a CD player, and cassette player and often occupy a central place in the living room.

11. José attended an Assembleia de Deus in Visionário.

12. As Maxwell Pinheiro Fajardo (2015) notes, many conservative adherents of the Assembleia de Deus considered television a threat to their spiritual well-being until the 1970s, although progressive adherents had pleaded to use the medium for evangelical purposes before that time.

13. R. R. Soares, whom I will describe in more detail in the next chapter, is the leader of the neo-Pentecostal church Igreja Internacional da Graça de Deus.

14. *Arrastão* is a type of collective robbery that happens from time to time on the beaches of Rio de Janeiro. *Arrastar* can be translated as "dragging."

15. While Brazilian gospel music has incorporated many styles and genres (rap/hip-hop, hard rock, forró) during the last few decades, most Brazilian gospel music demonstrates a distinctive influence of North American gospel music, which itself is influenced primarily by jazz, rock, and pop.

16. Cassiane was born in 1975. Her family took her to the Assembleia de Deus de Nova Iguaçu, where she still congregates today. Most of Cassiane's songs are low-tempo ballads that express great emotional experience in relation to life and God.

17. *Conexão Gospel* is a gospel music television program broadcast on CNT. Many Assembleia de Deus congregants mentioned this program as one of their favorites.

18. Although Pastor Marcelo Crivella is affiliated with a different record company, he also recorded the duet "Glória a Jesus" with Cassiane on his CD *Ajuda Teu Irmão do Sertão* (Help your brother from the Sertão [dry hinterland]). Most of his songs are low-tempo ballads.

19. See http://www.melodia.com.br/pages/programacao.php.

20. For a detailed analysis of the word *amigo/amiga* in the discourse of Edir Macedo and pastors of the Igreja Universal, see Kramer 2001b, 151.

21. Bispo Rodrigues of the Igreja Universal, cited in Fonseca 1997, 195.

22. Arolde de Oliveira, owner of 93 FM, cited in ibid., 194.

23. For people who attend the Assembleia de Deus, the wish to be baptized by the Holy Spirit often follows their acceptance of Jesus and baptism in water. Since not all people experience such a baptism immediately after their decision to accept Jesus, some feel they need to make an extra effort to live according to biblical norms.

24. What may be experienced by some as a very intimate experience with the Word (or sound) of God, others experience as an intrusion in their private space. The emphasis on separation in the religious

sense also points to the quality of radio as an electroacoustic instrument that may help separate someone in the physical sense of the word, much as electroacoustic devices block other sounds in the environment.

25. Jay David Bolter and Richard Grusin (1999, 5) argue that contemporary culture is characterized by the twin logic of hypermediacy and immediacy: "Our culture wants to multiply its media and to erase all traces of mediation: ideally, it wants to erase its media in the very act of multiplying them."

26. Several writers on "religion and/as media" (Stolow 2005) have suggested a more complex relation between the production of (religious) truth, mass media, and the senses (Hirschkind 2004; Eisenlohr 2009; Meyer 2006; Schmidt 2000).

27. The emphasis on the ear in this chapter is not to say that electroacoustic media do not invoke other senses. In fact, the senses appear firmly entangled with one another (see Bull 2004; Hirschkind 2001; Marks 2000).

28. See Campos 1997; Kramer 2001b; Mafra 2002.

29. Mostly in relation to an *oferta* (the donation of money). I will not go into the important place of money in the Igreja Universal in depth. For further reading, see Oro and Semán 1999; Mariano 1999; Campos 1997; Kramer 2001b.

30. See, for example, Steven Connor's (1999) work on the mirroring of communicational technologies in Spiritualism in the nineteenth and twentieth centuries.

31. The distinction between música evangélica and música do mundo does not imply that people no longer listen to pagode music; such classifications are contingent and therefore change constantly.

32. As we will see in the next chapter, this also holds for television, though in a slightly different manner.

33. See also Novaes 1985; Burdick 1993; Mafra 2001.

34. This argument resembles Bourdieu's (1984, 19) insistence on seeing (musical) taste in relation to the drive for distinctions among social classes. Yet there are considerable differences. People who distinguish between música evangélica and música do mundo generally belong to the same economic class and have enjoyed the

same kind of schooling as those from whom they want to distance themselves. It is therefore not socioeconomic class or scarcity of cultural capital that inspires the appropriation of a different musical taste.

35. How Brazilian gospel funk artists critique and rework carioca funk bears many resemblances to how Trinidadian gospel dancehall artists use lyrics to "warn against the very issues that so concern church leaders" (Rommen 2007, 112).

36. At certain points in her work, Luhrmann's interlocutors use similar electroacoustic metaphors to describe their sonic relation to God: "One man explained how much his experience of God had changed since coming to the Vineyard. 'God's voice is like a fuzzy radio station, 95.2, 94.9, that needs more tuning. You're picking up the song, and it's not so clear sometimes. It's clearer to me now'" (Luhrmann 2012, 114).

Chapter 6

1. See the work of Eric Kramer (2001a) about the court case, in which lawyers and judges had to argue over the status of the statue as either a religious or a profane object for the bispo who kicked it, in relation to the status it held for a large part of the Brazilian society.

2. Protestants made ample use of imagery in their evangelizing practices in a colonial context, as David Morgan (2005) and Isabel Hofmeyr (2004) have shown.

3. R. Laurence Moore (1994) and Colleen McDannell (1995) have both emphasized form and style in North American Christian movements in relation to the commoditization of Christianity.

4. For further reading on the place of these objects and their relation to other Brazilian religious practices, see Campos 1997. According to Campos (61–112), these objects are important features of the constitution of the church as *templo-teatro* (theater-temple).

5. See http://www.cpad.com.br.

6. For discussions on the history of the telenovelas, see Hamburger 1998.

7. Record and Globo both aired news programs, but only Record broadcast *Cidade Alerta* (Watchful city), which featured

spectacular police operations (see also chapter 3). SBT and Globo each offered a reality show, *Casa dos Artistas* on SBT and *Big Brother Brasil* on Globo. Record and Globo both offered soccer matches. The rest of the television stations offered similar programs.

8. SBT featured the popular program *Ratinho* (Little Mouse), a talk show that revolved around people who accused one another of all sorts of things, including dramatized fights over legal paternity. In these programs the DNA of men and babies were compared to decide whether alimony had to be paid.

9. Some people mentioned Silas Malafaia's program *Vitória em Cristo*, broadcast on Rede TV, and others the gospel music program *Conexão Gospel*.

10. Most people watched his program *Show da Fé* on CNT (channel 9) or on TV Band (channel 7). *Show da Fé* features R. R. Soares preaching in church.

11. As Fonseca (2003) also confirms, the programs *Fala que Eu te Escuto* (Speak and I will listen), broadcast in the afternoon, and *Despertar da Fé* (The awakening of faith), broadcast in the early morning, were both replaced by *Ponto de Luz* in 2001.

12. Programs such as *Ponto de Luz* seemed to be aimed primarily at those who did not yet attend the Igreja Universal. This would seem to confirm the work of both Kramer (2005) and Fonseca (2003), who conclude that the main object of the Igreja Universal is to attract people to its churches for revenue.

13. The title of the program is a direct reference to George Orwell's novel *Nineteen Eighty-Four*, in which citizens are victims of continuous television surveillance by the state, whose leader goes by the name "Big Brother."

14. The television program *Big Brother* was created by the Dutch media corporation John de Mol Produkties and first broadcast in the Netherlands in 1999. The show achieved worldwide popularity when it was sold in other countries, such as the United States and Brazil.

15. The program *Big Brother* was "Brazilianized" from the outset. When it was introduced in Brazil, the group of contestants consisted of a carefully selected variety of "Brazilians": people from different Brazilian states and cities with different

regional accents, backgrounds, and religious affiliations. The program reproduced an image of unity in diversity, giving spectators from different regions and backgrounds the possibility of identifying with the contestants. A common critique was that in fact the majority of the contestants of *BBB* were white, middle-class individuals whose appearances matched the beauty ideals reproduced in popular magazines and advertisements.

16. According to the newspaper *O Globo*, *Big Brother Brasil* attracted an average of 41.5 million viewers per minute, which is 57 percent of possible viewers. See *"Big Brother Brasil* bate recorde no horário," *O Globo*, April 4, 2002.

17. Pedro Paulo Pitto, *O Pasquim 21*, March 26, 2002.

18. See "A programação de mal a pior," *Carta Capital*, March 6, 2002. Before Globo introduced *Big Brother Brasil*, the format of the program had already been "copied" by the broadcast company SBT, which named its program *Casa dos Artistas* (House of artists). Though not as interactive as *BBB*, *Casa dos Artistas* also showed a group of people enclosed in a house under constant camera surveillance.

19. Arguably, this stance of the critics was also paternalistic.

20. Fernando Barbosa Lima, *Jornal do Brasil*, March 27, 2003.

21. *Enfoque*, no. 7 (2002): 41.

22. Pastor Carlos Rodrigues, *Folha Universal*, March 10, 2002. Emphasis added.

23. See the website of Silas Malafaia, "O lixo do big brother; veja comentário do Pr.," *Verdade Gospel*, January 20, 2012, http://www.verdadegospel.com/o-lixo-do-big-brother-veja-comentario-do-pr-silas-malafaia/.

24. TV Record broadcasts evangelical programs but also screens Hollywood movies and telenovelas.

25. Pedro Bial, journalist and host of *Big Brother Brasil*, TV Globo, February 26, 2002.

26. In particular, the nightly broadcasts of the Igreja Universal on TV Record enforced this spectator position. The Igreja Universal has developed a visual technique by which to present the work of the devil and the work of God. In small clips, the work of the devil is visualized by showing "real" images of the lives of "real" people who testify that they have been possessed by demons and therefore lived in misery until they started attending the Igreja Universal. During these testimonies, "flashbacks" show unhappy people in miserable conditions. The clips, filmed in black and white or with vague and blurred camerawork, represent the "dark" period, when the people were still under the spell of the demons. These images are followed by colorful images of the lives of people "illuminated" by the presence of the Holy Spirit.

27. André Bakker (2007) encountered a very similar engagement with television among the evangélicos on Ilha Grande, Brazil. His informants generally described being firm (*firme*) in relation to the televisual temptations of the devil as being "structured in the Word."

28. Take, for example, the study *A leitura social da novela das oito* by Ondina Fachel Leal (1986).

29. The telenovela *Malhação* differs considerably from other telenovelas in that it pictures the lives of Brazilian high school students, is aimed at that age group, and has returned to the screen each year since 1995.

30. See also Freedberg 1989; Gordon and Hancock 2005; Morgan 2005.

31. See the article by Anna Weiss, "Game of Bíblia," *IstoÉ*, June 19, 2015, http://www.istoe.com.br/reportagens/423415_GAME+OF+BIBLIA?.

32. After having worked at TV Globo for a long time, Xuxa signed a contract with TV Record in March 2015. According to Chico Felitti, Xuxa's contract states that she cannot speak about religion on television. See "'Só não posso falar de religião,' diz Xuxa sobre seu programa na Record," *Folha de S. Paulo*, August 11, 2015, http://www1.folha.uol.com.br/ilustrada/2015/08/1667163-so-nao-posso-falar-de-religiao-diz-xuxa-sobre-seu-programa-na-record.shtml.

Bibliography

Abreu, Maria José Alves de. 2002. "On Charisma, Mediation and Broken Screens." *Etnofoor* 15 (1–2): 240–58.

———. 2005. "Breathing into the Heart of the Matter: Why Padre Marcelo Needs No Wings." *Postscripts* 1 (2–3): 325–49.

Abumanssur, Edin S. 2015. "Faith and Crime in the Construction of Social Coexistence in the Outskirts of São Paulo." *Social Compass* 62 (3): 396–411.

Agamben, Giorgio. 1998. *Homo Sacer: Sovereign Power and Bare Life.* Stanford, CA: Stanford University Press.

———. 2005. *State of Exception.* Chicago: University of Chicago Press.

Althouse, Peter, and Michael Wilkinson. 2015. "Musical Bodies in the Charismatic Renewal: The Case of Catch the Fire and Soaking Prayer." In *The Spirit of Praise: Music and Worship in Pentecostal-Charismatic Christianity*, edited by Monique M. Ingalls and Amos Yong, 29–44. University Park: Pennsylvania State University Press.

Alvito, Marcos. 1998. "Um bicho-de-sete-cabeças." In *Um século de favela*, edited by Alba Zaluar and Marcus Alvito. Rio de Janeiro: Editora Fundação Getulio Vargas.

———. 2001. *As cores de Acari, uma favela carioca.* Rio de Janeiro: Editora FGV.

Amin, Ash, and Nigel Thrift. 2002. *Cities: Reimagining the Urban.* Cambridge, UK: Polity Press.

Amorim, Carlos. 1993. *Comando vermelho: A história secreta do crime organizado.* Rio de Janeiro: Editora Record.

Anderson, Allan, Michael Bergunder, André F. Droogers, and Cornelis van der Laan, eds. 2010. *Studying Global Pentecostalism: Theories and Methods.* Berkeley: University of California Press.

Antoniazzi, Alberto. 1994. "A Igreja Católica face a expansão do Pentecostalismo." In *Nem anjos nem demônios: Interpretações sociológicas do pentecostalismo*, edited by Alberto Antoniazzi, 17–23. Rio de Janeiro: Editora Vozes.

Appadurai, Arjun. 1996. *Modernity at Large: Cultural Dimensions of Globalization.* Minneapolis: University of Minnesota Press.

Appleby, R. Scott. 2000. *The Ambivalence of the Sacred: Religion, Violence, and the Sacred.* Lanham, MD: Rowan and Littlefield.

Arias, Enrique Desmond. 2006. *Drugs and Democracy in Rio de Janeiro: Trafficking, Social Networks, and Public Security.* Chapel Hill: University of North Carolina Press.

Arias, Enrique Desmond, and Daniel M. Goldstein, eds. 2010. *Violent Democracies in Latin America.* Durham, NC: Duke University Press.

Asad, Talal. 1993. *Genealogies of Religion: Discipline and Reasons of Power in Christianity and Islam.* Baltimore: Johns Hopkins University Press.

———. 1996. "Comments on Conversion." In *Conversion to Modernities: The Globalization of Christianity*, edited by Peter van der Veer, 263–73. New York: Routledge.

———. 2003. *Formations of the Secular: Christianity, Islam, Modernity.* Stanford, CA: Stanford University Press.

Attali, Jacques. 1985. *Noise: The Political Economy of Music.* Minneapolis: University of Minnesota Press.

Austin-Broos, Diane. 2003. "The Anthropology of Conversion: An Introduction." In *The Anthropology of Religious Conversion*, edited by Andrew Buckser and Stephen D. Glazier, 1–12. Lanham, MD: Rowman & Littlefield.

Avelar, Idelber, and Christopher Dunn. 2011. "Introduction: Music as Practice of Citizenship in Brazil." In *Brazilian Popular Music and Citizenship*, edited by Idelber Avelar and Christopher Dunn, 1–27. Durham, NC: Duke University Press.

Bakker, André. 2007. "God, Devil, and the Work of Television: Modern Mass Media and Pentecostal Christianity in an Evangelical Community in Brazil." Master's thesis, Vrije Universiteit Amsterdam.

Banck, Geert A. 1998. "Personalism in the Brazilian Body Politic: Political Rallies and Public Ceremonies in the Era of Mass Democracy." *European Review of Latin American and Caribbean Studies* 65: 25–43.

Barcellos, Christovam, and Alba Zaluar. 2014. "Homicides and Territorial Struggles in Rio de Janeiro Favelas." *Revista de Saúde Pública* 48 (1): 94–102.

Bauman, Zygmunt. 2000. *Liquid Modernity.* Cambridge, UK: Polity Press.

Baumann, Gerd. 1996. *Contesting Culture: Discourses of Identity in Multi-Ethnic London.* Cambridge, UK: Cambridge University Press.

Bellotti, Karina Kosicki. 2003. "Uma luz para o seu caminho: A mídia Presbiteriana no Brasil no caso de 'luz para o caminho' (1976–2001)." Master's thesis, University of Campinas.

———. 2009. "'Delas é o reino dos céus': Mídia evangélica infantil e o supermercado cultural religioso no Brasil (Anos 1950 a 2000)." *História* 28 (1): 621–52.

Berger, Peter L., and Thomas Luckmann. 1966. *The Social Construction of Reality: A Treatise in the Sociology of Knowledge.* Harmondsworth, UK: Penguin.

Bessire, Lucas, and Daniel Fischer. 2013. "The Anthropology of Radio Fields." *Annual Review of Anthropology* 42 (1): 363–78.

Beyer, Peter. 2006. *Religions in Global Society.* London: Routledge.

Bialecki, Jon. 2015. "Tongues, Academic, and Ecstatic: Affect as Key to Neo-Charismatic Language, Embodiment, and Genre." In *The Anthropology of Global Pentecostalism and Evangelicalism*, edited by Simon Coleman and Rosalind I. J. Hackett, 95–108. New York: New York University Press.

Birman, Patricia. 2006. "Future in the Mirror: The Media, Evangelicals, and Politics in Rio de Janeiro." In *Religion, Media, and the Public Sphere*, edited by Birgit Meyer and Annelies Moors, 52–72. Bloomington: Indiana University Press.

———. 2008. "Favela é comunidade?" In *Vida sob cerco: Violência e rotina nas favelas do Rio de Janeiro*, edited by Luiz Antonio Machado da Silva, 99–114. Rio de Janeiro: Nova Fronteira.

Birman, Patricia, and David Lehmann. 1999. "Religion and the Media in a Battle for Ideological Hegemony: The Universal Church of the Kingdom of God and TV Globo in Brazil." *Bulletin of Latin American Research* 18 (2): 145–64.

Birman, Patricia, and Marcia Pereira Leite. 2000. "Whatever Happened to What Used to Be the Largest Catholic Country in the World?" *Daedalus* 129 (2): 271–91.

Blacking, John. 1987. *A Commonsense View of All Music: Reflections on Percy Grainger's Contribution to*

Ethnomusicology and Music Education. Cambridge, UK: Cambridge University Press.

Bolter, Jay David, and Richard Grusin. 1999. *Remediation: Understanding New Media.* Cambridge, UK: MIT Press.

Boudewijnse, Barbara, André Droogers, and Frans Kamsteeg, eds. 1998. *More Than Opium: An Anthropological Approach to Latin American and Caribbean Pentecostal Praxis.* Lanham, MD: Scarecrow Press.

Bourdieu, Pierre. 1984. *Distinction: A Social Critique of the Judgement of Taste.* Cambridge, MA: Harvard University Press.

Boyer, Paul S. 2005. "Biblical Prophecy and Foreign Policy." In *Quoting God: How Media Shape Ideas About Religion and Culture*, edited by Claire Hoertz Badaracco, 107–22. Waco, TX: Baylor University Press.

Brito, F., and J. A. Carvalho. 2006. "As migrações internas no Brasil e as novidades sugeridas pelos Censos Demográficos de 1991 e 2000 e pelas PNADs recentes." *Parcerias Estratégicas* 22: 441–55.

Brubaker, Rogers. 2004. *Ethnicity Without Groups.* Cambridge, MA: Harvard University Press.

Bucci, Eugênio. 1997. *Brasil en tempo de TV.* São Paulo: Boitempo Editorial.

Buckser, Andrew, and Stephen D. Glazier. 2003. *The Anthropology of Religious Conversion.* Lanham, MD: Rowman & Littlefield.

Bull, Michael. 2004. "Thinking About Sound, Proximity, and Distance in Western Experience: The Case of Odysseus's Walkman." In *Hearing Cultures: Essays on Sound, Listening and Modernity*, edited by Veit Erlmann, 173–90. Oxford, UK: Berg.

Burdick, John. 1993. *Looking for God in Brazil: The Progressive Catholic Church in Urban Brazil's Religious Arena.* Berkeley: University of California Press.

——. 1998. *Blessed Anastácia: Women, Race, and Popular Christianity in Brazil.* New York: Routledge.

——. 2013. *The Color of Sound: Race, Religion, and Music in Brazil.* New York: New York University Press.

Butler, Judith. (1990) 1999. *Gender Trouble: Feminism and the Subversion of Identity.* New York: Routledge.

——. 2004. *Precarious Life: The Powers of Mourning and Violence.* London: Verso.

Cabral, Sergio. 1996. *A MPB na era do rádio.* São Paulo: Moderna.

Caldeira, Teresa P. R. 2000. *City of Walls: Crime, Segregation, and Citizenship in São Paulo.* Berkeley: University of California Press.

Caldeira, Teresa P. R., and James Holston. 1999. "Democracy and Violence in Brazil." *Comparative Studies in Society and History* 41 (4): 691–729.

Campbell, Heidi. 2010. *When Religion Meets New Media: Media, Religion, and Culture.* London: Routledge.

Campos, Leonildo Silveira. 1997. *Teatro, templo e mercado: Organização e marketing de um empreendimento neo-pentecostal.* Rio de Janeiro: Vozes.

Carroll, Noël. 1998. "Is the Medium a (Moral) Message?" In *Media Ethics*, edited by Matthew Kieran, 135–51. London: Routledge.

Casanova, José. 1994. *Public Religions in the Modern World.* Chicago: University of Chicago Press.

Cavalcanti, Mariana. 2008. "Tiroteios, legibilidade e espaço urbano: Notas etnográficas de uma favela carioca." *Dilemas: Revista de Estudos de Conflito e Controle Social* 1: 35–59.

Cecchetto, Fátima Regina. 1998. "Galeras funk Cariocas: Os bailes e a constituição do ethos guerreiro." In *Um Século de Favela*, edited by Alba Zaluar and Marcus Alvito, 145–66. Rio de Janeiro: Editora Fundação Getulio Vargas.

Coimbra, Cecilia. 2001. *Operação Rio: O mito das classes perigosas.* Niterói, Brazil: Intertexto.

Coleman, Simon. 2000. *The Globalisation of Charismatic Christianity: Spreading the Gospel of Prosperity.* Cambridge, UK: Cambridge University Press.

Coleman, Simon, and Rosalind I. J. Hackett, eds. 2015. *The Anthropology of Global Pentecostalism and Evangelicalism.* New York: New York University Press.

229

Connor, Steven. 1999. "The Machine in the Ghost: Spiritualism, Technology, and the 'Direct Voice.'" In *Ghosts: Deconstruction, Psychoanalysis, History*, edited by Peter Buse and Andrew Stoll, 203–25. London: Macmillan.

———. 2004. "Edison's Teeth: Touching Hearing." In *Hearing Cultures: Essays on Sound, Listening, and Modernity*, edited by Veit Erlmann, 153–72. Oxford, UK: Berg.

Comaroff, Jean, and John L. Comaroff. 1991. *Of Revelation and Revolution, Volume 1: Christianity, Colonialism, and Consciousness in South Africa*. Chicago: University of Chicago Press.

———. 2000. "Millennial Capitalism: First Thoughts on a Second Coming." *Public Culture* 12 (2): 291–343.

Conrado, Flávio Cesar. 2001. "Política e mídia: A Igreja Universal do Reino de Deus nas eleições." *Religião e Sociedade* 21 (2): 85–111.

Corbin, Alain. 2000. *Village Bells: Sound and Meaning in Nineteenth-Century French Countryside*. New York: Columbia University Press.

Corten, André, and Ruth Marshall-Fratani. 2001. "Introduction." In *Between Babel and Pentecost: Transnational Pentecostalism in Africa and Latin America*, edited by André Corten and Ruth Marshall-Fratani, 1–21. Bloomington: Indiana University Press.

Cox, Harvey. 1995. *Fire from Heaven. The Rise of Pentecostal Spirituality and the Reshaping of Religion in the Twenty-First Century*. Cambridge, MA: Da Capo Press.

Csordas, Thomas. 2009. "Global Religion and the Reenchantment of the World: The Case of the Catholic Charismatic Renewal." In *Transnational Transcendence: Essays on Religion and Globalization*, edited by Thomas J. Csordas, 73–96. Berkeley: University of California Press.

Cunha, Christina Vital da. 2002. "'Ocupação Evangélica': Efeitos do Crescimento Pentecostal na Favela de Acari." Master's thesis, Universidade Federal do Rio de Janeiro.

———. 2008. "'Traficantes evangélicos': Novas formas de experimentação do sagrado em favelas cariocas." *Plural* 15: 23–46.

Cunha, Magali do Nascimento. 2007. *A explosão gospel: Um olhar das Ciências Humanas sobre o cenário Evangélico no Brasil*. Rio de Janeiro: Mauad.

Dant, Tim. 2012. *Television and the Moral Imaginary: Society Through the Small Screen*. New York: Palgrave.

Dantas, José Guibson. 2008. "O Deus televisivo da IURD: Análise de um programa-modelo para a corrente Neopentecostal." *Caligrama* 4 (1): 7–15.

Davis, Mike. 2004. "Planet of Slums." *New Left Review* 26 (37): 5–34.

Deleuze, Gilles, and Félix Guattari. 1987. *A Thousand Plateaus: Capitalism and Schizophrenia*. Minneapolis: University of Minnesota Press.

Derrida, Jacques. 2001. "Above All, No Journalists!" In *Religion and Media*, edited by Hent de Vries and Samuel Weber, 56–93. Stanford, CA: Stanford University Press.

Dolghie, Jacqueline Ziroldo. 2007. "Por uma sociologia da produção e reprodução musical do presbiterian-ismo brasileiro: A tendência gospel e sua influência no culto." PhD diss., Methodist University of São Paulo.

Douglas, Mary. (1966) 2002. *Purity and Danger: An Analysis of Concepts of Pollution and Taboo*. New York: Routledge.

Douglas, Susan, J. 1999. *Listening In: Radio and the American Imagination, from Amos 'n' Andy and Edward R. Murrow to Wolfman Jack and Howard Stern*. New York: Times Books.

Dowdney, Luke. 2003. *Crianças do tráfico: Um estudo de caso de crianças em violência armada organizada no Rio de Janeiro*. Rio de Janeiro: 7 Letras.

Droogers, André. 1998. "Paradoxical Views on a Paradoxical Religion: Models for the Explanation of Pentecostal Expansion in Brazil and Chile." In *More Than Opium: An Anthropological Approach to Latin American and Caribbean Pentecostal Praxis*, edited by Barbara Boudewijnse, André Droogers, and

Frans Kamsteeg, 1–34. Lanham, MD: Scarecrow Press.

———. 2001. "Globalisation and Pentecostal Success." In *Between Babel and Pentecost: Transnational Pentecostalism in Africa and Latin America*, edited by André Corten and Ruth Marshall-Fratani, 41–61. Bloomington: Indiana University Press.

Eisenlohr, Patrick. 2006. *Little India: Diaspora, Time, and Ethnolinguistic Belonging in Hindu Mauritius*. Berkeley: University of California Press.

———. 2009. "Technologies of the Spirit: Devotional Islam, Sound Reproduction, and the Dialectics of Mediation and Immediacy in Mauritius." *Anthropological Theory* 9 (3): 273–96.

Enders, Armelle. 2002. *A História do Rio de Janeiro*. Rio de Janeiro: Gryphus.

Engelke, Matthew. 2004. "Discontinuity and the Discourse of Conversion." *Journal of Religion in Africa* 34 (1–2): 82–109.

———. 2007. *A Problem of Presence: Beyond Scripture in an African Church*. Berkeley: University of California Press.

Erlmann, Veit. 2004. "But What of the Ethnographic Ear? Anthropology, Sound, and the Senses." In *Hearing Cultures: Essays on Sound, Listening and Modernity*, edited by Veit Erlmann, 1–20. Oxford, UK: Berg.

Fairclough, Norman. 1995. *Media Discourse*. London: Arnold.

Fajardo, Maxwell Pinheiro. 2015. "'Onde a luta se travar': A expansão das Assembleias de Deus no Brasil urbano (1946–1980)." PhD diss., São Paulo State University.

Fausto, Boris. 1999. *A Concise History of Brazil*. Cambridge, UK: Cambridge University Press.

Feld, Steven. 1994. "From Schizophonia to Schismogenesis: On the Discourses and Commodification Practices of 'World Music' and 'World Beat.'" In *Music Grooves: Essays and Dialogues*, edited by Charles Keil and Steven Feld, 257–89. Chicago: University of Chicago Press.

———. 1996. "Waterfalls of Song: An Acoustemology of Place Resounding in Bosavi, Papua New Guinea." In *Senses of Place*, edited by Steven Feld and Keith H. Basso, 91–135. Santa Fe: School of American Research Press.

Fernandes, Rubem César, et al. 1998. *Novo nascimento: Os evangélicos em casa, na igreja e na política*. Rio de Janeiro: Mauad.

Fiske, John. 1989. *Understanding Popular Culture*. London: Routledge.

Flausino, Cristina Valéria. 2003. "Chorro gratuito: A violência no tele-jornalismo Brasileiro." Paper presented at the annual conference of the Brazilian Association of Communication Sciences, Belo Horizonte, Brazil.

Flordelis. 2011. *Flordelis: A incrível história da mulher que venceu a pobreza e o preconceito para ser mãe de cinquenta filhos*. Rio de Janeiro: Thomas Nelson Brasil.

Fonseca, Alexandre. 1997. *Evangélicos e a mídia no Brasil*. Rio de Janeiro: IFCS/UFRJ.

———. 1998. "Lideranças evangélicas na mídia: Trajetorias na política e na sociedade civil." *Religião e Sociedade* 19 (1): 85–111.

———. 2003. "Fé na tela: Características e ênfases de duas estratégias evangélicas na televisão." *Religião e Sociedade* 23 (2): 33–53.

———. 2008. "Religion and Democracy in Brazil: A Study of the Leading Evangelical Politicians." In *Evangelical Christianity and Democracy in Latin America*, edited by Paul Freston, 163–206. New York: Oxford University Press.

Foucault, Michel. 1978. *The Will to Knowledge: The History of Sexuality, Vol. 1*. London: Penguin.

———. (1978) 1991. "Governmentality." In *The Foucault Effect: Studies in Governmentality*, edited by Graham Burchell, Colin Gordon, and Peter Miller, 87–104. Chicago: University of Chicago Press.

Freedberg, David. 1989. *The Power of Images: Studies in the History and Theory of Response*. Chicago: University of Chicago Press.

231

Freston, Paul. 1994. "Popular Protestants in Brazilian Politics: A Novel Turn in Sect-State Relations." *Social Compass* 41 (4): 537–70.

———. 1995. "Pentecostalism in Brazil: A Brief History." *Religion* 25 (2): 119–33.

———. 2005. "The Universal Church of the Kingdom of God: A Brazilian Church Finds Success in Southern Africa." *Journal of Religion in Africa* 35 (1): 332–65.

———. 2008. "Introduction: The Many Faces of Evangelical Politics in Latin America." In *Evangelical Christianity and Democracy in Latin America*, edited by Paul Freston, 3–36. New York: Oxford University Press.

Frith, Simon. 1996. "Music and Identity." In *Questions of Cultural Identity*, edited by Stuart Hall and Paul du Gay, 108–27. London: Sage.

Garmany, Jeff. 2010. "Religion and Governmentality: Understanding Governance in Urban Brazil." *Geoforum* 41 (6): 908–18.

Garnham, Nicholas. 1992. "The Media and the Public Sphere." In *Habermas and the Public Sphere*, edited by Craig Calhoun, 359–76. Cambridge, MA: MIT Press.

Garrard-Burnett, Virginia, and David Stoll, eds. 1993. *Rethinking Protestantism in Latin America*. Philadelphia: Temple University Press.

Gay, Robert. 1994. *Popular Organization and Democracy in Rio de Janeiro: A Tale of Two Favelas*. Philadelphia: Temple University Press.

———. 2005. *Lucia: Testimonies of a Brazilian Drug Dealer's Woman*. Philadelphia: Temple University Press.

———. 2010. "Toward Uncivil Society: Causes and Consequences of Violence in Rio de Janeiro." In *Violent Democracies in Latin America*, edited by Daniel M. Goldstein and Enrique Desmond Arias, 201–25. Durham, NC: Duke University Press.

———. 2015. *Bruno: Conversations with a Brazilian Drug Dealer*. Durham, NC: Duke University Press.

Gershon, Ilana. 2010. "Media Ideologies: An Introduction." *Journal of Linguistic Anthropology* 20 (2): 283–93.

Gillespie, Marie. 1995. *Television, Ethnicity and Cultural Change*. London: Routledge.

Goldstein, Donna. 2003. *Laughter Out of Place: Race, Class, Violence, and Sexuality in a Rio Shantytown*. Berkeley: University of California Press.

Gomes, Edlaine de Campos. 2009. "Ser única e universal: Materializando a autenticidade na cidade do Rio de Janeiro." In *Religiões e cidades: Rio de Janeiro e São Paulo*, edited by Clara Mafra and Ronaldo de Almeida, 111–32. São Paulo: Terceiro Nome.

Gonçalves, Honorilton da Costa. 1996. *Lágrimas de perdão*. Rio de Janeiro: Editora Gráfica Universal.

Gordon, Colin. 1991. "Governmental Rationality: An Introduction." In *The Foucault Effect: Studies in Governmentality*, edited by Graham Burchell, Colin Gordon, and Peter Miller, 1–52. Chicago: University of Chicago Press.

Gordon, Tamar, and Mary Hancock. 2005. "'The Crusade Is the Vision': Branding Charisma in a Global Pentecostal Ministry." *Material Religion* 1 (3): 386–404.

Gormly, Eric Kevin. 1999. "The Study of Religion and the Education of Journalists." *Journalism and Mass Communication Educator* 54 (2): 24–40.

———. 2003. "Evangelizing Through Appropriation: Toward a Cultural Theory on the Growth of Contemporary Christian Music." *Journal of Media and Religion* 2 (4): 251–65.

Guimarães, Patricia. 1997. "Ritos do Reino de Deus: Pentecostalismo e invenção ritual." Master's thesis, Universidade do Estado do Rio de Janeiro.

Hackett, Rosalind I. J. 1998. "Charismatic/Pentecostal Appropriation of Media Technologies in Nigeria and Ghana." *Journal of Religion in Africa* 28 (3): 258–77.

Hamburger, Esther. 1998. "Diluindo fronteiras: A televisão e as novelas no cotidiano." In *História da vida privada no Brasil: Contrastes da intimidade contemporânea*, edited by Fernando A.

Novaes and Lilia Moritz Schwarcz, 439–88. São Paulo: Companhia das Letras.

Hancock, Mary, and Smriti Srinivas. 2008. "Spaces of Modernity: Religion and the Urban in Asia and Africa." *International Journal of Urban and Regional Research* 32 (3): 617–30.

Hansen, Thomas Blom, and Finn Stepputat. 2006. "Sovereignty Revisited." *Annual Review of Anthropology* 35: 295–315.

Harding, Susan. 1993. "The Born-Again Telescandals." In *Culture/Power/History: A Reader in Contemporary Social History*, edited by Nicholas B. Dirks, Geoff Eley, and Sherry B. Ortner, 539–56. Princeton, NJ: Princeton University Press.

———. 2000. *The Book of Jerry Falwell: Fundamentalist Language and Politics.* Princeton, NJ: Princeton University Press.

Hayward, Keith. 2010. "Opening the Lens: Cultural Criminology and the Image." In *Framing Crime: Cultural Criminology and the Image*, edited by Keith Hayward, and Mike Presdee, 1–16. London: Routledge.

Hefner, Robert W. 1993. "World Building and the Rationality of Conversion." In *Conversion to Christianity: Historical and Anthropological Perspectives on a Great Transformation*, edited by Robert W. Hefner, 3–44. Berkeley: University of California Press.

Hendy, David. 2000. *Radio in the Global Age.* Cambridge, UK: Polity Press.

Hervieu-Leger, Daniele. 2002. "Space and Religion: New Approaches to Religious Spatiality in Modernity." *International Journal of Urban and Regional Research* 26 (1): 99–105.

Hirschkind, Charles. 2001. "The Ethics of Cassette-Sermon Audition in Contemporary Egypt." *American Ethnologist* 28 (3): 623–49.

———. 2004. "Hearing Modernity: Egypt, Islam, and the Pious Ear." In *Hearing Cultures: Essays on Sound, Listening, and Modernity*, edited by Veit Erlmann, 131–52. Oxford, UK: Berg.

———. 2006. *The Ethical Soundscape: Cassette Sermons and Islamic Counterpublics.* New York: Columbia University Press.

———. 2011. "Media, Mediation, Religion." *Social Anthropology* 19 (1): 90–98.

Hirschkind, Charles, and Brian Larkin. 2008. "Introduction: Media and the Political Forms of Religion." *Social Text* 26 (3): 1–9.

Hjarvard, Stig. 2008. "The Mediatization of Religion: A Theory of the Media as Agents of Religious Change." *Northern Lights* 6 (1): 9–26.

Hofmeyr, Isabel. 2004. *The Portable Bunyan: A Transnational History of the Pilgrim's Progress.* Princeton, NJ: Princeton University Press.

Holstein, James A., and Jaber F. Gubrium. 2000. *The Self We Live By: Narrative Identity in a Postmodern World.* New York: Oxford University Press.

Holston, James. 2008. *Insurgent Citizenship: Disjunctions of Democracy and Modernity in Brazil.* Princeton, NJ: Princeton University Press.

Hoover, Stewart. 1998. *Religion in the News: Faith and Journalism in American Public Discourse.* Thousand Oaks, CA: Sage.

———. 2002. "The Culturalist Turn in Scholarship on Media and Religion." *Journal of Media and Religion* 1 (1): 25–36.

———. 2006. *Religion in the Media Age.* London: Routledge.

Hoover, Stewart, and Lynn Schofield Clark, eds. 2002. *Practicing Religion in the Age of Media: Explorations in Media, Religion and Culture.* New York: Columbia University Press.

Hoover, Stewart, and Knut Lundby, eds. 1997. *Rethinking Media, Religion, and Culture.* Thousand Oaks, CA: Sage.

Howard, Jay R., and John M. Streck. 1999. *Apostles of Rock: The Splintered World of Contemporary Christian Music.* Lexington: University Press of Kentucky.

Hughes, Stephen P. 2002. "The 'Music Boom' in Tamil South India: Gramophone, Radio, and the Making of Mass Culture. *Historical Journal of Film, Radio and Television* 22 (4): 445–73.

Hunt, Stephen. 2010. "Sociology of Religion." In *Studying Global Pentecostalism: Theories and Methods,* edited by Allan Anderson, Michael Bergunder, André Droogers, and Cornelis van der Laan, 179–201. Berkeley: University of California Press.

Huxley, Margo. 2008. "Space and Government: Governmentality and Geography." *Geography Compass* 2 (5): 1635–58.

Ingalls, Monique M., and Amos Yong, eds. 2015. *The Spirit of Praise: Music and Worship in Pentecostal-Charismatic Christianity.* University Park: Pennsylvania State University Press.

Jewkes, Yvonne. 2004. *Media and Crime.* London: Sage.

Jovchelovitch, Sandra. 2000. *Representações sociais e esfera pública: A construção simbólica dos espaços públicos no Brasil.* Rio de Janeiro: Editora Vozes.

Keane, Webb. 2007. *Christian Moderns: Freedom and Fetish in the Mission Encounter.* Berkeley: University of California Press.

Keil, Charles, and Steven Feld. 1994. *Music Grooves: Essays and Dialogues.* Chicago: University of Chicago Press.

Koonings, Kees, and Dirk Kruijt. 2004. "Armed Actors, Organized Violence and State Failure in Latin America: A Survey of Issues and Arguments." In *Armed Actors: Organised Violence and State Failure in Latin America,* edited by Kees Koonings and Dirk Kruijt, 5–15. London: Zed Books.

Kottak, Conrad Phillip. 1990. *Prime-Time Society: An Anthropological Analysis of Television and Culture.* Belmont, CA: Wadsworth.

Kramer, Eric W. 2001a. "Law and the Image of a Nation: Religious Conflict and Religious Freedom in a Brazilian Criminal Case." *Journal of the American Bar Foundation* 26 (1): 35–62.

———. 2001b. "Possessing Faith: Commodification, Religious Subjectivity, and Collectivity in a Brazilian Neo-Pentecostal Church." PhD diss., University of Chicago.

———. 2002. "Making Global Faith Universal: Media and a Brazilian Prosperity Movement." *Culture and Religion* 3 (1): 21–47.

———. 2005. "Spectacle and the Staging of Power in Brazilian Neo-Pentecostalism." *Latin American Perspectives* 32 (1): 95–120.

Krell, Marc A. 2003. *Intersecting Pathways: Modern Jewish Theologians in Conversation with Christianity.* Oxford, UK: Oxford University Press.

Lacey, Kate. 2000. "Towards a Periodization of Listening: Radio and Modern Life." *International Journal of Cultural Studies* 3 (2): 279–88.

Landim, Leilah. 2013. "Violência e organizações civis na periferia do Rio de Janeiro: Novas cartografias?" In *Sobre periferias: Novos conflitos no Brasil contemporâneo,* edited by Neiva Vieira da Cunha and Gabriel de Santis Feltran, 69–86. Rio de Janeiro: Lamparina and Faperj.

Lanz, Stephan. 2007. "Favelas regieren: Zum Verhältnis zwischen Lokalstaat, Drogenkomplex und Favela in Rio de Janeiro." *Zeitschrift für Wirtschaftsgeographie* 51 (2): 93–107.

Latour, Bruno. 2005. *Reassembling the Social: An Introduction to Actor-Network-Theory.* Oxford, UK: Oxford University Press.

Leal, Ondina Fachel. 1986. *A leitura social da novela das oito.* Petrópolis, Brazil: Vozes.

Leeds, Elizabeth. 1996. "Cocaine and Parallel Polities in the Brazilian Urban Periphery: Constraints on Local Level Democratization." *Latin American Research Review* 31 (3): 47–83.

Lefebvre, Henri. 1991. *The Production of Space.* Malden, MA: Blackwell.

Lehmann, David. 1996. *Struggle for the Spirit: Religious Transformation and Popular Culture in Brazil and Latin America.* Cambridge, UK: Polity Press.

———. 2001. "Charisma and Possession in Africa and Brazil." *Theory, Culture and Society* 18 (5): 45–74.

Leite, Márcia Pereira. 1997. "Da metáfora da guerra à mobilização pela paz: Temas e imagens do Reage Rio." *Cadernos de Antropologia e Imagem* 4: 121–45.

Lemke, Thomas. 2001. "'The Birth of Bio-Politics': Michel Foucault's Lecture at the Collège de France on Neo-Liberal Governmentality." *Economy and Society* 30 (2): 190–207.

234

Lima, William da Silva. 1991. *Quatrocentos contra um: Uma história do comando vermelho*. Rio de Janeiro: Vozes.

Lopes, Adriana Carvalho. 2011. *Funk-se quem quiser: No batidão negro da cidade carioca*. Rio de Janeiro: Bom Texto.

Lorenz, Aaron. 2011. "Embodying the Favela: Representation, Mediation, and Citizenship in the Music of Bezerra da Silva." In *Brazilian Popular Music and Citizenship*, edited by Idelber Avelar and Christopher Dunn, 172–87. Durham, NC: Duke University Press.

Luhrmann, Tanya Marie. 2012. *When God Talks Back: Understanding the American Evangelical Relationship with God*. New York: Knopf.

Macedo, Edir. 1999. *Doutrinas de Igreja Universal do Reino de Deus 2*. Rio de Janeiro: Editora Gráfica Universal.

———. 2000. *Orixás, caboclos e guias: Deuses ou demônios?* Rio de Janeiro: Editora Gráfica Universal.

Machado, Carly Barbosa. 2013. "'É muita mistura': Projetos religiosos, políticos, sociais midiáticos, de saúde e segurança pública nas periferias do Rio de Janeiro." *Religião e Sociedade* 33 (2): 13–36.

Machado, Maria das Dores Campos, and Silvia Regina Alves Fernandes. 1998. "Mídia pentecostal: Saúde feminina e planejamento familiar em perspectiva." *Cadernos de Antropologia e Imagem* 7 (2): 19–39.

Machado, Maria das Dores Campos, and Cecília Loreto Mariz. 2004. "Conflitos religiosos na arena política: O caso do Rio de Janeiro." *Ciencias Sociales y Religión* 6 (6): 31–50.

Maffesoli, Michel. 1996. *The Contemplation of the World: Figures of Community Style*. Minneapolis: University of Minnesota Press.

Mafra, Clara. 1998. "Drogas e símbolos: Redes de solidariedade em contextos de Violência." In *Um século de favela*, edited by Alba Zaluar and Marcus Alvito, 277–98. Rio de Janeiro: Editora Fundação Getulio Vargas.

———. 2001. *Os evangélicos*. Rio de Janeiro: Jorge Zahar Editor.

———. 2002. *Na posse da palavra: Religião, conversão e liberdade pessoal em dois contextos nacionais*. Lisbon: Imprensa de Ciências Socias.

Mahmood, Saba. 2005. *The Politics of Piety: The Islamic Revival and the Feminist Subject*. Princeton, NJ: Princeton University Press.

———. 2009. "Religious Reason and Secular Affect: An Incommensurable Divide?" *Critical Inquiry* 35 (4): 836–62.

Mainwaring, Scott. 1986. "The Catholic Church and the Popular Movement in Brazil: Nova Iguaçu, 1974–1985." In *Religion and Political Conflict in Latin America*, edited by Daniel Levine, 124–55. Chapel Hill: University of North Carolina Press.

Manovich, Lev. 2001. *The Language of New Media*. Cambridge, MA: MIT Press.

Mariano, Ricardo. 1999. *Neopentecostais: Sociologia do novo Pentecostalismo no Brasil*. São Paulo: Loyola.

———. 2007. "Pentecostais em ação: A demonização dos cultos Afro-Brasileiros." In *Intolerância religiosa: Impactos do neopentecostalismo no campo religioso Afro-Brasileiro*, edited by Vagner Gonçalves da Silva, 119–48. São Paulo: EDUSP.

Mariz, Cecília Loreto. 1994. *Coping with Poverty: Pentecostals and Christian Base Communities in Brazil*. Philadelphia: Temple University Press.

Marks, Laura U. 2000. *The Skin of the Film: Intercultural Cinema, Embodiment, and the Senses*. Durham, NC: Duke University Press.

Marshall, Ruth. 2009. *Political Spiritualities: The Pentecostal Revolution in Nigeria*. Chicago: University of Chicago Press.

Martin, David. 1990. *Tongues of Fire: The Explosion of Protestantism in Latin America*. Oxford, UK: Basil Blackwell.

———. 2002. *Pentecostalism: The World Their Parish*. Oxford, UK: Blackwell.

Martín-Barbero, Jesús. 2002. "The City: Between Fear and the Media." In *Citizens of Fear*, edited by Susana Rotker, 25–36. New Brunswick, NJ: Rutgers University Press.

Massumi, Brian. 2002. *Parables for the Virtual: Movement, Affect, Sensation*. Durham, NC: Duke University Press.

Mazzarella, William. 2004. "Culture, Globalization, Mediation." *Annual Review of Anthropology* 33 (1): 345–68.

235

McDannell, Colleen. 1995. *Material Christianity: Religion and Popular Culture in America*. New Haven, CT: Yale University Press.

McGuire, Meredith B. 2008. *Lived Religion: Faith and Practice in Everyday Life*. New York: Oxford University Press.

McLuhan, Marshall. 1964. *Understanding Media: The Extensions of Man*. New York: Signet Books.

McQuail, Denis. 1994. *Mass Communication Theory: An Introduction*. London: Sage.

Mendonça, Joêzer de Souza. 2008. "O evangelho segundo o gospel: Mídia, música pop e neopentecostalismo." *Revista do Conservatório de Música da UFPel* 1: 220–49.

Menezes, Palloma Valle. "'Entre o 'fogo cruzado' e o 'campo minado': Uma etnografia do processo de 'pacificação' de favelas cariocas." PhD diss., Rio de Janeiro State University, 2015.

Merriam, Alan P. 1964. *The Anthropology of Music*. Evanston, IL: Northwestern University Press.

Mesquita, Wânia. 2008. "'Tranqüilidade' sob a ordem violenta: O controle da 'mineira' em uma favela carioca." In *Vida sob cerco: violência e rotina nas favelas do Rio de Janeiro*, edited by Luiz Antonio Machado da Silva, 227–48. Rio de Janeiro: Nova Fronteira.

Meyer, Birgit. 1996. "Modernity and Enchantment: The Image of the Devil in Popular African Christianity." In *Conversion to Modernities: The Globalization of Christianity*, edited by Peter van der Veer, 199–230. London: Routledge.

———. 1998. "'Make a Complete Break with the Past': Memory and Post-Colonial Modernity in Ghanaian Pentecostalist Discourse." *Journal of Religion in Africa* 28 (3): 316–49.

———. 1999. *Translating the Devil: Religion and Modernity Among the Ewe in Ghana*. Edinburgh: Edinburgh University Press.

———. 2003. "Visions of Blood, Sex, and Money: Fantasy Spaces in Popular Ghanaian Cinema." *Visual Anthropology* 16 (1): 15–41.

———. 2006. "Impossible Representations: Pentecostalism, Vision, and Video Technology in Ghana." In *Religion, Media, and the Public Sphere*, edited by Birgit Meyer and Annelies Moors, 290–312. Bloomington: Indiana University Press.

———. 2009. "Introduction: From Imagined Communities to Aesthetic Formations: Religious Mediations, Sensational Forms, and Styles of Binding." In *Aesthetic Formations: Media, Religion, and the Senses*, edited by Birgit Meyer, 1–28. New York: Palgrave.

———. 2010. "Aesthetics of Persuasion: Global Christianity and Pentecostalism's Sensational Forms." *South Atlantic Quarterly* 109 (4): 741–63.

Meyer, Birgit, and Annelies Moors, eds. 2006. *Religion, Media, and the Public Sphere*. Bloomington: Indiana University Press.

Meyrowitz, Joshua. 1993. "Images of Media: Hidden Ferment—and Harmony—in the Field." *Journal of Communication* 43 (3): 55–66.

Miller, Donald E., and Tetsunao Yamamori, eds. 2007. *Global Pentecostalism: The New Face of Christian Social Engagement*. Berkeley: University of California Press.

Misse, Michel, Carolina Christoph Grill, Cesar Pinheiro Teixeira, and N. E. Neri. 2013. *Quando a polícia mata: Homicídios por "autos de resistência" no Rio de Janeiro (2001–2011)*. Rio de Janeiro: Booklink.

Mitchell, Timothy. 1988. *Colonising Egypt*. Berkeley: University of California Press.

Montes, Maria Lúcia. 1998. "As figuras do sagrado: Entre o público e o privado." In *História da vida privada no Brasil: Contrastes da intimidade contemporânea*, edited by Fernando A. Novaes and Lilia Moritz Schwarcz, 63–171. São Paulo: Companhia das Letras.

Moore, R. Laurence. 1994. *Selling God: American Religion in the Marketplace of Culture*. New York: Oxford University Press.

236

Moores, Shaun. 1993. *Interpreting Audiences: The Ethnography of Media Consumption*. London: Sage.

———. 2004. "The Doubling of Place: Electronic Media, Time-Space Arrangements and Social Relationships." In *MediaSpace: Place, Scale and Culture in a Media Age*, edited by Nick Couldry and Anna McCarthy, 21–37. London: Routledge.

Morgan, David. 1998. *Visual Piety: A History and Theory of Popular Religious Images*. Berkeley: University of California Press.

———. 2005. *The Sacred Gaze: Religious Visual Culture in Theory and Practice*. Berkeley: University of California Press.

Novaes, Regina Reyes. 1985. *Os Escolhidos de Deus: Pentecostais, Trabalhadores e Cidadania*. Rio de Janeiro: Marco Zero.

———. 2002. "Crenças religiosas e convicções politicas: Fronteiras e passagens." In *Política e cultura: Século XXI*, edited by Luis Carlos Fridman, 63–98. Rio de Janeiro: Relume Dumará.

Nunes, Guida. 1976. *Rio, metrópole de 300 favelas*. Petrópolis, Brazil: Vozes.

Oliveira, Anazir Maria de, and Cíntia Paes Carvalho. 1993. *Favelas e as organizações comunitarias*. Petrópolis, Brazil: Vozes.

Oro, Ari Pedro. 2003. "A política da Igreja Universal e seus reflexos nos campos religioso e político Brasileiros." *Revista Brasileira de Ciências Sociais* 18 (53): 53–69.

Oro, Ari Pedro, and Pablo Semán. 1999. "Neopentecostalismo e conflitos éticos." *Religião e Sociedade* 20 (1): 39–54.

Orsi, Robert A. 1999. "Introduction: Crossing the City Line." In *Gods of the City: Religion and the American Urban Landscape Religion in North America*, edited by Robert A. Orsi, 1–78. Bloomington: Indiana University Press.

Ortiz, Renato. 1988. *A moderna tradição Brasileira: Cultura Brasileira e indústria cultural*. São Paulo: Brasiliense.

Perlman, Janice. 1977. *O mito da marginalidade*. Rio de Janeiro: Editora Paz e Terra.

———. 2003. "Marginalidade: Do mito à realidade nas favelas do Rio de Janeiro." City Studies Collection, Rio Estudos 102.

———. 2010. *Favela: Four Decades of Living on the Edge in Rio de Janeiro*. Oxford, UK: Oxford University Press.

Perrone, Charles A., and Christopher Dunn, eds. 2001. *Brazilian Popular Music and Globalization*. Gainesville: University Press of Florida.

Pinheiro, Márcia Leitão. 1998. "O proselitismo evangélico: Musicalidade e imagem." *Cadernos de Antropologia e Imagem* 7 (2): 57–67.

Pinney, Christopher. 2001. "Piercing the Skin of the Idol." In *Beyond Aesthetics: Art and the Technologies of Enchantment*, edited by Christopher Pinney and Nicholas Thomas, 157–80. Oxford, UK: Berg.

Poewe, Karla. 1989. "On the Metonymic Structure of Religious Experiences: The Example of Charismatic Christianity." *Cultural Dynamics* 2 (4): 361–80.

Port, Mattijs van de. 2005. "Candomblé in Pink, Green, and Black: Re-scripting the Afro-Brazilian Heritage in the Public Sphere of Salvador, Bahia." *Social Anthropology* 13 (1): 3–26.

———. 2011. *Ecstatic Encounters: Bahian Candomblé and the Quest for the Really Real*. Amsterdam: Amsterdam University Press.

Prandi, Reginaldo. 1996. *Herdeiras do axé: Sociologia das religiões Afro-Brasileiras*. São Paulo: Hucitec.

Prandi, Reginaldo, and Antônio Flávio Pierucci. 1995. "Religiões e voto: A eleição presidencial de 1994." *Opinião Pública* 3 (1): 32–63.

Putman, Daniel A. 1985. "Music and the Metaphor of Touch." *Journal of Aesthetics and Art Criticism* 44 (1): 59–66.

Rambo, Lewis R. 1993. *Understanding Religious Conversion*. New Haven, CT: Yale University Press.

Ramos, Silvia, and Anabela Paiva. 2007. *Mídia e violência: Tendências na*

237

cobertura de criminalidade e segurança no Brasil. Rio de Janeiro: IUPERJ.

Robbins, Joel. 2004. "The Globalization of Pentecostal and Charismatic Christianity." Annual Review of Anthropology 33 (1): 117–43.

Robeck, Cecil M., Jr., and Amos Yong, eds. 2014. The Cambridge Companion to Pentecostalism. New York: Cambridge University Press.

Rommen, Timothy. 2007. "Mek Some Noise": Gospel Music and the Ethics of Style in Trinidad. Berkeley: University of California Press.

Rondelli, Elizabeth. 1994. "Media, representações sociais da violência, da criminalidade e ações políticas." Communição e Política 1 (2): 97–108.

Sá Martino, Luís Mauro. 2002. "Mercado político e capital religioso." In Comunicação na pólis: Ensaios sobre mídia e política, edited by Clóvis de Barros Filho, 312–31. Petrópolis, Brazil: Vozes.

Sánchez, Rafael. 2008. "Seized by the Spirit: The Mystical Foundation of Squatting Among Pentecostals in Caracas (Venezuela) Today." Public Culture 20 (2): 267–305.

Sansone, Livio. 2001. "Não-trabalho, consumo e identidade negra: Uma comparação entre Rio e Salvador." In Raça como retórica, edited by Yvonne Maggie and Claudia Barcellos Rezende, 155–84. Rio de Janeiro: Civilização Brasileira.

Santana, Luther King de Andrade. 2005. "Religião e mercado: A mídia empresarial-religiosa." Revista de Estudos da Religião 1: 54–67.

Santos, Myrian Sepúlvada dos. 1998. "Mangueira e Império: A carnavalização do poder pelas escolas de samba." In Um Século de Favela, edited by Alba Zaluar and Marcus Alvito, 114–44. Rio de Janeiro: Editora Fundação Getulio Vargas.

Schäfer, Murray R. 1994. The Soundscape: Our Sonic Environment and the Tuning of the World. Rochester, VT: Destiny Books.

Scheper-Hughes, Nancy. 1992. Death Without Weeping: The Violence of Everyday Life in Brazil. Berkeley: University of California Press.

Schmalzbauer, John. 2002. "Between Objectivity and Moral Vision: Catholics and Evangelicals in American Journalism." In Practicing Religion in the Age of Media: Explorations Media, Religion, and Culture, edited by Stewart Hoover and Lynn Schofield Clark, 165–87. New York: Columbia University Press.

Schmidt, Leigh Eric. 2000. Hearing Things: Religion, Illusion, and the American Enlightenment. Cambridge, MA: Harvard University Press.

Schofield Clark, Lynn. 2003. From Angels to Aliens: Teenagers, the Media, and the Supernatural. New York: Oxford University Press.

Schultze, Quentin J. 1991. Televangelism and American Culture: The Business of Popular Religion. Grand Rapids, MI: Baker Book House.

Schwartz, Vanessa R. 1995. "Cinematic Spectatorship Before the Apparatus: The Public Taste for Reality in Fin-de-Siècle Paris." In Cinema and the Invention of Modern Life, edited by Leo Charney and Vanessa R. Schwartz, 297–319. Berkeley: University of California Press.

Shilling, Chris. 2005. The Body in Culture, Technology, and Society. London: Sage.

Silva, Luiz Antonio Machado da. 2008. "Introdução." In Vida sob cerco: Violência e rotina nas favelas do Rio de Janeiro, edited by Luiz Antonio Machado da Silva, 13–26. Rio de Janeiro: Nova Fronteira.

Silva, Vagner Gonçalves da. 2007. "Prefácio ou notícias de uma guerra nada particular: Os araques neopentecostais às religiões afro-brasileiras e aos símbolos da herança Africana no Brasil." In Intolerância religiosa: Impactos do neopentecostalismo no campo religioso Afro-Brasileiro, edited by Vagner Gonçalves da Silva, 9–28. São Paulo: Editora da Universidade de São Paulo.

Silverstone, Roger. 2002. "Complicity and Collusion in the Mediation of Everyday Life." New Literary History 33 (5): 761–80.

238

Slater, Don, and Jo Tacchi. 2004. *Research: ICT Innovations for Poverty Reduction*. New Delhi: UNESCO.

Smilde, David. 2003. "Skirting the Instrumental Paradox: Intentional Belief Through Narrative in Latin American Pentecostalism." *Qualitative Sociology* 26 (3): 313–29.

———. 2007. *Reason to Believe: Cultural Agency in Latin American Evangelicalism*. Berkeley: University of California Press.

Sneath, David, Martin Holbraad, and Morten Axel Pedersen. 2009. "Technologies of the Imagination: An Introduction." *Ethnos* 74 (1): 5–30.

Sneed, Paul. 2007. "Bandidos de Cristo: Representations of the Power of Criminal Factions in Rio's Proibidão Funk." *Revista de Música Latinoamericana* 28 (2): 220–41.

Soares, Luiz Eduardo. 1995. "Criminalidade e violência: Rio de Janeiro, São Paulo e perspectivas internacionais." *Comunição e Política* 1 (2): 15–34.

———. 2000. *Meu casaco de general: Quinhentos dias no front da segurança pública no Rio de Janeiro*. São Paulo: Companhia das Letras.

Sobchack, Vivian. 2004. *Carnal Thoughts: Embodiment and Moving Image Culture*. Berkeley: University of California Press.

Sontag, Susan. 2003. *Regarding the Pain of Others*. New York: Picador.

Souto de Oliveira, Jane, and Maria Hortense Marcier. 1998. "A Palavra é favela." In *Um século de favela*, edited by Alba Zaluar and Marcus Alvito, 61–114. Rio de Janeiro: GTV.

Souza, Marcelo Lopes de. 2008. *Fobópole: O medo generalizado e a militarização da questão urbana*. Rio de Janeiro: Bertrand Brasil.

Spitulnik, Debra. 2001. "The Social Circulation of Media Discourses and the Mediation of Communities." In *Linguistic Anthropology: A Reader*, edited by Alessandro Duranti, 93–113. Oxford, UK: Blackwell.

Stamps, Donald C., and J. Wesley Adams, eds. 1995. *The Full Life Study Bible New Testament*. Grand Rapids, MI: Zondervan.

Stokes, Martin. 1994. "Introduction: Ethnicity, Identity and Music." In *Ethnicity, Identity and Music: The Musical Construction of Place*, edited by Martin Stokes, 1–27. Oxford, UK: Berg.

Stoll, David. 1990. *Is Latin America Turning Protestant? The Politics of Evangelical Growth*. Berkeley: University of California Press.

Stolow, Jeremy. 2005. "Religion and/as Media." *Theory, Culture and Society* 22 (2): 137–63.

———. 2006. "Communicating Authority, Consuming Tradition: Jewish Orthodox Outreach Literature and Its Reading Public." In *Religion, Media, and the Public Sphere*, edited by Birgit Meyer and Annelies Moors, 73–90. Bloomington: Indiana University Press.

Straubhaar, Joseph. 1995. "Brazil." In *The International World of Electronic Media*, edited by Lynne Schafer Gross, 61–85. New York: McGraw-Hill.

Swatowiski, Claudia Wolf. 2009. "Dinâmicas espaciais em macaé: Lugares públicos e ambientes religiosos." In *Religiões e cidades: Rio de Janeiro e São Paulo*, edited by Clara Mafra and Ronaldo de Almeida. São Paulo: Terceiro Nome.

Tacchi, Jo. 2000. "The Need for Radio Theory in the Digital Age." *International Journal of Cultural Studies* 3 (2): 289–98.

Taussig, Michael T. 1980. *The Devil and Commodity Fetishism in South America*. Chapel Hill: University of North Carolina Press.

Teixeira, Cesar Pinheiro. 2011. *A construção social do "ex-bandido": Um estudo sobre sujeição criminal e pentecostalismo*. Rio de Janeiro: 7 Letras.

Tolson, Andrew. 1996. *Mediations: Text and Discourse in Media Studies*. London: Arnold.

Turino, Thomas. 2008. *Music as Social Life: The Politics of Participation*. Chicago: University of Chicago Press.

Tweed, Thomas A. 2006. *Crossing and Dwelling: A Theory of Religion*. Cambridge, MA: Harvard University Press.

Valladares, Licia do Prado. 1978. *Passa-se uma casa: Análise do programa de remoção de favelas do Rio de Janeiro.* Rio de Janeiro: Zahar Editores.

Vargas, Lucila. 1995. *Social Uses and Radio Practices: The Use of Participatory Radio by Ethnic Minorities in Mexico.* Boulder, CO: Westview Press.

Veer, Peter van der. 1996. "Introduction." In *Conversion to Modernities*, edited by Peter van der Veer, 1–22. New York: Routledge.

Velho, Otavio. 2009. "Missionization in the Postcolonial World: A View from Brazil and Elsewhere." In *Transnational Transcendence: Essays on Religion and Globalization*, edited by Thomas J. Csordas, 31–54. Berkeley: University of California Press.

Verrips, Jojada. 2002. "Haptic Screens and Our 'Corporeal Eye.'" *Etnofoor* 15 (1–2): 21–46.

Vianna, Hermano. 1999. *The Mystery of Samba: Popular Music and National Identity in Brazil.* Chapel Hill: University of North Carolina Press.

Vink, Nico. 1988. *The Telenovela and Emancipation: A Study on Television and Social Change in Brazil.* Amsterdam: Royal Tropical Institute.

Voegelin, Salome. 2014. *Sonic Possible Worlds: Hearing the Continuum of Sound.* London: Bloomsbury.

Vries, Hent de. 2001. "In Media Res: Global Religion, Public Spheres, and the Task of Contemporary Religious Studies." In *Religion and Media*, edited by Hent de Vries and Samuel Weber, 3–42. Stanford, CA: Stanford University Press.

Waiselfisz, Julio Jacobo. 2004. *Mapa da violência IV: Os jovens do Brasil.* Brasilia, BR: UNESCO.

Warner, Michael. 1992. "The Mass Public and the Mass Subject." In *Habermas and the Public Sphere*, edited by Craig Calhoun, 377–401. Cambridge, MA: MIT Press.

Weber, Max. (1958) 2003. *The Protestant Ethic and the Spirit of Capitalism.* New York: Dover.

Williams, Raymond. 1961. *The Long Revolution.* London: Chatto & Windus.

Wolseth, Jon. 2008. "Safety and Sanctuary Pentecostalism and Youth Gang Violence in Honduras." *Latin American Perspectives* 35 (4): 96–111.

Zaluar, Alba. 1985. *A máquina e a revolta: As organizações populares e o significado da pobreza.* São Paulo: Brasiliense.

———. 1998. "Para não dizer que não falei de samba: Os enigmas da violência no Brasil." In *História da vida privada* 4, edited by Lilia Moritz Schwarcz, 245–318. São Paulo: Companhia das Letras.

Zaluar, Alba, and Isabel Siqueira Conceição. 2007. "Favelas sob o controle das milícias no Rio de Janeiro." *São Paulo em perspectiva* 21 (2): 89–101.

Index

242

245

Typeset by
REGINA STARACE

Printed and bound by
SHERIDAN BOOKS

Composed in
FREIGHT TEXT AND WHITNEY

Printed on
NATURES NATURAL

Bound in
ARRESTOX

www.ingramcontent.com/pod-product-compliance
Lightning Source LLC
Chambersburg PA
CBHW032127020426
42334CB00016B/1072